ENDORSEMENTS

Secure the Gates is a clarion call to the believer who is willing to hear and obey. Dr. Janet Shuler strategically crafts the command to apostolically build and secure the gates in order to forcefully advance the Kingdom of God. Biblical principles are passionately expressed and clearly articulated for practical application. Along with your marching orders you'll receive the principles, especially as an intercessor, that will impact your life and expand your Kingdom's influence. Dr. Janet Shuler is a prolific writer as well as a woman of trusted character—I just love her!

Dr. Melodye Hilton
Author: *Double Honor: Uprooting Shame in Your Life, Higher Living Leadership, Higher Living Leadership Biblical Edition*

Dr. Janet Shuler brings a message as a General in the Kingdom of God within *Secure the Gates!* that will mobilize Kingdom intercessors and prophetic voices. Keys of authority have been given to the believer that will secure their lives in the things of God, and this message will help you effectively utilize your Holy Spirit given keys. Dr. Janet gives practical tools with a prophetic edge. If you have ever wondered how to be a troop for God, you will learn with no doubt, how to arise to this calling as a believer.
Dr. Janet is a proven woman of integrity, grace, power, and a true friend! Let her message impact your life.

Apostle Harold Williams, Jr.
Activation International, Inc.
Author: Dancing with Wolves

This book is a crisp prophetic charge. Dr. Shuler has written a timely, in season exhortation to the Church of the United States of America. I pray we have ears to hear.

John Kuebler
Elder of Abundant Life Worship Center and Principal of Abundant Life Academy, Nutley, NJ

Secure the Gates is strong meat, rich with content that is very important for all of us to grab a hold of and understand.

Seer David Fang,
Seer, of Christian International,
Santa Rosa, Fl.

SECURE THE GATES!

SECURE THE GATES!

Dr. Janet Shuler

XULON PRESS

Xulon Press
2301 Lucien Way #415
Maitland, FL 32751
407.339.4217
www.xulonpress.com

Printed in the United States of America.

ISBN-13: 9781545622001

Dedication

To my husband Jim thank you for your love, wisdom and support. I love you!
To our children and grandchildren you sincerely are my greatest joy. I'm so proud of each of you. Thank you for your love and support.
I *so* love my family! I am one blessed woman.

Acknowledgements

> "The people who influence you are the people who believed in you."
>
> – Henry Drummond

I WANT TO ACKNOWLEDGE APOSTLES STEVEN & Dr. Melodye Hilton for their wisdom, love and covering in the Lord. Your guidance and prophetic encouragement have truly anchored, inspired and encouraged me forward.

Christina Jeffers, Publisher and Editor-in-Chief of A Word of Encouragement (AWE) your professionalism, input and sound recommendations in editing were so on target and helpful. I also value your friendship and encouragement so much.

To the men and women of God who have inspired, encouraged, guided, listened when I needed to talk, invested in praying for me, and have simply 'been there': Apostle Harold Williams, Jr., Prophetess Janice Mixon, Torrey Marcel Harper, Pastor Bill von Husen, Pastor/Chaplain Karen Lomax, Pastors Ruth & Marcel Langhorn, David Fang, John Kuebler, and more.

To Bishop Bill Hamon we are thankful to be under Christian International. Thank you for the soundness, humility, and excellence that you have built, established and multiplied.

I'm so grateful for the support, encouragement and inspiration of so many.

Thank you for believing in me! For all you do, for who you are, I will be forever grateful you are in my life.

A Note About the Front Cover:

The cover was designed by prophetic artist David Munoz (www.davidmunozart.com). Grateful for your prayer and in what you saw in the design, as you said,

"It is time to walk in our identity in Christ! Wearing our crown as we carry and use the sword to defend. We are not passive, but vigilant warriors and worshippers. For such a time as this, we are the defenders of the Gates of the kingdom. The Crown and His Word (the Sword) will rule! It is a time to advance!"

Contents

Introduction

ON MY WAY TO A corporate prayer meeting, the cry, "Secure the Gates!" resounded urgently in my spirit. Later that evening Jennifer LeClaire prophecied over me, "I hear kairos time over you! Put your pen to paper in this kairos time. Share boldly! I break every intimidation of the enemy off of your life. Rise up!" In obedience to God I began writing on securing gates. That is how *Secure the Gates* was birthed and developed – prophetically and prayerfully.

Prophetic revelation is so important. It is the 'now', proceeding word of God (rhema) to us. True prophecy always agrees with the Bible (logos), if it doesn't then it's illegitimate. Because it is God-breathed it carries His authority to shift atmospheres. Prophecy gives us revelation, warning, divine guidance and encouragement that helps navigate our steps into our future with godly wisdom and insight. Our response to prophetic revelation (His rhema word) prepares the way of the Lord. Secure the Gates contains prophetic revelation for us in these times.

"Secure the Gates" will encourage you to move in your identity in Christ defending gates and advancing His kingdom on earth. May you see with the eyes of the Spirit, while becoming more informed of current events in the context of prophetic revelation.

I'm simply a watchman on the wall, a gatekeeper, sounding the alarm, "Secure the Gates"!

May you be inspired, equipped, and empowered, to secure your gates, possessing the land in your; family, neighborhood, town/city and beyond.

CHAPTER 1

Advance & Secure – Secure & Advance!

IT'S TIME TO TAKE BACK our land! The Church has done a sub-par job at best of being the voice of influence in recent decades. We either sounded religious, judgmental, or made no sound at all. America, the country where: "In God We Trust" is engraved upon our currency, 'one nation under God' is uttered daily by millions in schools across our nation, reciting the pledge of allegiance, has become a god-less nation. The silent majority was silent for decades, while other voices screamed for attention, jockeyed for position, and took ground. We, the Church, didn't want to make waves or offend anyone; while our families, government, and the moral fabric of society unraveled and began to slip away.

The Church is finally awakening! "Silent No Longer" should be a banner that we hang over Main Street, USA. Once again, His Bride is awakening, coming out of the captivity of inertia, rising to the forefront to be who she's called to be: salt and light. We are finding and re-discovering our voice. As importantly we're learning HOW to use our voice. Embracing that "mercy triumphs over judgement" (James 2:13) we are speaking with love, but we are not muzzled any longer. Facing our own fears, we're counting the cost and declaring truth(s) anyway. No longer slaves to fear. We are an army of reformers, arising as integral movers and shapers taking hold of the land of the free and home of the brave once again.

"From the days of John the Baptist until now the kingdom of heaven suffers violence, and violent men take it by force." (Matthew 11:12, NASB) As ground is gained the enemy is constantly at war to take it back. Perhaps you've experienced set-backs or the sense of taking 2 steps forward, but 5 steps backward? Gaining ground, followed by attacks and then a feeling of regression. We can minimize this sense of losing ground as we learn how to diligently, vigilantly 'hold the fort' and secure our gates.

Significant prophetic voices are in agreement. Jennifer LeClaire decreed, "The Lord is mantling you with new boldness to go into territories that you have not gone into before in the Spirit, to take on enemies you have not fought before, by the Spirit, led by the Holy Ghost. He's putting a new boldness on you to tackle issues in society like abortion, perversion, things that have come to infiltrate the Church." [1]

Across the globe there's a great and mighty outpouring of His Spirit evidenced by miracles, signs, and wonders. A major shift has taken place. His radical, Reformation Army is arising, advancing His kingdom on earth as it is in heaven! Pay attention to the 3 R's in this season: Remnant, Reform, Revival. A remnant is arising; those who have been overlooked, passed by, ostensibly hidden, for such a time as this. The remnant are those who have, remained pure and true, and have gone through a great deal of fiery testing. They paid a price being hidden and overlooked for several seasons. They aren't famous or well-known, but they're faithful and willing to do what He says do. They will be forerunners of reformation, simply because they're willing to take the church out of the box of tradition, get out of the seats into the streets, and impregnate the very fabric of society (business, the arts, media, education, etc.) with kingdom principles, biblical living – Christ-like, without being religious. (Which makes sense because Jesus wasn't religious.) These reformers will have an authentic voice and be void of the fear of man. They're radical, willing to do and say what He says, when and how He says. This remnant of reformers will scale to the top of each of the 7 mountains (Family, Church, Marketplace, Media, Government, Education, Arts & Entertainment) and reclaim the ground. The kingdoms of this world will become the kingdoms of our Lord and Savior! (Revelation 11:15)

Coming from this modern-day reformation, led by the Church, will be the greatest global revival ever known to man. It won't be a sudden flash fire that burns out quickly. It will be more of a slow burn that has a longer duration than most revivals of the past. It will have a longer burn because it will be carried and sustained through the reformation. It will reach into every layer of society. NOW is the time to secure our gates!

If we do not secure the gates we will not be able to sustain and maintain the ground we gain in on-going reform and revival.

If we do not secure the gates we will not be able to sustain and maintain the ground we gain in on-going reform and revival. "The Lord wants the Church to take back as much territory as it has the maturity to hold." [2] We have a mandate to action that must be commensurate with maturity, evidenced by *securing*/ holding the new ground we lay hold of. To advance without securing ground is like trying to fill a tub without shutting the drain all the way. The tub will only hold water if the drain is completely closed.

Rebuilding is a needed part of securing. Our gates are badly broken and in need of repair. Family, the most important social unit in society, has suffered greatly. The American family is a mess; divorce, fatherlessness, abortion, domestic violence, addiction, identity and gender confusion, etc.. When Family is in disarray, it is reflected in every aspect of society. We need healing as a nation, from the grassroots up. "Righteousness exalts a nation, but sin is a disgrace to any people." (Proverbs 14:34)

"... if my people, who are called by my name, will humble themselves and pray and seek my face and turn from their wicked ways, then I will hear from heaven, and I will forgive their sin and will heal their land." 2 Chronicles 7:14)

The call to prayer is rising; believers are organizing and uniting in increasing manner. Believers in Christ of all denominations and backgrounds coming together to pray, repent, humble themselves, worship, prophecy, utter prophetic decrees and declarations in the name of Jesus over our nation and the nations. Before all else I am an intercessor and love corporate prayer. Something very special takes place when, the body of Christ operates in unity! "For there the LORD commanded the blessing." (Psalm 133:1-3)

The week of the 15th anniversary of 9-11 there were many regional and national prayer rallies held across America. I attended several of them.

Interestingly, the number 15 has biblical, prophetic meaning as the number for 'acts of divine grace'. 15 is also the number of years that were given/graced to Hezekiah from the Lord:

"Hezekiah became ill and was at the point of death. The prophet Isaiah son of Amoz went to him and said, "This is what the LORD says: Put your house in order, because you are going to die; you will not recover."

"Hezekiah *turned his face to the wall and prayed* to the LORD, "Remember, LORD, how I have walked before you faithfully and with wholehearted devotion and have done what is good in your eyes." And Hezekiah wept bitterly. (Isaiah 38:1-3)

Intercessors stand in the gap, as Hezekiah did, repenting, humbling ourselves before the Lord, on behalf of a sinful, wayward America. God has moved on the heart of other nations to cry out for America in prayer. The nation of Australia came together to pray for America, for over 5 years now. [2] Oh Lord, truly our faces are turned to the wall in prayer!

"Then the word of the LORD came to Isaiah: "Go and tell Hezekiah, 'This is what the LORD, the God of your father David, says: I have heard your prayer and seen your tears; I will add fifteen years to your life. And I will deliver you and this city from the hand of the king of Assyria. I will defend this city." (Isaiah 38:4-6)

Could it be that America has been given an additional 15 years of grace rather than judgment "? Or is this a Nineveh turn-around time? Where judgment was completely reversed by God. " When God saw what they did and how they turned from their evil ways, he relented and did not bring on them the destruction he had threatened." (Jonah 3:10)

Whichever it is; a 15 year Hezekiah-like extension or a Nineveh reversal of judgement, *one thing is for certain – it is a turn-around season!*

A Personal Glimpse Back at 911

Indulge me for a moment. They (historians) say that 9-11 marked a new era. It marked me personally.

September 11, 2001 the date commonly referred to as 9-11. Terrorism hit American soil. It was a day that rocked the world. I live in NJ, in the shadow of NYC. It is like our backyard, we see the NYC skyline daily. The day of 9-11 we reeled in shock, stunned, in the pit of our stomach we felt sucker-punched.

The world was stunned, incredulous and we in the area, in the midst of the fall out were dazed. Cell phone connectivity was shut down, intensifying the raw anxiety that was almost palpable. Unable to verify if our loved ones were alive or where they were added an eerie, gnawing anxiety, uncertainty, confusion, and fear – swept in and gripped the region. Those working in schools (such as myself) had to make decisions; whether to send students home at the end of the school day, or not. Would they be going home to an empty, parent-less home? If their parents were ok were they stranded in NYC, unable to get home, unable to make a call? Phones lines were shut down. What to do with students whose parents we couldn't contact? (We held them until they were picked up by a family member.) Crossing guards came in from the street corners, asking how they could assist us, while an Army helicopter hovered overhead. The school was near Teterboro, a small airport in NJ, adjacent to NYC. It was being guarded against the possibility of additional attacks.

My son, Joshua, was on a roof working, looking toward the NYC skyline, when at 8:46am the World Trade Center (WTC) was struck and went down. He kept rubbing his eyes; his mind could not comprehend what he was seeing and what was happening. He said, "Everyone thinks it went down instantly, it didn't, it easily took 20-30 minutes. I couldn't believe what I was seeing. I thought I was hallucinating or going crazy or something." My other son, Michael, burst through the door as after work that day, exclaiming, "That's it, I'm joining the Marines! I'm not going to sit back and watch this happen and do nothing!!!"

The view of smoke rising from the remains of the smoldering World Trade Center lingered, for another 6 weeks afterward, clearly visible to us each day.

My daughter's friend Darlene, from Queens, NY, was coming to visit us that day. Her subway connection was directly under the WTC – because of the phone blackout we couldn't make contact with her for several anxious hours. We were on pins and needles not knowing where or how she was. Finally, communications were restored later that evening, by the grace of God she was ok. She had overslept and was going to take a later train. My co-worker's brother was to be working in the WTC at the time the planes hit. It was hours before she knew if her brother was alive or not. His car had a flat tire, he was delayed on the side of the highway. As he was fixing his tire the towers were struck. There are so many testimonies like these. The death toll could have been much higher.

God wants to encourage you: Some delays are divine delays. We often give the devil way too much credit for the inconvenient delays that we encounter. His hand is on you – even in, especially in the delay.

One of our pastors, Pastor Willie Freeman, was in the WTC as it was collapsing. He and many others scurried down staircases, on cell phones (before communications were shut down) to let his wife and family know he loved them. Pastor Freeman, literally shared Jesus with people as they were in the stairwell, fleeing the building, leading them to the Lord. Yet others that I know personally, one of my graduate professors lost her son, and fellow church members lost loved ones in the WTC that day.

We continued to move forward, immediately, going about our usual jobs and activities, not wanting to give the terrorists a 'win'. Although business went on 'as usual' nothing was 'usual'. We were all functioning on 'automatic pilot' as in the background smoke still rose above the skyscrapers across the river.

Dazed and numbed, the day after 9-11 I drove through a stop sign. Surprisingly, people had an added measure of compassion and understanding. The other cars, that I almost plowed into as I ran the stop sign, simply nodded their heads and made way for me. (Usually in this congested, metro area one is given the NJ sign for 'bird' with car horns blaring and loud tirades following.) There was evident compassion one for another in the air. Even in this tragedy His mercy and grace were present.

Churches offered memorial services and special prayer meetings. But to be honest, post 9-11 America and the Church blew it! What should have been the biggest wake-up call ever to repentance, salvation and revival became not much more than a temporary shock wave.

The Present & the Future

Our gates have been broken down and are in disrepair. They'd been deteriorating for years, we just didn't realize how much ground had slipped away. This Scripture describes the Church in the last 3 decades or so:

> How long will you lie down, O sluggard?
> When will you arise from your sleep?
> "A little sleep, a little slumber,
> A little folding of the hands to rest"—
> Your poverty will come in like a vagabond
> And your need like an armed man.
> (Proverbs 6:9-11)

We're waking up and feeling the impoverished value system and godlessness of our society. The past left its imprint on our today. I love the insight of this secular reporter, Cindy Rodriguez, back in 2006, "People say 9-11 is the day America lost its innocence. To me, it was the beginning of a wake-up call. Terrorism was a problem over there. But this, the first major attack of civilians on U.S. soil, prompted us to start asking questions. ... We may have lost our innocence, but we're also losing, thankfully, our ignorance." [3] **We are not defined by our past, but we must learn from it, and move forward with insight, courage, decisiveness, and commitment.**

Fifteen years later, under an open heaven, at the site of the World Trade Center (WTC) memorial, we stood, praying and repenting for America and the Church. Fred Rowe (of Global Prayer Watch) shared, "I hear the Holy Spirit saying, '**Church don't blow it this time**.' 9-11 had taken this nation, the world, and the Church by surprise. We missed seizing upon perhaps the greatest opportunity/ open door to move America into repentance and revival. The Church is awakening, arising to build and reform. **The legacy that we will be known by is not the failure of yesterday, but will be determined by our decisions, actions and obedience today – that will shape tomorrow**.

Kim Clement prophesied, in April 2007, "I will raise up the Trump to become a trumpet and I will not forget 9-11. I will not forget what took place that day and I will not forget the gatekeeper that watched over New York who will once again stand and watch over this nation." [5]

"Shift!", has been proclaimed prophetically for several years (2011-2017). There is a shaking and a shifting taking place on every level; personally, corporately, locally, regionally, nationally, internationally; touching all 7 mountains and various platforms of influence. We see governments shaken and challenged. Even the way we 'do church' is shifting; traditional ways are changing for His Bride to shine, relevant reformers *in every* stratosphere of society. The Church had been a silent majority for too long. She is now awakening, finding her voice, and moving into action!

First the natural then the spiritual: The spiritual did not come first, but the natural, and after that the spiritual. (1 Corinthians 15:46) Major international current events are causing significant shifts in our natural world. In 2011 the 5th largest earthquake recorded since 1900, with a magnitude of 9.0 hit Japan, triggering a massive tsunami. These events caused a literal shift in the earth's axis (of about 17 cm. or 6.5 inches) which scientists say has literally shortened the length of earth's days. Scientists calculate that various earthquakes (such as the 2004 Sumatran quake and the 2010 Chilean quake) have effected shifts in the earth's axis and shortening the length of days. [6] Interestingly, Jesus spoke of the distress of the end times, "If those days had not been cut short, no one would survive, but for the sake of the elect those days will be shortened." (Matthew 24:22)

Shifting continues throughout all of creation, like the contractions of a woman in childbirth, coming closer and closer together before delivery, thick and furious. In a short period there has been tumultuous change with the: Brexit (Great Brittain leaving the European Union), Syrian refugee crisis, ISIS radicalization, escalating global terrorism ripping through Europe (most notably France, Germany, Belgium, and Great Britain), Asia (India & Pakistan), Egypt, and more. Within the same year: Donald Trump won the USA presidency, Fidel Castro passed away, generals of the faith, such as; C. Peter Wagner, Miles Monroe, John Paul Jackson and Kim Clements transitioned into glory, and others. C. Peter Wagner charged Chuck Pierce to carry the baton as he transitioned. A 'changing of the guard' is taking place. New diverse leadership, across generations, is rising with fire and passion both in the world and in the Church.

A clashing of kingdoms reverberates as never before. Pastor Isaac Pitre prophetically exclaimed in 2011, "The pressure of heaven is coming down and is colliding with the corruption of earth. .... God is about to take over and YOU are going to be the ones who are going to bring it to pass!" [7] There is an urgency to secure our gates now, as thoroughly as possible, if we are going to gain, sustain and maintain ground! He who possesses the gates will possess the

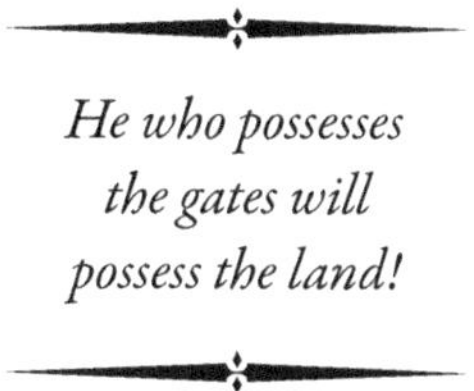

land! Possessing the gates is synonymous with possessing the city. (Genesis 22:17, see multiple translations) The gates of hell will not prevail! (Matthew 16:18)

This clash, is the division of light and darkness; good versus evil; heaven and hell. The clash of kingdoms is more apparent than ever. We are learning how to fight the good fight, to be united and strategic; loving our enemies, without compromising or losing our voice. The kingdom of heaven suffers violence, and violent men take it by force. (Matthew 11:12, NASB) We are taking back ground and advancing His kingdom.

"The kingdom of God is a real realm that operates throughout and over the realms and kingdoms of this world. It is about ruler-ship in one individual at a time as its power and authority are not derived from human structures rather from a realm above human-endorsed ones. It is contrary to how human power structures operate today. The kingdom of God was not meant to compete with existing empires or kingdoms of the world. Its operation cannot be state-controlled, or free market based,"[8] "Allegiance to the Kingdom of God does not mean to rebel against mammon-based power structures of today rather knowing and applying the authority of God over all systems."[9]

Do not mistake entering the land, or occupying the land with possessing the land and gaining new territory – they're not the same. Possession first secures the gates; to remain in possession the gates must be vigilantly, daily secured. Newly entered territory will be occupied and possessed *if* the gates are first secured.

There is a progression that leads to possession.

1. Spy Out
2. Enter
3. *Secure the Gates*
4. Occupy
5. Possess

Sending out the spies means to research, assess, and discern the report of the Lord. Then, develop a plan of action. As we 'spy out the land' it's important to have the eyes of the spirit, in order to keep the 'opposition' in perspective; lest we see the task ahead of us as too great and ourselves as grasshoppers. The opposition will see us as we see ourselves. (Numbers 13:33) We must be knowledgeable about the land we are entering; know its assets, strengths, weaknesses, geography, etc.

Upon entering the land, implement His battle plan; whether it is with a shout, sword and trowel or all of the above. Hear His voice, use discernment, and ACT upon it implementing His plan of action.

Securing gates and occupying the land should occur almost simultaneously. If gates are not properly secured the tenure of occupancy will be sabotaged and short-lived. **It's at the gates that safety is ensured, that which doesn't belong is expelled, boundaries are established, secured and held.** Occupying is the equivalent of setting up residency and becoming inextricably intertwined and entrenched in the fabric, composition/reformation of society and culture.

When I go shopping for a car I 'spy out the land', by determining what my needs are, researching about different types of cars, reading consumer reports, talking with friends, etc. before I decide upon which one I want. Then I'll look for sales, in-stock selection, and proximity to me as I choose which dealership to go to. I do a lot of research before I occupy or purchase a new vehicle. Once I'm at the dealership I'll sit in the car, examine, touch it, schmooze with the car salesman, and take a car or two for a test drive. But I have not secured, occupied or possessed it yet. True occupancy is only established through daily usage or abiding and dwelling in it. When you get into a car that's been occupied by a family with children you know it; signs of occupancy are all over, wrappers, clothing, books, sports equipment, and the like. They 'infiltrate' placing their mark upon it.

Before I own my new vehicle (aka take possession, and it becomes mine) I'll work to negotiate the best deal that I can. Possession is more than occupancy, it carries with it responsibility, i.e: car payments, care, and maintenance. Possession is ruling, dwelling, maintaining all that has been established in occupancy and then some. Ownership/possession has its privileges and responsibilities. The car is always there for me, I have immediate transportation access whenever needed.

Once we have possession of the gates, we can become too comfortable and lazy. That is what happened when the Church became the 'silent majority'. It was presumed that this nation, founded on principles of Judeo-Christian faith and ethics, would always remain of that persuasion. Christians assumed that in a country where the all daily declare in the pledge of allegiance, "One nation under God", where, "In God We Trust" is inscribed on all of our currency, surely this nation was secure and established as Judeo-Christian. Possessing means to maintain due diligence; sitting in the seat of authority, vigilantly subduing and reigning should enemies arise. Possession should NOT bring us to complacency, but continually advancing His kingdom, on earth as it is in heaven.

In legal terminology there is a difference between ownership and possession. The **main difference** between ownership and possession is that **possession is having physical custody or control of an object whereas ownership is a right by which something belongs to someone**. Usually both possession and ownership are held by the same person. To understand the term possession more clearly imagine that you are the owner of a car and you lend your car to a friend. Your friend has possession of the car, but you have ownership. The same can be said of a stolen object, i.e. a thief has the possession of an object, not the ownership. [I experienced this year's ago I lent my car to someone for 2 weeks. They didn't tell me that due to a parking violation it had been towed and impounded. The bill after well over 2 weeks of daily impound charges was huge! I found out about it as the towing company summoned me to court. Yikes! The judge was abundantly plain that I was legally responsible for the bill, as the owner it was mine.] I'm so thankful that Christ has paid our debt in full! I couldn't afford a towing bill, much less the debt of my sins over a lifetime!!!

In some countries' rulers have 'ownership' of the country. But because they rule corruptly, they are always in danger of losing possession through a hostile take-over. The people under them perpetually look to overthrow them. The rulers 'own' but their possession of their kingdom is always at risk, because of their oppressive rule. It's God's will for kingdom occupation, possession and righteousness to advance and prevail "The scepter of the wicked will not remain over the land allotted to the righteous, for then the righteous might use their hands to do evil." (Psalm 125:3)

"The kingdom of the world has become the kingdom of our Lord and of his Messiah, and he will reign for ever and ever." (Revelation 11:15) "The earth is the Lord's and everything in it." (Psalm 24:1) Spiritually speaking we have been given legal, covenantal, blood bought ownership through Jesus Christ, because we share in His inheritance and are fellow-partakers with Him in all things. (Ephesians 3:6). Legally we have been given ownership to rule and reign with Him, but warfare takes place for possession. Godly possession involves guarding, tending, and must be established and maintained in the gates. As gates are secured we occupy and establish through godly reformation that requires daily, on-going vigilance.

Then, kingdom *possession* is fully realized. The problem in Christian circles is that after prayer and travail we see breakthrough, we put everything on hold to celebrate. Christians are famous for storming the gates, breaking them down – but too often we stop there to have a Hallelujah party and then go home. We go in strong and then fizzle. I'm all for giving God thanks, praise and glory, however, we must press and keep on pressing in. Good can be the enemy of best. Good, better, best – do not rest, until the good is better and the better is best. Keep pressing! Until we see what Hosea proclaimed, that,

> "the earth is filled
> With the knowledge of the glory of the LORD,
> As the waters cover the sea." (Hosea 2:14)

> Chuck Pierce gave a prophetic directive, "The LORD is saying this is a time to know our boundaries and secure them! We are living in a season of contending for boundaries and borders. *The Border Wars* **we face this year will establish where we'll be three years from now. Therefore, it's imperative that we understand God's desire for establishing our boundaries.**"[10] One of my favorites, Sun Tzu (author of the Art of War, a classic since the 5th century BC) said, "Don't depend on the enemy not coming; rather depend on being ready for him."

Boundaries are only kept secure through vigilance! The gates and gatekeepers are key. What are the gates? I propose to you that the gates of the 21st century are the access points to each of the 7 mountains. I would add one more gated mountain, the mountain of SELF.

Lord, show us the gates of the 21st century and how to secure them. Father, let each of us see clearly Your purposes and the keys that will open closed doors. Show us our gate(s), call, mountain, and territory that You have for each of us. Show us how to be effectual individually and corporately to establish Your kingdom, on earth as it is in heaven. We want to know where we fit as living stones on the wall to fulfill Your call. Let us lay hold of that which You have laid hold of us for! (Philippians 3:12)

The World Trade Center (1973-2001), NYC, before 9-11. The Statue of Liberty is situated in the midst of the gateway of America on the east, in between NY and NJ. (Taken from the NJ side facing NYC.

The day that rocked the world, marking the beginning and end of an era in history. The 9-11 terror attack (9/11/01) viewed through the Brooklyn Bridge, NYC.

Boots on the ground! Our small but powerful prayer group met to repent and pray for America at the site of the WTC Memorial. The site is adjacent to the Freedom Tower. This picture was taken on the 15th anniversary after 9-11, on Sept. 10, 2016). Wherever 2 or 3 gather, united in Jesus' name, He's in their midst.

At the Gateway of America, 911 Memorial at Liberty State Park in Jersey City NJ. On the day of 911 ferries transported NYC school children being evacuated, away from the city that was burning, to safety across the river – here at this site. (Note: In the foreground is a beam from what remained of the WTC, to the left is the Freedom Tower. The Hudson River is in between NJ and NY in the gateway, the Statue of Liberty is in the water just a bit further to the right.

CHAPTER 2

THEN: Gates and Gatekeepers of the Old Testament

The one who enters by the gate is the shepherd of the sheep. The gatekeeper opens the gate for him, and the sheep listen to his voice. He calls his own sheep by name and leads them out.

(John 10:2, CEV)

GATES ARE STRATEGIC ACCESS AND exit points. They are the point of passage for commerce, people, and supplies. Daily, everything went through the gates: laborers, farmers, families, livestock, grain, food, foreigners, etc. It is where the elders of the city sat. They were literal, geographic places, guarded and monitored.

Every city had two or several gates. Prestigious city gates were made of strong, fortified materials such as wood, iron, brass, and bronze. Most gates were wooden with strong locks that securely bolted shut. Temple gates were ornate, designed by skilled artisans, such as the temple gate in Jerusalem, called Beautiful. (Acts 3:2) Heavenly gates, described in the Bible, are made of precious stones, pearl and gold. (Isaiah 54:12, Revelation 21:21)

Everything happened at the gates: commerce, civic matters, legal disputes, murder plots and gossip. These matters were brought to the elders at the gates. **Eldership in the gates was a high honor.** (Proverbs 31:23) Kings such as King David, gave directives and made official appearances at the gates. (2 Samuel 19:1-8)

It was in the gates that the elders of the city determined Boaz was to be Ruth's kinsman-redeemer in marriage; unruly children's discipline was decided. (Dt. 21:18-21) Where are today's gates? Where does everyone bring their 'stuff' nowadays? Very few are bringing their personal life disputes to the mouth of the

Lincoln Tunnel or the Golden Gate Bridge, etc. Things transpire via the gates of the Internet. (More about this in chapter 8.) Today's gates are more ethereal and metaphorical, making them harder to guard and secure.

Whatever went on in the city, eventually made its way to the gates, including political corruption and injustice. (God knew this would be the case and commanded in His Word, "Do not rob the poor, because he is poor, or crush the afflicted *at the gate*." (Dt. 24:14; Proverbs 22:22, ESV) It was in the gates that Mordecai learned about the plot to kill King Xerxes. (Esther 2:19-23)

Increase & Prevailing

Controlling the gates of one's enemies was equal to conquering their city. A significant part of God's blessing to Abraham was, "Your offspring shall possess the gates of his enemies" (Genesis 22:17, ESV) A similar blessing was spoken over Rebekah, "And they blessed Rebekah and said to her, "Our sister, may you become thousands of ten thousands, **and may your offspring possess the gates of those who hate him!**" (Genesis 24:60, ESV)

There's a pattern over those He favored of (a) increase and multiplication, and (b) possessing the gates of their enemies.

God's favor is on you. Dear one, pause for a moment to declare a powerful blessing over yourself, out-loud:

"*The blessing of God is over my life, my family, career and ministry. He is increasing me! I will possess the gates of my enemies. The Church will possess the gates of all of the mountains of influence for the glory of the Lord*!"

To possess the gates is to possess the city. Securing them is an essential, on-going process of due diligence.

To possess the gates is to possess the city. Securing them is an essential, on-going process of due diligence.

Old Testament gates were particularly subject to attack. "Whether in the natural or in the spiritual there is perpetual warfare at the gates – they're key access points. The gate became a symbol of strength, power, and dominion (Ps.24:7), but it was also the weakest point of defense (2Chr.14:7; 26:9; 32:5; Ps.48:12) and therefore heavily defended. At night the gates were closed, barred and guarded (Josh.2:5,7; Neh.7:3), secured by locks with big keys." [1]

"From the days of John the Baptist until now, the kingdom of heaven has been subjected to violence, and violent people have been raiding it." (Matthew 11:12)

The enemy enjoys instilling paralyzing fear, at the gates. "Your enemy the devil prowls around like a roaring lion looking for someone to devour." (1 Peter 5:8) The roaring is geared at intimidation, to stop the people of God from moving forward.

> "So that hearts may melt with fear
> and the fallen be many,
> I have stationed the sword for slaughter
> at all their gates.
> Look! It is forged to strike like lightning,
> it is grasped for slaughter. (Ezekiel 21:15)

The enemy tries to bind with fear because he is fearful of what you carry. Your authority in Christ secures and possesses gates, gains territory and advances other kingdom influencers. (Matthew 16:18) There will be trials, warfare and battles – but hell will not prevail whether in physical or metaphorical gates, no Satanic plan will stand to defeat the Church! Those in Christ are positioned to prevail in the gates!

Scripture does not say 'the gate' (singular) of hell will not prevail, but rather that the *gates* (in its plural form, there's more than one) of hell will not prevail!

Take a moment to absorb the enormity of what this promise means! The gates of hell *will* come against us. Like it or not there is a spiritual battle that rages 24/7 for control of your soul, your family, your sphere of influence, and the kingdoms of this world. Jesus reigns and give us strategic, kingdom keys needed to prevail.

Today we have *many* gates to secure. Our metaphorical walls are broken down and our gates have been burnt with fire: families are broken, gang activity is on the rise, gender confusion, moral decay, corruption, etc. are widespread. We are called and positioned for such a time as this to restore our gates!

NEHEMIAH – An Era of Strategic Reformation

The Church is awakening today, as the Jews of Ezra and Nehemiah's time had re-awakened from captivity. (The Jews had been exiled to Babylon for 70 years under the Medo-Persian Empire.)

> "Those who survived the exile and are back in the province are in great trouble and disgrace. The wall of Jerusalem is broken down, and its gates have been burned with fire." (Nehemiah 1:3)

The burden of the Lord had gripped Nehemiah, practically overwhelming him. He fasted and prayed, carrying the burden of his people to the Lord in prayer. God met him and filled him with vision and boldness. Nothing happens without prayer.

The next day, as the cupbearer of King Artaxerxes, king of the Medo-Persian empire, Nehemiah went into the king's presence, continuing to pray without ceasing, asking God:

> "Give your servant success today by granting him favor in the presence of this man." (Nehemiah 1:11)

[Note: Culturally his perspective alone was radical. Most people thought of kings as god-like, not as mere mortal men. Also, when one was in the presence of a king such as Artaxerxes one was to be well-groomed, having a positive countenance. Being unkept or looking depressed was punishable.]

> "I had not been sad in his presence before, so the king asked me, "Why does your face look so sad when you are not ill? This can be nothing but sadness of heart."
>
> I was very much afraid, but I said to the king, "May the king live forever! Why should my face not look sad when the city where my ancestors are buried lies in ruins, and its gates have been destroyed by fire?"
>
> The king said to me, "What is it you want?"
>
> Then I prayed to the God of heaven, and I answered the king, "If it pleases the king and if your servant has found favor in his sight, let him send me to the city in Judah where my ancestors are buried so that I can rebuild it." (Nehemiah 2:1-5)

Nehemiah had both eyes, the natural and the spiritual, open. He got 'his ducks in a row' *before* he left the king's presence. He got everything he could out of his, unexpected, moment of exceptional, divine favor. He maximized the offer of favor with this 'homefield advantage'. It's rare that the king of the empire asks you, "What is it you want?" Nehemiah, was ready and seized the day with a detailed list of requests:

> "If it pleases the king, may I have letters to the governors of Trans-Euphrates, so that they will provide me safe-conduct until I arrive in Judah? And may I have a letter to Asaph, keeper of the royal park, so he will give me timber to make beams for the gates of the citadel by the temple and for the city wall and for the residence I will occupy?" And because the gracious hand of my God was on me, the king granted my requests. So

> I went to the governors of Trans-Euphrates and gave them the king's letters. The king had also sent army officers and cavalry with me." (Nehemiah 2:7-9)

How many of us would be as poised and ready as Nehemiah was? He *wanted* permission to go and rebuild, what he *needed* was documentation from the government, supplies, and a residence. Before the king asked him what he wanted Nehemiah had spent hours of thought, meditation and prayer on the rebuilding of the wall. (Nehemiah 1:4) Perhaps he had detailed dreams regarding it, we don't know for sure. One thing is for certain – he capitalized on his answer to one simple question, making the most of his moment of favor. The king exceeded all of Nehemiah's requests offering to provide a cavalry for protection. The heart of the king not only trusted Nehemiah, he could see he was a worthwhile investment; possessing vision, leadership, and a plan.

Know what you want and what you need; they're not necessarily the same thing. Nehemiah wanted to rebuild the wall of Jerusalem. He was ready in season to answer the king with a targeted, clear, and specific reply. He was not naïve, but shrewd. He presumed they would have opposition from their enemies and planned for it in advance to minimize enemy interference.

Father give us clarity of Your vision, purpose and mission for our lives. We want to be effectual, laying hold of that which You've laid hold of us for. If our boss or someone with means and power asked you in the middle of your work day, 'What do you want? What can I do for you?' What will your answer be? Would you be ready with an articulate response? There's a very real possibility of not knowing what to say or needing time to pray and think about it, before replying. Lord grant us grace to be ready in and out of season.

Once you hear Him clearly write the vision *and* plan of action down. "Write down the revelation and make it plain on tablets so that a herald may run with it. For the revelation awaits an appointed time." (Habakkuk 2:2-3)

Getting permission was only half of the battle to rebuilding the walls of Jerusalem. He still had to get there! Nehemiah as a captive of the Babylonian Empire was in the citadel of Susa. (Nehemiah 1:1) Jerusalem was not around the corner, it was of 800-1,000 miles away! The drive from Susa to Jerusalem, by car, over paved roads and highways is about a 20 hour drive. Nehemiah, the cavalry, officers, and attendants traveled dirt roads and trails. It was arduous, challenging terrain between Susa and Jerusalem. Thankfully the king gave him cavalry to accompany him! He had counted the cost and was all in. The journey by horseback, a processional, loaded with supplies, would have taken about 30–50 days, 1-2 months, just to get there. (This assumes a rate of 20-30 miles per day by horse).

Nehemiah's journey

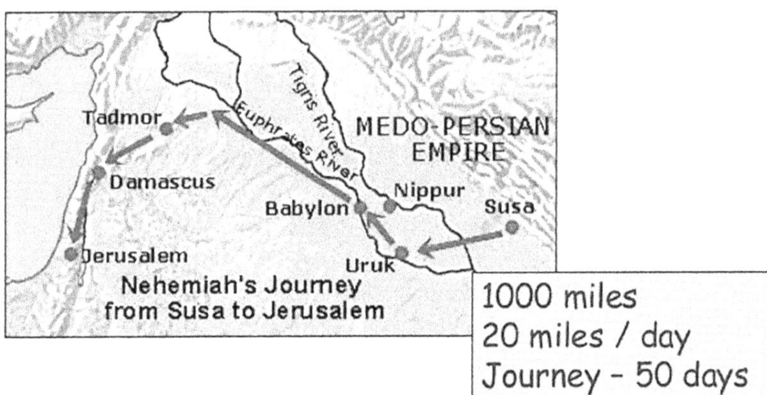

Map of Nehemiah's Journey (Fuller, Paul. https://www.slideshare.net/paulmfuller/nehemiahs-prayers-david-muller)

PRAYER: Lord, make me ready in season and out of season to spring into action, to know what You want, as well as what I need. Make me brave, to face my fears and move past the snare of comfort and familiarity.

First things first, Nehemiah didn't start rebuilding on day 1, he first:

1. Re-established and re-acquainted himself with his 'home' that was a foreign land to him, the area that he was to rebuild.
2. His identity was transformed, and he shifted into a new role.
3. He didn't tip his hand to the enemy, he kept things on a 'need to know' basis
4. Shared vision as he enlisted support and gained buy-in

Nehemiah had spent his life in captivity, during the Exile. He had lived in the king's palace and was not familiar with Jerusalem. He gave himself a few days to re-connect.

> "I went to Jerusalem, and after staying there three days, I set out during the night ..." (Nehemiah 2:11)

Scripture doesn't elaborate on what Nehemiah did during those three days. I envision him observing, studying, researching, and praying. I believe Nehemiah got an eye-opening education in those 3 days of mingling and observing in Jerusalem. He probably learned what people thought about the Jews, their status in Jerusalem, who their friends were, who their enemies were, area customs, where to get supplies, etc.

Then perhaps the most amazing transformation of all took place – Nehemiah made an identity shift. He went from a slave mentality as an exiled captive, to a great, respected, visionary leader. He took initiative, was shrewd, strategic. He was not only a man who was under authority (that of the king) but he was also a man *of* authority. The spirit of God was at work within him from the moment he embraced the burden of the Lord and let the burden of the Lord embrace him. (Nehemiah 1:1-4) That was the transitional point in Nehemiah's life. He was never the same after prayer and fasting, taking on the burden of the Lord.

The spirit of God was at work within him from the moment he embraced the burden of the Lord and let the burden of the Lord embrace him.

As my spiritual Mom, Dr. Melodye Hilton says, "Loving life is a by-product of discovering your mission and becoming the person able to walk it out." [2]

Being a cupbearer is a high-ranking position, for a slave/servant, but God destined Nehemiah for greatness *as a leader* in the kingdom of God. As prestigious as being a cup-bearer was, it was simply a stepping stone in the design of heaven for where God would bring him, what God had for him, who he was becoming. For years Nehemiah was 'up close and personal' with King Artaxerxes of the Medo-Persian Empire, the largest, most powerful kingdom of that era. He learned leadership lessons with 'on the job training', observing a top-notch world leader daily; present for kingdom dinners with dignitaries of the Medes and Persians, and surrounding kingdoms.

Nehemiah's character was formed in humility as a servant among rulers preparing him for leadership and greatness. The Lord had positioned Nehemiah to encounter divine, kingly alliance and favor that would open doors of opportunity to rebuild and restore the land, heritage and freedom of God's chosen people. His purpose was bigger than he was. Leaving behind the known, comfortable, secure palace for uncertainty, risk, relocation and responsibilities. He didn't shrink back. Passion stirred within him. He fasted and prayed. He was in the vein, pulsing with the heartbeat of heaven. It changed how he saw himself, how he carried himself, from the inside out.

May His spirit ignite and transform each of us from the inside out. You are uniquely fashioned and destined for His kingdom purposes. No one can fulfill what He has called *you* to, nor can you fulfill what another has been called to. We each must find our place 'on the wall' as living stones. (1 Peter 2:5) Child of God pray this simple prayer: "Lord show me clearly Your vision and purpose, that I will pursue it wholeheartedly, following hard after You."

Nehemiah is a biblical model for rebuilding. He worked smarter not harder! First, he inspected the gates, he was an informed leader. He developed a plan of action and implemented it. This summarizes his rebuilding process. **The process is God's crucible. It's His means of pruning and refining us, as He accomplishes His purpose through us.**

5 step Nehemiah model:

1. Face the fear and do it anyway.
2. KNOW – actively flow in prophetic revelation (know & do) :
   a. know what you're called to do,
   b. know what you want,
   c. know what you need.
3. Procure and Prepare (Get supplies & support *before* you get there.)
4. Inspect, survey, and strategize –
5. Implement the plan. (Build & War while you War & Build – Just do it!)

The rebuilding of the wall of Jerusalem was miraculous. Their enemies opposed and mocked them, "What are those feeble Jews doing? Will they restore their wall? Will they offer sacrifices? Will they finish in a day? Can they bring the stones back to life from those heaps of rubble—burned as they are?" (Nehemiah 4:2)

Nehemiah had a God-given revelation knowledge of WHO he truly was in God. He understood his; *purpose*, wants and needs were for rebuilding, and moved in the confidence of his identity. Knowledge is power with prophetic revelation it is dunamis/dynamo, magnified God-power.

STRATEGIC, DISCIPLINED & READY

Nehemiah exercised great self-restraint, he knew how to be secretive and covert. As a servant-cupbearer he over-heard a LOT of private governmental transactions taking place at the table. He had learned to be close-mouthed. It was expected and required by the king.

> "... I set out during the night with a few others. *I had not told anyone* what my God had put in my heart to do for Jerusalem. There were no mounts with me except the one I was riding on. ... The officials did not know where I had gone or what I

> was doing, because *as yet I had said nothing* to the Jews, or the priests, or the nobles, or any others who would be doing the work." (Nehemiah 2:11-12, 16)

Loose lips sink ships. Very few of us could be as tight-lipped as Nehemiah. We would be tempted to post on social media a selfie of us standing by our horse at midnight, or post a "Nehemiah just checked into the Valley Gate" with a map pointing every friend, foe and Internet predator to our location. I truly believe that if Nehemiah had shared the vision and plans prematurely, there would have been a pre-emptive strike from the enemy, and the rebuilding of the wall would have ended before it began.

Next, Nehemiah stepped fully into his role as a leader. NOW he shared the vision, got buy-in *with those who would be doing the work* and began building. (Nehemiah 2:17-18) He shared the vision with his people, closing with words on how gracious the king had been toward him. This sealed buy-in for the people. They were under the authority, and covering of the king, with documentation to back that up!

Nehemiah was shrewd, he knew they had enemies and would experience opposition. He might have known their names from his 3 days of observing, watching and praying while in Jerusalem. No sooner did he share the vision to rebuild, get willing volunteers, and begin the work, then the opposition started. As the saying goes, the wolf only comes to the house where something is cooking.

> "But when Sanballat the Horonite, Tobiah the Ammonite official and Geshem the Arab heard about it, they mocked and ridiculed us. 'What is this you are doing?' they asked. 'Are you rebelling against the king?'" (Nehemiah 2:19-20)

It's not the punch that hits you the hardest that takes you out, it's the one you didn't see coming. God kept Nehemiah a step ahead of the enemy. The workers already knew that the king had sanctioned their work, so Sanballat's words didn't have any adverse impact on them at all. This initial strategy of the enemy did not deter them.

I love Nehemiah's reply! He exercised biblical principles of wisdom. "Do not answer a fool according to his folly, or you yourself will be like him. Answer a fool according to his folly, or he will be wise in his own eyes." (Proverbs 26:4-5) He did not ignore them, but did not answer their question. *He answered out of his identity, under the authority of the King of Kings,* as he said,

> "The God of heaven will give us success. We His servants will start rebuilding, but as for you, you have no share in Jerusalem or any historic right to it." (Nehemiah 2:20)

Nehemiah was strategic, he didn't begin with a random section of wall, he began with the gates – the only legitimate, daily entrance and exit points of access. Not only did Nehemiah begin by inspecting and rebuilding the gates, *he began with the lowest access point*, the Valley Gate. 'You're only as strong as your weakest link.' Nehemiah began inspection at their most vulnerable gate. We must keep this in mind as we rebuild our broken gates of today. **Nehemiah didn't start at the top, he began in the valley**.

Strategically, Nehemiah assigned different families to work on specific gates, 10 in total. The number 10 represents the perfection of divine order. God was rebuilding and re-establishing Jerusalem, representing His Church, in His divine order.

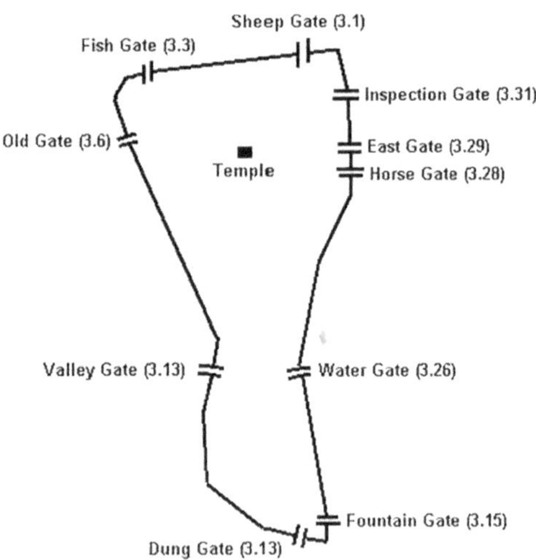

http://www.jesusplusnothing.com/studies/online/nehem3.htm

The enemy was relentless in continued attacks on Nehemiah and those building the wall. Mocking, ridicule, jeering, magnifying how broken-down the walls were. Their enemies worked to attack and shake their personhood, self-image, and confidence. Each time their enemies came at them they pressed into God in prayer. The rebuilding continued and flourished despite the opposition. Their enemies were incensed seeing the progress that the Jews were making, so they stepped up their game attacking them. **Has the enemy stepped up his attack? Perhaps**

even changed how he attacks you? It may be that you're making progress and moving closer to fulfilling His purposes in and through you! Satan is afraid.

Nehemiah was a leader of character with integrity and justice. He was in tune with what was going on among the people. He caught wind of the poor being oppressed among the workers and would have none of it. He was a strong leader, not afraid to stand up among his own people. (Nehemiah 5:1-13) He helped the poor, insisting on ways of justice and righteousness.

The Jews remained united in their resolve to press on and build despite threats, exhaustion and even hunger. Not everyone is called to be Nehemiah. There was only 1 Nehemiah, but there were many workers. Often you will serve and fulfill your purpose in securing gates by serving under a godly, noble leader who already has a plan in action. Serve well.

God gave the Jews strength and strategies to meet every challenge. They used the trumpet to sound the alarm and rally together as needed. They worked in shifts. Guards were posted at night, while others worked by day. In one hand was a sword to fight with and in the other a trowel to build. (Nehemiah 4:16-18) They built while they warred and warred while they built. Their enemy appeared relentless, but God is unstoppable. As we move in our true identity in Christ, we are more than conquerors!

They built while they warred and warred while they built. Their enemy appeared relentless, but God is unstoppable. When His people realize their true identity, and move in Him He makes them more than conquerors!

The best revenge is success! Overcoming the attacks and residue of reproach from their enemies: seeds of doubt, ridicule, threats on their lives, etc. The sheer enormity and feasibility of the task alone was great. Jerusalem's wall was: 2.5 miles around, 40 ft. high, 8 ft. thick, containing 34 watchtowers, and 7 main gates for traffic. Voile! The gates and walls were completely restored, without power tools, in record time, only 52 days! (Nehemiah 6:15)

Now that the gates and walls were restored, the people needed to be restored to their God-ordained purpose and function. God was re-establishing their identity in Him, not as slaves and servants, but as chosen, free men and women of worship. The gate keepers were among the first to be re-established.

The Gate Keepers

Gatekeepers held a sacred, position of trust and calling. One didn't apply to be a gatekeeper. There wasn't an ad placed in the paper, no job interviewing process, or letters of recommendation. There were many gatekeepers, over 200 in Jerusalem alone.

There were 3 criteria to be a gatekeeper, be:

1. a Levitical priest
2. a trusted, trustworthy individual
3. appointed by the king and prophet of the land

> *"Altogether, those chosen to be gatekeepers at the thresholds numbered 212. They were registered by genealogy in their villages. The gatekeepers had been assigned to their positions of trust by David and Samuel the seer.* [23] *They and their descendants were in charge of guarding the gates of the house of the LORD—the house called the tent of meeting. The gatekeepers were on the four sides: east, west, north and south. Their fellow Levites in their villages had to come from time to time and share their duties ..." (1 Chronicles 9:22-25)*

Levitical priests came from the tribe of Levi. In other words, you were born into it, or not. It was a matter of proven genealogy, requiring documentation. This became increasingly difficult over time as the Jews were displaced in the Babylonian exile for 70 years. Over time, hardships and captivity some Levites lost all or part of their documentation. (Ezra 2:62)

The name Levi means: attached, intertwined, unite, abide with, join and cleave to. A priest was to abide with and cleave to the Lord; representing the people to the Lord, and the Lord to the people.

The securing of city and temple gates was a priestly, holy calling and duty.

They (the Levites) and their descendants were in charge of guarding the gates of the house of the LORD—the house called the tent of meeting. The gatekeepers were on the four sides: east, west, north and south. Their fellow Levites in their villages had to come from time to time and share their duties for seven-day periods. But the four principal gatekeepers, who were Levites, were entrusted with the responsibility for the rooms and treasuries in the house of God. They would spend the night stationed around the house of God, because they had to guard it; and they had charge of the key for opening it each morning. (1 Chronicles 9:23-27)

Gatekeepers were given specific, designated responsibilities.

Some of them were in charge of the articles used in the temple service; they counted them when they were brought in and when they were taken out. Others were assigned to take care of the furnishings and all the other articles of the sanctuary, as well as the special flour and wine, and the olive oil, incense and spices. But some of the priests took care of mixing the spices. A Levite named Mattithiah, the firstborn son of Shallum the Korahite, was entrusted with the responsibility for baking the offering bread. Some of the Kohathites, their fellow Levites, were in charge of preparing for every Sabbath the bread set out on the table.

Those who were musicians, heads of Levite families, stayed in the rooms of the temple and were exempt from other duties because they were responsible for the work day and night.

All these were heads of Levite families, chiefs as listed in their genealogy, and they lived in Jerusalem. (1 Chronicles 9:28-34)

Gatekeepers are also referred to as watchmen in Scripture. The primary purpose and responsibility of the watchmen in the Old Testament were to:

- watch, guard
- warn
- grant access – or not
- worship

An intercessor is also considered a watchman, a prophetic priest of the Lord. Watchmen guard cities, are stationed on their walls and gates. (The walls of Jerusalem contained 34 watchtowers.)

> "when the watchman sees the sword coming against the land and blows the trumpet to warn the people, then if anyone hears the trumpet but does not heed the warning and the sword comes and takes their life, their blood will be on their own head. Since they heard the sound of the trumpet but did not heed the warning, their blood will be on their own head. If they had heeded the warning, they would have saved themselves. But if the watchman sees the sword coming and does not blow the trumpet to warn the people and the sword comes and takes someone's life, that person's life will be taken because of their sin, but I will hold the watchman accountable for their blood. Son of man, I have made you a watchman for the people of Israel; so hear the word I speak and give them warning from me." (Ezekiel 33:2-7)

Ezekiel 33 is a directive from the Lord letting watchmen/ intercessors know that if they see danger in the spirit they must do their part, and warn others. If they don't, whatever danger comes the Lord will hold them personally accountable. Conversely if people don't listen, that's not the intercessor's problem. Their duty before God is simply to give voice to it and warn others. Each individual is accountable before God.

That may seem easy, and on one level it is, but it can be very intimidating. Faithfully giving words of warning got Jeremiah beaten and held as a captive. (Jeremiah 38)

As a pastor and an intercessor, I have had to face down my own fears to give voice to what God has shown me. There was a couple in our church, Mike and Mindy (fictitious names) they were going through a very difficult period, frankly it looked like their marriage was rapidly approaching the 'end of the road'. God gave me a prophetic word to share with Mike and Mindy. He was putting His finger on the heart of their issue.

It wasn't an easy word that I had to share, but one that would bring healing if they could receive it. The Lord reminded me of Ezekiel 33. I spoke to my spirit and prayed, "If we lose them we lose them. But as their pastor I need to love them enough to speak the truth in love. I can't withhold what has the power to heal, even though it may hurt first. Fear can't be the basis of my decision making. Lord give me Your words, Your heart to share with." I faced the fear and shared anyway. It was hard, for me as well as for them, but they received the word. That was a decisive, turning point for them. They received the admonishment as from the Lord and ran with it. They are now doing well and have grown so much! My responsibility before God was simply to love them and be faithful to Him. They were responsible for their response; and the Lord takes responsibility to perform His word when we obey it.

PRACTICAL INSIGHT ABOUT PHYSICAL GATES

A gate is only as good as the framework and hardware it is constructed with. The framework that the gates are operating in is Family, the hardware is Communication. As in Nehemiah's day the gates framework and hardware needed repair.

The challenge with every gate is to build one that not only is stable and secure, but also can be opened and closed repeatedly without losing its structural integrity. The design must be strong and durable, the framework sturdy and the hardware, (screws, etc.) hinges, must be made of durable, long-lasting materials (ie; galvanized steel) – providing long-lasting security. [3]

Different types of real-life, physical gates are constructed differently, based upon their purpose, various security considerations must be made. There are yard gates, alley gates, highway gates/toll plazas, gates by bridges. Rarely does one see a literal city gates today. The most difficult part of securing a yard-gate is positioning it property between your fence posts so that the latch, lock or bolt lines up perfectly, making the gate secure. Now, with an alley-way gate there's nothing decorative about it. No handles, no hinges, on the outside of it – there's nothing for anyone to tamper with to enter the property. (The hinges are accessible from the inside only.)

All gates; physical, spiritual, metaphorical must have a framework that can properly handle what they are designed and constructed for. The strength of the gate is affected by what it is attached to on either side.

> <u>Fast fact</u>:
> It is much easier to install a gate with two people, with one person holding the gate, while the other person confirms alignment or uses shims as needed to adjust placement.

Two are better than one, because they have a good return for their labor. (Ecclesiastes 4:9) "One will chase a thousand, and two put ten thousand to flight". (Deuteronomy 32:30)

In addition to the materials gates are attached to, quality hardware is vital. My father was a general contractor, he built the house that I grew up in. The quality of his workmanship was outstanding. His workshop was in our basement, there was always the smell of sawdust in the air and it was filled with premium power tools. One day, when I was hanging with him, he said to me, "Janet, I want you to remember a life-lesson, whatever you do, invest in your tools, buy quality at the start. If you don't you'll spend twice as much money repairing and replacing the lesser expensive ones. It's worth it in the long run to have quality." He lived what he spoke. We weren't rich by any standards, but the tools of his trade were top of the line. I honestly don't remember them breaking or having down time.

With our tools we both build and war. Nehemiah also built with sword and trowel; building supplies and weapons of war. We advance likewise, standing on His promises:

> I will make your battlements of rubies,
> your gates of sparkling jewels,
> and all your walls of precious stones.
> All your children will be taught by the LORD,
> and great will be their peace.

In righteousness you will be established:
Tyranny will be far from you;
you will have nothing to fear.
See, it is I who created the blacksmith
who fans the coals into flame
and forges a weapon fit for its work.
no weapon forged against you will prevail,
and you will refute every tongue that accuses you.
(Isaiah 54:12-14, 16-17)

CHAPTER 3

PRAYER

I have posted watchmen on your walls, Jerusalem;
they will never be silent day or night.
You who call on the LORD, give yourselves no rest,
and give him no rest till he establishes Jerusalem
and makes her the praise of the earth (Isaiah 62:6-7)

INTERCESSORS ARE GATEKEEPERS AND WATCHMEN on the walls. **Securing the gates of a city can only be successfully accomplished through prayer.** It is a holy, priestly calling and duty.

The strongest place to stand in prayer is in humility, acknowledging we don't know how to pray as we ought. Jesus' disciples could ask Him anything – they asked "Lord, teach us how to pray." (Luke 11:1)

E.M. Bounds said, "**Prayer is the best school for learning how to pray**." Sometimes we have so much to lay down, it takes a while to quiet our Spirit. "Seek first His kingdom and His righteousness, and all these things will be added to you." (Matthew 6:33)

Someone asked is there a difference between someone who prays and an intercessor. The answer is yes and no. We're all called to pray, but not everyone is an intercessor. There are many types of prayer, such as supplication, asking God for things. Many don't go beyond supplication. **Intercession goes beyond asking for things into the heartbeat of heaven**.

Jesus, the greatest intercessor of all time is interceding for you and I! Covering us in love, He is our role-model and standard.

> *"Therefore, he is able to save completely, those who come to God through him, because <u>he always lives to intercede for them</u>." (Hebrews 7:25)*

> *"My intercessor is my friend as my eyes pour out tears to God; <u>on behalf of a man he pleads with God as one pleads for a friend</u>." (Job 16:20-21)*

> *"because the Spirit intercedes for God's people in accordance with the will of God. ... Who then is the one who condemns? No one. Christ Jesus who died—more than that, who was raised to life—is <u>at the right hand of God and is also interceding for us</u>." (Romans 8:27, 34)*

An intercessor is a priest, carrying the burden of the people to the Lord in prayer, and the heart and voice of the Lord to the people. "He who dwells in the secret place of the Most High, shall abide under the shadow of the Almighty." (Psalm 91:1)

Once in the 'secret place' an intimate exchange takes place, God shares His heart and plans as He communes with us. Then we are no longer simply 'boots on the ground infantryman'. **We are fellow partakers that direct and administrate His will, on earth as it is in heaven; according to His say-so, revealed as we are seated with Him in heavenly places.** (Ephesians 2:6) We then move in our God-given authority to invoke and advance His kingdom here on earth. Knowing His heart and voice we decree and declare it, and command the day! (Job 38:12)

> *"Fellow heirs and fellow members of the body, and fellow partakers of the promise in Christ Jesus ... so that the manifold wisdom of God might now be made known through the church to the rulers and the authorities in the heavenly places."* (Ephesians 3:6, 10)

> *"His divine power has given us everything we need for a godly life through our knowledge of him who called us by his own glory and goodness. For by these He has granted to us His precious and magnificent promises, so that by them you may become partakers of the divine nature,"* (2 Peter 1:3-4, NASB)

> *"Your kingdom come, Your will be done, on earth as it is in heaven."* (Matthew 6:10)

Intercession is one of the primary roles of priests. Who is called to be a priest? All who are believers in Jesus Christ. For "you are a chosen people, *a royal priesthood,* a holy nation, God's special possession, that you may declare the praises of him who called you out of darkness into his wonderful light." (1 Peter 2:9)

An intercessor is like a Marine, one of the first ones in and the last ones out! Intercessors are birthing agents! Nothing happens without prayer, but through prayer we establish His will on earth as it is in heaven. Through prayer we are forerunners, fellow-partakers, sharing in His divine nature, ruling and reigning with Him! Intercessors are modern-day, pioneer trail-blazers. **Through prayer; watchmen receive prophetic revelation and empowerment to advance and secure the kingdom**.

"I need My intercessors. You have entered into a time of the Tabernacle of David being exemplified and emerging in the earth. All religious culture across the earth must now shift. Be willing to be the Judah expression that creates MY prototype for the future. ... If you will shift into a new time of worship and declaration, I will set 'ambushments' for your enemies. If not, they will ambush you. By My hand, I have set things for you to discover as you walk out your day. From the new prototype of war, praise, and leadership that I am arising in the earth, I WILL have a harvest of your enemies. The structure is in the Blood and My Blood overcomes every other structure. But My Blood must be appropriated! I will have a people who bind the strongman and take his captured wealth."[3] (Excerpted word by Chuck Pierce.)

Many are called, but few are chosen. (Matthew 22:14, NASB) Why is that? Not everyone makes the investment of time, focus and self-discipline that it will require of them. Many want the robes, title and position, but not the cost.

CONSECRATION as PRIESTS

There is a consecration of ourselves that needs to take place. Moses consecrated Aaron and his sons, the very first Levitical priests.

> "*the ram of ordination*, ... Moses then took some of its blood and put it on Aaron's right earlobe, on the thumb of his right hand, and on the big toe of his right foot." And then did the same with Aaron's sons. (Leviticus 8:23-27)

Why was a ram used as the priests were ordained? In many ancient societies the ram was a symbol of: determination, action, initiative, and leadership. In the Bible the ram represents protection as the ram protected the herd. It also symbolizes sacrifice as the ram was one of the first animals to be sacrificed on altars. The ram was the substitute for Isaac.

Why not a lamb? Both the lamb and ram are symbolic of Christ. The ram is more aggressive. The Lamb that was slain was docile, peaceful, submitted unto death – the Lamb that was slain for the forgiveness of our sins. **God's priestly intercessors take on the many characteristics of God, including that of a warrior.**

"God is a warrior." (Exodus 15:3) **Intercessors have determination and tenacity to press in and do battle in spiritual warfare.** The enemy is not rolling over and playing dead. Satan is at war, there is a clashing of kingdoms. Jack Hayford says, "True intercession is actually twofold. One aspect is asking God for divine intervention; the other is destroying the works of Satan." [1]

Ed Silvoso said, "**Without God you can't. Without you He won't.**" [2] The gates of hell shall not prevail! *Obtain your keys and strategies for securing victory in the secret place.*

Consecrate yourself for godliness and intercession as Moses consecrated Aaron and his sons. The blood of the ram was smeared *on ear, hand & foot.* This was a prophetic act of consecration as priests, who were intercessors, were ordained.

> Ear – hearing and discerning the voice of God. Jesus would only do what He heard the Father say. (John 5:19) He set a high standard as a priest according to the order of Melchizedek.
>
> Hand – represents ministry. Jesus told us that whatever our hand finds to do, do so with all of our might as unto the Lord, not men. The Lord establishes the work of our hands. (1 Samuel 10:7; Ecclesiastes 9:10; Colossians 3:23; Psalm 90:17)
>
> Foot – When we walk it should be as the foot print of God. With our feet God increases the dominion of His kingdom on earth. Wherever the sole of your foot will tread I have given it to you. It was as priests stepped foot in the Jordan River that the waters, which were at flood stage, parted. (Joshua 3)

Set apart, set aside as holy our ears, hands and feet. Many are called, but few are chosen. We are created to be called *and* chosen – the choice is ours. How committed are you?

Intense intercession and repentance has always been a noted precursor to revival. Repentance and intercession are primary keys to: secure gates, strengthen a people, bring divine favor, unlock strategies, receive blessing, gain ground, loose a mighty outpouring of His Spirit and Presence. There are other keys but identity is the master key and prayer is the other essential key.

"I have looked down upon My cities," says the Lord. "I am placing the eagles over My cities as the watchmen who tower into the skies. Every city will have watchmen on the walls, watchmen from within, and watchmen in the skies. I am sending My eagles up into the skies to see far out in advance in order to warn My people of distant trouble. **As prophetic voices, we must speak into the nations, political realms, states, and regions where we reside. Natural battles are always won through the power of prayer joined with unified hearts."**[4] (Excerpted prophetic word by Andy Sanders.)

Repentance and intercession are primary keys to: secure gates, strengthen a people, bring divine favor, unlock strategies, receive blessing, gain ground, loose a mighty outpouring of His Spirit and Presence.

Abiding in the secret place of the Most High, we are in alignment with Him. (Psalm 91:1) In His Presence our sense of self and identity become anchored in Him.

"In short, our vulnerabilities and weaknesses as a nation—economically, spiritually, morally or otherwise, have a deeper root than the failures of human management or policy.

... Unless a **reawakening** of Christ's body in America occurs, of **prayer and intercession** for leaders, peoples and nations, no administration or political party will be capable of a solution to our nation's essential problems.

... Unless the church ... humbles ourselves, seeking God's presence (more than it demonstrates our skill at making music)—no degree of programming or growth will be able to regain the place of influence the once-effective voice the church historically has had in the U.S. as 'salt', to neutralize the toxic issues existing in the arena of morality, justice and family life." [5]

Through prayer and intercession, the church is empowered to take back and bear fruit in her inherent, God-given dynamic to affect the spiritual climate of our nation and effect a harvest of the 'fruit of righteousness' ... to leave a deep enough stamp on the national life to indicate a credible, spiritual presence.

Prayer is on the rise in our nation! Springing up increasingly over the last decade are national and global prayer watches, networks, and houses of prayer. I have participated in some of these. Listed here is a sampling of houses of prayer and networks. (This is not a comprehensive list.):

- Large organized prayer movements such as Reformation Prayer Network, Global Prayer Network, One Cry, and many others (visit www.project-pray.org/links-to-prayer-organizations for a more extensive list)

- National prayer & fasting events such as: Facedown 40, Asuza Now/ The Call, Esther Fast & Prayer, On The Wall, and numerous others
- Houses of Prayer (Bethel, International House Of Prayer, Kansas City House of Prayer, Eastern Gate House of Prayer, Times Square House Of Prayer, and more) for a broader list visit www.ihopnetwork.com
- Intercessors, organized and networked are on the rise. The more we are united in prayer the greater the yoke that will be broken. Father God says, "I am raising groups of strategic, prophetic intercessors across the land and in the nations to take back the gates."

However, **it doesn't take large numbers to be effectual**; bringing down corruption and deception, establishing His kingdom on earth. **Small micro-groups of fearless intercessory warriors hearing from heaven, praying with humility, authority, in one accord are dismantling strongholds**. These micro-groups are akin to our elite forces, ie; Navy Seals, Green Berets, Delta, Force, and others. 2-5 believers of world shaking history-makers humbly, fervently praying in Jesus' name behind closed doors. The Father takes great delight in that type of intercession, where the only One who is glorified is Jesus. The power of one is mighty, with God you are a majority!

There is great reward for your labor of love and faithful prayers of intercession, that are poured out before the Father in secret. He sees, He knows, and your reward will be from Him. (Revelation 22:12) Cornelius received angelic visitation because his prayers and offering to the poor came up before God. (Acts 10:4) The most important reward of all is intimacy with HIM.

God wants vessels of His presence! For example, in the book of Daniel there was a mark of excellence upon Daniel, Shadrach, Meshach and Abednego. They moved with extraordinary wisdom, understanding, and outright revelation that was recognized by the secular power-players of Babylon. They outperformed, outshined everyone else around them. They had creative, revelatory answers and solutions that their peers didn't. They were a united group of fervent, praying believers, who walked in their God-given identity. They wouldn't compromise, even if it meant their life. In unparalleled unity and one accord they had each other's back. A handful of believers coming together in intercession can dramatically impact the world!

PRAYING FOR THOSE IN LEADERSHIP

First of all, then, I urge that entreaties and prayers, petitions *and thanksgivings, be made on behalf of all men, for kings and all who are in authority, so that we may lead a tranquil and quiet life in all godliness and dignity. (1 Timothy 2:1-2)*

A clashing of kingdoms, a type of 'civil war' has commenced. It is seen in the natural, but is spiritual in nature. It has created a 'dividing line', even within the Church. I was taken aback when a pastor emphatically told me that they would NOT pray for President Trump. We can't pick and choose which part of the Word we want to embrace while ignoring others. It is time to be all-in, not for a person or a candidate, for the Lord and His ways! God told us to pray for ALL who are in authority. Not necessarily the ones we like, or voted for – He simply said for ALL in authority. He said what He meant.

Startlingly about a month after President Donald Trump took office witches publicly gathered to cast a mass spell/curse on him. The witches pledged to cast a spell under each crescent moon until Trump would no longer be president. [6] Whatever your position in politics is or is not, as Christians we do not want to find ourselves praying in agreement with witches, warlocks, and their spells!

Whatever your position in politics is or is not, we do not want to find ourselves as Christians praying in agreement with witches, warlocks, and their spells!

"You will reap what you sow" (Galatians 6:7). Do you want to receive a double portion of blessings or curses? We are in a season of the double portion. The double portion can be a double-edged sword. (Galatians 6:7) If you sow blessing you reap a double portion of blessing, if cursing, you reap a double portion of evil.

Warning – Bless and do not curse. God is not playing!

It's also a turn-around season where curses are being reversed! A time when situations, organizations and systems change in a positive direction. God has drawn a line, this far and no further. "Do not touch my anointed ones and do my prophets no harm!" (1 Chronicles 16:22 ; Psalm 105:15)

CAUTION: Pay attention to how you are praying.

There are consequences for witchcraft prayers. Witchcraft prayers invoke evil upon the head of others, they malign and slander.

CAUTION: Pay attention to how you pray.

There are consequences for witchcraft prayers. Witchcraft prayers invoke evil upon the head of others, they malign and slander.

"Woe to those who draw sin along with
cords of deceit,
and wickedness as with cart ropes, ...
Woe to those who call evil good
and good evil,
who put darkness for light
and light for darkness,

> who put bitter for sweet
> and sweet for bitter.
> Woe to those who are wise in their own eyes
> and clever in their own sight." (Isaiah 5:18,20-21)

> "Woe to the obstinate children,"
> declares the LORD,
> "to those who carry out plans that are not mine,
> forming an alliance, but not by my Spirit,
> heaping sin upon sin;
> who go down to Egypt
> without consulting me;
> who look for help to Pharaoh's protection,
> to Egypt's shade for refuge.
> But Pharaoh's protection will be to your shame,
> Egypt's shade will bring you disgrace." (Isaiah 30:1-3)

Be careful. **Let's keep our prayers pure by keeping emotions and personal preferences in check.** Before we can repent on behalf of our family or a nation we must first repent for ourselves, or we may be off-center in our praying. Whether we're right wing, left wing, broken wings – get into His Presence until the only wing we see is that of the Holy Spirit. **"For my thoughts are not your thoughts, neither are your ways my ways," declares the LORD. As the heavens are higher than the earth, so are my ways higher than your ways and my thoughts than your thoughts."** (Isaiah 55:8-9) Good, better, best – best isn't our way, it's His. True and pure intercession is being in His Presence, hearing, Him and giving voice to the heart, desire of God above our own desires! Declaring what He says and calling it forth.

True and pure intercession is being in His Presence, hearing, Him and giving voice to the heart of God above your own Thy will be done, not my will be done!

UNITY

Divine synergy occurs in unity. **Unity reflects a key divine attribute of the Godhead.** The Trinity, three in One; Father, Son and Holy Spirit. God gave Man authority to rule, He did so in the context of Unity. As it is written, "Then God said, "Let *us* make mankind *in our image*, *in our likeness*, so *that they may rule* over the fish in the sea and the birds in the sky, over the livestock and all the wild animals, and over all the creatures that move along the ground." (Genesis

1:26) **When the Church, moves in unity, His image and likeness are more fully reflected.**

Wearing our crown, carrying the sword of the Spirit *as one*, we will change the world. "One of us can cause a thousand to flee and two of us 10,000." The best sports coaches, and military personnel, cultivate this principle. "The strength of team is each individual. The strength of each individual is team." (Phil Jackson)

God mantle us for a new season of prayer and intercession! An army of intercessors is arising, in diversity and unity; multi-racial, multi-cultural, multi-generational, male and female. **We are warriors on the frontlines**, not content to let our families, government, or any of the mountains slip away.

History and our Now

Past traumas and injustices leave a mark upon the land and its people. Unhealed hurt opens the door for demonic, Satanic activity. Know the history of the geographic area where you live and the land(s) you are called to.

In the USA our history is deep and wide; in addition to slavery and injustice against African-Americans, Native Americans experienced extreme injustices, Chinese-Americans were enslaved in order to build the trans-continental railroad, Japanese-Americans were prejudiced against and held in 'determent camps' during WWII, women were treated as 2nd class citizens (1920's won the right to vote, 1930's secured the right to an education), there's been racism against Mexican and Latino-Americans, and the list goes on. (More is said about this in chapters 5 & 7 on *Freedom* and *Prejudice in the Gates.*) Let's be specific when we pray naming the offenses and wounds that need healing in our lives, our families, cities, regions, and country. **As priestly intercessors we stand in the gap between heaven and earth, man and God. We can repent on behalf of our ancestors and our land.**

We cry out Father heal our land, but often our prayers are hindered by our own bitterness.

We cry out Father heal our land, but often our prayers are hindered by our own bitterness. **Forgiveness begins as a choice, not a feeling,** and continues as we pray.

Walking in forgiveness and righteousness brings greater effectualness in our prayers. "For if you forgive other people when they sin against you, your heavenly Father will also forgive you. But if you do not forgive others their sins, your Father will not forgive your sins." (Matthew 6:14-15)

Prayer:

"Lord where I have harbored hatred and/or bitterness in my heart, spoken and/or prayed against ___________ please forgive me. Disregard and void those hurtful, evil things I've thought in my heart and/or said. Wash me by the blood of Jesus. I need Your help to forgive them. I feel so hurt and violated, but I choose to forgive ______________. Please pour Your grace upon me, I need it. Uproot my bitterness and anger. Cleanse me. I choose Your will and Your way Lord Jesus."

Understanding our history gives insight into our 'now' and the territorial spirits vying for dominion over regions. That knowledge mixed with revelation and the prayer of faith is the TNT that can bring down strongholds.

Knowledge is power. I am amazed at how ill-informed Americans are on international affairs. The average American is ignorant of current events, especially on a global level. Our media keeps us ignorant and ill-informed of the culture and current events of Asia. We are largely ignorant of World powers such as China and India. A friend of ours in Bangladesh assisted victims of the worst flooding they've had in over 200 years. The flooding effected over 20 million, killing over 1,000. USA news scarcely made mention of it.

Amazing revival will be coming out of Asia. **We need to be conversant with the lands, nations and their people to pray effectively**. (Do not rely on USA news for international coverage, be sure to check out BBC and Al-Jazeera for more comprehensive international coverage. (Al-Jazeera however will contain an Arab, Islamic bias.)

On a national level most of the news we receive is loaded with bias. Use chapters 6-11 as food for prayer. They contain an overview of national and global current events of the shifting, a 'status of the world'. As you pray into the things in those chapters God will give you prophetic revelation. Become one of God's eagles in prayer. Pray prophetically over those areas – you will secure gates and become a world changer and kingdom shaker.

Warfare – Keep Pressing

When we see breakthroughs, praise Him and rejoice, but DON'T STOP! Press in all the more!

The Church, will be seeing many breakthroughs and turn-arounds! When we see breakthroughs, praise Him and rejoice, but DON'T STOP! Press in more! Watchmen are given a charge to, "give yourselves no rest, and give him no rest till he establishes Jerusalem and makes her the praise of the earth" (Isaiah 62:7) Too often Christians storm the gates, get lost in praise and celebration and then lose momentum. Keep pressing in! Please do not hear what I am not saying. It is good and fitting to praise and rejoice, in Him as victories are won, but if we stop there then we stop advancing. Picture storming castle gates. What self-respecting army would stop and have a party once the doors of the gates were battered in?! No, they'd storm through the gates, de-throne the old ruler, and possess it. Christians conversely storm the gates with great vigor and zeal. Then they stop have a Hallelujah party, relax and go home. Securing the gates, possessing and advancing is an *on-going*, God-ordained, responsibility we each have.

Jeremiah 51:30 speaks of enemy forces flagging in their warfare, "Babylon's warriors have stopped fighting; they remain in their strongholds. Their strength is exhausted; they have become weaklings." The picture here is of the enemy appearing as weaklings. Why? Because they stopped fighting and went back to their strongholds. **When breakthrough happens – go in for the kill! Have no mercy upon the enemy! That's when occupancy and possession, not just breakthrough, should become ours.**

"Those things you were not sure about in past seasons, the things you didn't know if you should step into, I'm going to show you. I'm going to show you how to step. I'm going to show you how to press. I'm going to teach your hands to battle and your fingers to war at a new level. I'm giving intercessors new strategies for this season. I'm giving intercessors new tactics in this season, even new weapons in this season. The righteous are as bold as a lion."[7] This was prophesied by Jennifer LeClaire.

We must be radical warriors in prayer, driving out kingdoms that are stronger than we are, but not stronger than He is! (Deuteronomy 7:1-9)

There are already multitudes of angels on assignment to shift the atmosphere across America and the world.

MINIMIZE CASUALTIES of WAR – Cover yourself, your family & your ministry

Each morning before your feet hit the floor say good morning to the Lover of your soul. Keep your relationship and intimacy with Father, Son and Holy Spirit fresh. In the natural one first puts on undergarments and clothing before protective gear. *Then*, put the full armor of God. (Ephesians 6) Look to the Lord who will guard your going out and your coming in (Psalm 121:7-8).

Its real warfare, in real warfare there can be injuries – cover yourself and your family first with the blood of Christ, especially *before* and *after* engaging in deliverance and/or warfare prayer. Cover the most vulnerable, or spiritually weakest member(s) of your family with the blood and name of Jesus Christ. We must be prudent and responsible warriors minimizing casualties of war while maximizing the reach and depth of our victories.

Wash our robes daily, in His blood, through repentance. "Blessed are those who wash their robes, that they may have the right to the tree of life and may *go through the gates* into the city." (Revelation 22:14)

We must be prudent and responsible warriors minimizing casualties of war while maximizing the reach and depth of our victories.

Be part of the bigger picture, rather than the lone ranger. Being in relationship, part of His family is God's design. In addition to being under and submitted to authority, we need the covering of our leaders.

Intentionally build intercessory teams. Ask others for their prayer support. **The greater your sphere of influence the greater the need for prayer.** Ministers I know have enlisted a large core of intercessors committed to praying for them. We need to have each other's back.

The gates are the points of entry and exit. Hell wants them. Anticipate attacks, keep your shield of faith up. (Ephesians 6:16) Don't be filled with fear, but don't be unwise – be proactive and strategize. When coming against strongholds walk in a corporate anointing whenever possible. When Jesus sent his disciples out He sent them out two by two. (Luke 10:1) One of us will cause a thousand to flee, but two of us 10,000. (Dt. 32:30)

After intense times of prayer saturate and bathe yourself in the word and worship.

DYING

Perhaps the most poignant prayer of Jesus' was simply, "My Father, if it is not possible for this cup to be taken away unless I drink it, *may your will be done*." (Matthew 26:42) Dying to self is a daily process. Pray, "Lord I will do what you say do. I will say what You say. I will go where You say 'Go.' I am Yours. I surrender my will to Your will. Have YOUR way in me Lord."

In the movie *Braveheart*, Mel Gibson played the part of William Wallace. At the end as he was awaiting his death, which he knew would be painful. William Wallace lifted his eyes heavenward, voicing a short, sincere prayer, "Lord help me to die well." Each of us are called to die to self. Jesus was plain, ""***Whoever wants to be my disciple must deny themselves and take up their cross daily and follow***

***me.*'"** (Luke 9:23) Let us echo William Wallace's prayer, "Lord, help me to die well." in this battle between the flesh and the spirit.

GETTING OUT of the BOX
Strategic & Prophetic Intercession

We are in a season of strategic, effectual praying. Where we pray, what we pray, when we pray, how we pray, who to pray with, when to fast, how to fast – strategic keys are being given. **An unprecedented gateway of prophetic revelation is opening-up.** God is not only raising an army of intercessors, within that army, some will be called into 'special forces' for special ops (operations).

Intercessors often are given a seer anointing showing them how to pray. *Decisive victories will be won in our families, our country and the nations, on our knees through revelation, in prophetic intercession.* His house is a house of prayer. He is building His church upon the rock of revelation! (Matthew 16:15-19)

<u>PRAYER WALKS</u>

> "Every place on which the sole of your foot treads shall be yours; ... No man will be able to stand before you; the LORD your God will lay the dread of you and the fear of you on all the land on which you set foot, as He has spoken to you." (Deuteronomy 11:24-25; Joshua 1:3)

This principle is like The Homestead Act of 1862 which allowed for citizens to claim land, with a mere ten dollars, claiming a homestead of up to 160 acres of government land, and "improve" the land by putting it to use as a family plot. This meant erecting a dwelling and farming the soil for a period of five years. If the claimant did so they could then gain ownership of their land free of charge.

Today we walk in our Father's shoes, and authority. He is in us and we are in Him. **Our footprints are His footprints, walking in divine mandate. We are placing the footprint of God on our land, staking our claim; taking back the kingdom in Jesus' name.**

As we walk we literally put our foot on the neck of our enemies. As Joshua said to his leaders in Joshua 10:24-25, "Come near, put your feet on the necks of these kings." So they came near and put their feet on their necks. Then Joshua said to them, "Do not fear or be dismayed! Be strong and courageous, for thus the LORD will do to all your enemies with whom you fight."

In authority we take ownership as we decisively, prayerfully put our foot on the land. We are taking territories and regions, one step at a time as we walk and pray! Prayer walks are organized by individuals, churches, and regions. Some of them are formally organized, others informally.

They range in size from 1-15 participants. (Large groups become more of a march.) For small groups you don't need to pull permits or get special permission from the city government. Prayer walks aren't loud, flashy events. The most important thing on a prayer walk is to walk and pray. Prophetically decree and declare as the Holy Spirit directs putting your foot on the land in the name of Jesus Christ.

One suggestion for a city prayer walk, is to have a prayer team stationed at each gate of your city, to the north, south, east ad west. It is ideal for prayer groups to represent diversity: various churches ethnicities, gender, etc. This is best to coordinate with local pastors. Let God show you what the focus for your city and each gate should be. Wow! The power of literally **securing every gate or access point in your city with diverse, but unified corporate prayer. You can shift your city for Jesus!**

There are many other prayer strategies for transforming our cities. One model includes 'adopt a street' and/or cop praying daily for them. Ed Silvoso, has initiated this powerfully at home and abroad. "We can change the spiritual climate through a lifestyle of prayer evangelism! Pray daily using Jesus' 4 simple steps outlined in the gospel of Luke, chapter 10." [8] (Learn more about prayer evangelism at www.transformourworld.org). Newark, NJ and many other cities saw a dramatic reduction and turn-around in crime, over 30% reduction, as streets were adopted and consistently prayed over.

- Bless – Speak peace to every house (Luke 10:5)
- Fellowship – Discover their felt need (Luke 10:7)
- Minister – Ask God to meet that need (Luke 10:9a)
- Proclaim – That the kingdom of God has come near (Luke 10:9)

Here are examples of 2 *strategic* prayer walks held in the NY and NJ area. There are myriads of prayer walks taking place across the nation. (It is important to note a prayer walk is not a million-man march. These prayer walks were with a handful of people 3-12.) One prayer walk only the facilitator showed up (me). I walked and prayed anyway. You and God are a majority.

1. Prayer walk in the Wall Street district of NYC:
   LOCATION: A key financial district in America and the world.
   DATE: The 1st day of Elul, a significant month on the Hebrew calendar. Elul is a significant month which led to the 40 days of repentance. It was

on the same month Jonah preached for 40 days and Nineveh repented, Jesus's 40 days in the wilderness and 40 days Moses in the mountain after the children of Israel sinned worshiping the Golden calf -all fell on the 1st of Elul. The month of Elul is marked by repentance and ends with the celebration of Rosh Hoshanah, the feast of trumpets, marking the Jewish new year.
TIMING: A solar eclipse also occurred ahead of the new moon on the 1st of Elul. The walk was planned during the historic solar eclipse.
FOCUS: The theme or focus of the walk was repentance on behalf of our nation.
ANCHOR SCRIPTURES: Hebrews 3:7-8; 2 Chronicles 7:14

2. Prayer walk at Liberty State Park, NJ
LOCATION: A key gateway in America. The Statue of Liberty, an iconic symbol for the nation and of liberty is there. It is on the harbor of the Hudson between NJ & NYC. Angelic presence is felt there in the winds.
DATE: Held just before Father's Day.
TIMING: high noon
FOCUS: To declare the Fatherhood of God over our nation.
ANCHOR SCRIPTURE: Malachi 4:6, *"He will turn the hearts of the parents to their children, and the hearts of the children to their parents; or else I will come and strike the land with total destruction."*

In each of these walks diverse groups of people came together: Asians, African-Americans, Latinos, whites; male, female, and a mix of various churches. The Lord declares His blessing in unity. (Psalm 133; Matthew 18:20) We were 'boots on the ground' placing the footprint of God on the land, reclaiming territory for His kingdom. We prophetically interceded, in the authority of the King of Kings and Lord of Lords declaring His decrees over the land.

If you've never been on a prayer walk I encourage and challenge you to move out of your comfort zone. **This is a strategic time and season to move beyond the walls and doors of the church building.** Out of the seats and into the streets! Put your foot on it. Charge the atmosphere with worship, praise and prophetic intercession – under an open sky. We're taking back our neighborhoods, schools, and government. **We can make a difference everyday right where we live, as we literally *walk* in Christ!**

Shifting Regions & Prophetic Acts

Prophetic acts are powerful, God inspired, visual declarative statements of authority that put the spirit realm into motion. A prophetic act is an action given by the Holy Spirit, done with faith and authority that becomes a sign and a decree to the spirit realm. We don't think it up on our own, or do it because someone else did it, it is a God breathed directive of action.

There are many examples of prophetic acts in the Bible. Here is a sampling of biblical prophetic acts. (This is not a comprehensive list.):

a. When the prodigal returned the Father threw his robe around him. He was tangibly expressing his son's complete redemption and restoration to the fullness of his position and covering, including that of royalty. (Luke 15:11-32)
b. Shooting and striking the ground with arrows was prophetically symbolic of victory over enemy armies. (2 Kings 13:17-19)
c. Jesus washes his disciples' feet, a prophetic act of serving and humility. (John 13)

Then, this prophetic act (from Joshua 4) God told His people to create a monument, by piling stones on top of one another. God did this as a testimony to Israel of His goodness and greatness, and as a declaration that they were about to dispossess nations in the Promised Land. (He caused all the other lands to dread and fear them. Dt. 2:25) This occurred as the Israelites crossed the Jordan to enter and take possession of the Promised Land, their God-given inheritance.

> "So Joshua called together the twelve men he had appointed from the Israelites, one from each tribe, and said to them, "Go over before the ark of the LORD your God into the middle of the Jordan. Each of you is to take up a stone on his shoulder, according to the number of the tribes of the Israelites, to serve as a sign among you. In the future, when your children ask you, *'What do these stones mean?' tell them that the flow of the Jordan was cut off before the ark of the covenant of the LORD. When it crossed the Jordan, the waters of the Jordan were cut off. These stones are to be a memorial to the people of Israel forever."*
>
> So the Israelites did as Joshua commanded them. They took twelve stones from the middle of the Jordan, according to the number of the tribes of the Israelites, as the LORD had told Joshua; and they carried them over with them to their camp, where they put them down. Joshua set up the twelve stones

> that had been in the middle of the Jordan at the spot where the priests who carried the ark of the covenant had stood. **And they are there to this day.**
>
> "In the future when your descendants ask their parents, 'What do these stones mean?' tell them, 'Israel crossed the Jordan on dry ground.' ... **He did this so that all the peoples of the earth might know that the hand of the LORD is powerful and so that you might always fear the LORD your God.**" (Joshua 4:4-9, 20-22, 24)

During some of our prayer walks the Holy Spirit has directed us in prophetic acts. It has been powerful, one could feel the shift in the atmosphere and the dominion of God established.

There isn't a chapter and verse for every prophetic act the Holy Spirit may lead you to do, but they will be aligned with and compliment the Word of God. For instance, during Rosh Hashana the eating of apple slices dipped in honey is a Jewish tradition. This is done as a declaration that the new year will be sweet, fruitful, healthy and prosperous. Eating apple slices dipped in honey is not delineated in the Word as part of the Feast of Trumpets, but it makes a poignant, spiritual impact as Rosh Hashana is observed.

Examples of prophetic acts that I or my contemporaries have participated in, on behalf cities and regions (These are examples, not a comprehensive list. Be led by the Spirit.):

1. A black man washing a white woman's feet as a white woman washes a black man's feet. Each stood as a representative of their race repenting with humility for prejudice and injustices committed.
2. Placing a peg or tent-stake in the ground on the property of the county seat of government, proclaiming and staking claim of God's promises and kingdom in the city and county.
3. Marching around a building 7x, while blowing the shofar – as we decreed that the barriers and walls of opposition would crumble.

There are many other examples of prophetic acts, these are just a few.

Hearing God In Order to Pray Effectively

Each time we enter the 'secret place' (Psalm 91:1) we hear Him. He speaks to us outside of prayer meetings as well as in: a song on the radio, a person's comment in the supermarket, imagery (ie; a reflection of a rainbow in a car window over a child), dreams and visions, physical manifestations, and more.

Dreams & Visions

God uses dreams to talk to us. They are a means of guidance that God has used for over 4,000 years. More guidance through dreams and visions will continue to flow in these end times. "*'In the last days, God says, I will pour out my Spirit on all people. Your sons and daughters will prophesy, your young men will see visions, your old men will dream dreams. Even on my servants, both men and women, I will pour out my Spirit in those days, and they will prophesy.*'" (Joel 2:28; Acts 2:17-18) Some dreams are a product of our subconscious, but many are from the Holy Spirit. May God sharpen our discernment to know which is which and accurately interpret what the Spirit is saying. When God speaks in a dream it is prophetic. Does God speak in dreams to some more than others? Yes. I'm open to however He wants to speak to me.

The first dream recorded in the Bible (not necessarily the first dream, but the first one recorded) is in Genesis 28:10-22. In that dream Jacob, "saw a stairway resting on the earth, with its top reaching to heaven, and the angels of God were ascending and descending on it." (Genesis 28:12) Through dreams you can ascend in the Spirit into another realm, beyond the1st heaven (earth's atmosphere), 2nd heaven (space), and even the 3rd heaven (before the throne of God).

God spoke audibly to Abraham, Isaac, and Jacob, but to Joseph He never spoke aloud, but communicated through dreams. Joseph is often referred to as 'the dreamer'. Joseph and Daniel were most noted for interpreting dreams. The ability to interpret dreams got Joseph out of prison and gained great favor among rulers.

God speaks to me in dreams. Some people have long dreams, with plots, etc. The dreams I have are usually more of a 'snapshot', a picture/ vision, or a short vignette. You've heard the saying a picture is worth 1,000 words. Sometimes I literally hear a phrase, without a visual, wake up and write it down. *(It is important to record or write your dreams down ASAP or you may forget and miss key revelation from the Lord.) There are times when the interpretation of the dream is lengthier than the image/description of it. For example:

> Table Dream:
>
> I saw myself sleeping on top of my dining room table. Although it looked weird, and uncomfortable; in the dream I was *very* comfortable and cozy.

Interpretation of Table Dream:

> Upon awakening I asked the Lord what this meant. He directed me to His Word, "Prepare the table, watch in the watchtower, eat, drink: arise, ye princes, and anoint the shield. For thus hath the Lord said unto me, Go, set a watchman, let him declare what he seeth." (Isaiah 21:5-6, KJV) The Lord was telling me not only am I an intercessor, but He will speak to me, giving me revelation in my dreams that will show me divine strategies/keys how to pray. He is preparing a banqueting table of revelation in dreams as I sleep. He will give me insight, revelation, and strategies that will bring down strongholds of the enemy. Dreams will be a key means of His communication to me. (I keep a recording device and a notebook by my bedside.) Furthermore, He told me that I am to DECLARE what He reveals to me in dreams. The declarations will be made with authority, because it is His decree that is going out. He's simply allowing me to be His mouthpiece. He further spoke to my spirit that as I rest in Him, He will do it and bring this to pass. (In quietness and trust is your strength. – Isaiah 30:15)

Since then I have had dreams of revelation for regions and nations, as well as personally. The interpretation isn't always obvious to me immediately. I write the dreams down and hold them before God. At the proper time the Holy Spirit gives me the interpretation then I know clearly how to administrate His will in prayer on earth as in heaven.

Some dreams are sent as a warning or a clarion call for urgent intercession. There have been times when I didn't even have a dream per se, I was simply awoken with a pressing concern for a certain family member. When I'm in the middle of a deep sleep I'm tired, sluggish and not with it. The Holy Spirit is so awesome and keeps shaking me awake. One of our family members was deployed in Afghanistan. In the middle of the night the Holy Spirit woke me up with an urgency that took my breath away. I sensed life and death danger. Was it an angel that woke me up? I don't know. I just knew and was certain that there was an urgent life and death situation. I began to pray and intercede. This very overwhelming sense persisted so I continued to pray until it lifted. I noted the date and time in my prayer journal. We didn't hear from him for almost another 2 weeks, which had me on pins and needles. When we connected he expressed that he'd been in many tense situations and close calls, but on that date, at that exact hour, was the closest ever in a true near-death scenario.

This is what is meant by standing in the gap.

What if I hadn't woken up? What if in my groggy, tired state I hadn't obeyed the promptings to pray, rolled over and went back to sleep? There is a responsibility to intercede, even when or especially when, its inconvenient for us. May God ever increase our sensitivity, to obey Him.

Personal Physical Manifestations and Intercession

There are times when I have carried a burden to the point of literally feeling the physical pain of others. I never asked for that, it just happens on occasion. For example: My Aunt Ginny had knee replacement surgery. I prayed for her recovery and then went to sleep. In the middle of the night a searing pain jarred me awake. Piercing, burning pain in one of my knees. It was unbearable. I was writhing and doubled up in a fetal position. What was happening to me?! Then I remembered my aunt, discerned that the Lord wanted me to pray for her. I prayed, the pain subsided, and I fell back asleep, only to be awoken again in excruciating pain. This happened several times for a couple of hours. When talking with my aunt I described the pain I'd experienced. She was amazed that I had described her pain to the tee. She further said that no one had understood her pain. She didn't know how she made it through the pain that night. I explained to her Jesus was with her and woke me to pray her through it.

What is interesting is that this type of manifestation of personal pain is now taking on territorial significance. There is a shift in the sphere and area of influence and authority that He is giving me to carry. I am now feeling the wrestling of regional principalities and powers.

Here's an example: The Lord directed me to take a prayer walk in what is called and known as 'the Gateway of America', in Liberty State Park – by the Statue of Liberty. I walked the ground, declaring His glory over America. I strongly sensed angelic presence, angels of the Lord spreading the decree of His glory over the land through the winds in the Gateway. The winds picked up and gusted as declarations were being made.

SHIFT! I know a shift occurred in the Spirit and angels were dispatched to spread His glory throughout the land during that humble time of prayer.

The very next day, my right heel felt badly bruised, I was limping and hobbling, having difficulty walking. I'd never had pain in my heel like that before. I discerned it was 'kick back' from the prayer walk. The spiritual correlation was obvious and direct. The Lord reminded me of the verse, "And I will put enmity between thee and the woman, and between thy seed and her seed; **it shall bruise thy head, and thou shalt bruise his heel.**" (Genesis 3:15, KJV). He had dealt a crushing, death-blow to Satan under His foot; killing/crushing the plans of the enemy, but His injury was minor, a bruised heel. (The pain lasted for almost 5 months, but has left completely.) I'm more determined than ever to keep walking and praying!

"For our struggle is not against flesh and blood, but against the rulers, against the powers, against the world forces of this darkness, against the spiritual *forces* of wickedness in the heavenly *places*." (Ephesians 6:12)

We went back to the Gateway of America at Liberty State Park several times since that first walk. God gave us very clear 'marching orders' each time. Other times with no agenda just to walk and pray, putting our feet in the gateway claiming America for the Lord and speaking revival over the land.

Tongues

I pray daily in the spirit (in tongues) as well as in English, intentionally building my stamina praying in tongues.

Why? Here's just a couple of reasons:

- You speak spiritual mysteries and build yourself up
- The spirit knows how to pray, we don't always
- When we pray in tongues we baffle the enemy, he doesn't know what we're saying
- We are speaking a heavenly language – there's a direct connect

Often, I don't fully understand what to pray for much less how to pray. The Spirit knew and prayed through me. I simply allowed Him to use me.

Also, have you ever been in another land where no one else speaks your language. Then you hear someone speaking in your language? You stop in your tracks and lean in to hear what they're saying. Tongues is a spiritual, heavenly language. It gets heaven's attention and the angels lean in to listen.

I'm so thankful to be under the covering of Christian International with the awesome example that Bishop Bill Hamon and his staff set. They pray daily for 1 hour in tongues. Praying for even half an hour in tongues takes spiritual discipline. It is vital for every Christian.

> *"We do not know what we ought to pray for, but the Spirit himself intercedes for us through wordless groans. And he who searches our hearts knows the mind of the Spirit, because the Spirit intercedes for God's people in accordance with the will of God." (Romans 8:26-27)*

Prophetic Intercession

We create lofty, spiritual terms, but prophetic intercession is simple. It is coming into His presence, knowing His heart and voice, then speaking it by His authority and say so. That is how we become fellow-partakers of the divine nature. We are transformed in His presence, reflect Him and pray it out. We are given opportunity to be His mouth, hands, and feet.

When a true prophet brings forth a word there is a shift in atmospheres, situations, healing, and mindsets that takes place. The prophetic word contains authority and creative power, because it is God-breathed. In the same way that God spoke and that which was not came into being each time He spoke. (Read Genesis 1.) One of my grandchildren was speech delayed as a young child. A prophet spoke a word over him saying, "And I thank you Lord for the gift of speech that he has. He will be used in speech and will be very articulate, moving the hearts of many." After he left I looked at my husband and said, "Well no one's 100% accurate all of the time." Oh, my little faith! From that point forward my grandson spoke in full sentences with an advanced vocabulary. I mean using 10 cent words, expressing sophisticated thought processes and rationales. The prophetic word spoken over him had God-ordained authority to accomplish the purpose that it was sent for.

> "*As the rain and the snow come down from heaven, and do not return to it without watering the earth and making it bud and flourish, so that it yields seed for the sower and bread for the eater, so is my word that goes out from my mouth: It will not return to me empty, but will accomplish what I desire and achieve the purpose for which I sent it.*" (Isaiah 55:11)

True prophetic words not only shift atmospheres, they heal, thwart the plans of the enemy, and activate the plans and purposes of God.

> "He sent His Word and healed them, He rescued them from the grave." (Psalm 107:20)

My husband received at least 3 prophetic words over a year's time regarding his heart. He was told prophetically that there was something in his heart that he wasn't even aware of that could be fatal, but God was intervening on his behalf, dissolving it. Just the other day he was told that he had an aneurism over his aorta, found 'accidentally' when they did a CT scan of his lungs. We know that the next CT scan will reveal that it is dissolved. Our God is awesome and is our Healer!

Prophetic words are weapons of war, stand on them, fight with them and be victorious. "Listen to me, Judah and people of Jerusalem! Have faith in the LORD your God and you will be upheld; have faith in his prophets and you will be successful." (2 Chronicles 20:20)

The Shofar & the Prophetic

There is a sound of worship, a sound of warning, a sound of war and a sound of triumph. God assigned the shofar as a priestly instrument to be blown by the priests and watchmen for each of those purposes. "When you hear the sound of the trumpet, rally together for the cause and fight as one!" (Nehemiah 4:20)

"The trumpet is always symbolic of the prophetic voice of the Lord that releases strategies from Heaven. At the sound of the trumpet, rally, unify, listen for the strategy and commands from Heaven and then fight!" [10] Leaders position your prophetic intercessors close to you. Nehemiah placed the watchmen close to him. "But the man who sounded the trumpet stayed with me." (Nehemiah 4:18) Watchmen, shofar players and worship leaders should literally be close at hand with their leaders; submitting, communicating what they see in the spirit.

(Intercessors are responsible to submit and share with leaders, *not* to usurp them. Leaders are accountable to carry the vision and build according to the Lord. Intercessors are responsible to watch, submit, share and pray.)

Prophetic Decrees Over Nations & Regions:

My friend, Apostle Linda Herbert, was stationed in Iraq with the Army. Daily she stood atop the palace walls that had once been Saddam Hussein's, prophesying and praying over the land. I believe her prophetic prayers are still reverberating, shifting the atmosphere, establishing His will and power in Iraq today.

Increasingly prophetic proclamations from the throne of heaven are being decreed across the globe. Because of greater digital connectivity the 'Amen' is being sounded in large numbers in agreement with heaven. I often participate in FaceBook-live prophetic prayer meetings held in India.

Waiting upon Him individually and corporately in prayer sharpens discernment and opens a greater flow of revelation. Standing in authority with marching orders from the throne, clothed in His armor, holding the sword of the Lord, we move in revelation in the name of Jesus! With the Word of the Lord in our mouth and a two-edged sword in our hand (Psalm 149:6; Hebrews 4:12) may His will be done on earth as in heaven.

"I have put my words in your mouth and covered you with the shadow of my hand" (Isaiah 51:16)

WORSHIP & PRAYER

Where does worship end and prayer begin? They should flow seamlessly in and out of one another. [*More is covered on worship in chapter12 as it is a weapon of warfare; therefore, part of God's military strategy in His Army and vital in prayer as well.*]

A NEW MOVEMENT of WORSHIP BIRTHED

Awaken the Dawn (ATD) was perhaps one of the most significant, and historical events spiritually, occurred in October 2017. It was the first gathering of its kind. I believe it has catapulted spiritual breakthrough and transformation in Washington, DC and our nation. Held on the National Mall, between Capitol Hill and the Washington Monument, there were 3 days of intensive 24/7 worship and prayer. It established a 'gateway portal' between heaven and earth strategically in our nation's capital.

Strategically timed, ATD was held during Sukkot, the Jewish Feast of Tabernacles, as with the feast of Tabernacles tents were set up. With over 50 tents set up on the National Mall, each state in the USA was represented in worship. This was the first (but not the last) event of its kind. **In the same way Woodstock marked an era in the secular world, Awaken the Dawn ushered in a new era in the Spirit.**

Melody Frazier-Morris said afterward, "I believe **prayer changes history**. And it's proven over and over. Wars were ended through prayer. Nations were founded. Israel was founded in 1948 through prayer: the people crying out for a land and they got a land, amen?" [11]

ATD will be remembered for generations to come. It was an epic time, changing the atmosphere of a nation, creating a gateway, like Jacob's ladder, of angels ascending and descending

In addition to worship, there was a hallmark of tremendous *unity*, as one people prayer arose: repentance for racial prejudice, injustice and a moral outcry for the reversal of abortion legislation (Roe v. Wade) in our country.

It comes as no surprise that the mainstream media didn't cover this event. There are plans to expand these events into state capitals, cities, and schools. ATD kicked off what will become a worship and outreach movement.", remarked Hannah Ford. [12]

STRATEGIC WORSHIP & PRAYER
Under an Open Sky

It's time to *go outside* to worship, pray, and share. The Lord God says, **Strategically it is time to literally be outside, where there are no walls. Penetrate, infiltrate, and permeate the air and the land with His presence**. Be bold, fearless, and assertive! Take the homefield advantage. Move out under an open sky in the freedom you have in this nation. Be atmosphere changers, seize the day while it is today!" Don't waste this opportune time moving in these freedoms that are ours.

Satan is called the 'prince of the powers of the air'. There is a special dynamic as we worship, praise and pray under an open heaven. Infiltrate the air!

> *"wherein ye once walked according to the course of this world, according to the prince of the powers of the air, of the spirit that now worketh in the sons of disobedience" (Ephesians 2:2, ASV)*

The clash of kingdoms takes place in the 2nd heaven and is felt on earth. Now sons and daughters of obedience exalt and intercede in His name, in masse, under an open sky rallying angelic hosts, literally worshipping our way into Revival.

Filling the air with His Presence, His Spirit, in the very air that is inhaled. People will be filled with "*the breath of life. ... Then the* L*ORD* God formed a man from the dust of the ground and breathed into his nostrils the breath of life" (Genesis 1:30; 2:7)

Powerful, dynamic transformation is happening as the ekklesia, the Church of the Lord God Almighty, goes outside of the walls, under an open heaven to: worship, pray, walk, and touch the world. His image will be felt as His breathes upon the land and its people.

> *I looked, and tendons and flesh appeared on them and skin covered them, but there was no breath in them.*
>
> *Then he said to me, "Prophesy to the breath; prophesy, son of man, and say to it, 'This is what the Sovereign* L*ORD* says: Come, breath, from the four winds and breathe into these slain, that they may live.'" So I prophesied as he commanded me, and breath entered them; they came to life and stood up on their feet—a vast army. (Ezekiel 37:8-10)

Thrones of worship and intercession are being established throughout our land, *under an open sky*, opening Gateway portals of connection, like Jacob's ladder, between heaven and earth. There is a unique dynamic of freedom and majesty that occurs under an open sky, as well as upon the waters. One of the most memorable conferences I attended was on a ferry on the Chesapeake Bay. (... and the Spirit of God was hovering over the waters. Genesis 1:2) He works through His people and fills all in all – the land, waters, sky and peoples.

The Humble, the Few, the Fervent, and the Faithful

Call a gathering for worship with great music or a fiery speaker and a crowd comes. Call a prayer meeting and the numbers are few.

There is a special place in the Father's heart for intercessors. One of the significant things about the ministry of intercession is that it is unseen by man. Rarely is there a platform, pulpit or spotlight for an intercession before men. It's all about the secret place.

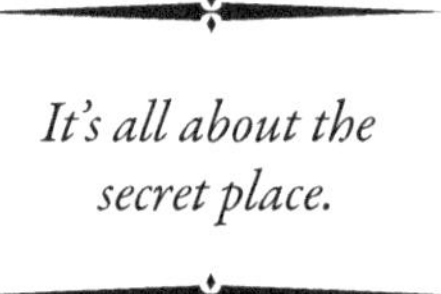

Intercession is rich with the intimacy of the Lord. Intercessors are brought into the inner chambers of the King. Deep calls to deep. Secrets and revelation are entrusted to you. Not everything that is shared in the secret place is for the public.

Conversely, intercessors guard against becoming introverted or exclusive. Know when to go into your prayer closet/war room and when to reach out and draw others in – or step out. Submit revelation(s) to those in authority; this will be your greatest safeguard to keep from the deception of Satan, or thinking of yourself more highly than you ought.

There is a new breed of prophet and intercessor arising. Brave men and women who hear Him clearly, move according to His plan in His timing, unafraid to speak and fear only the Lord. An Army that is multi-racial, multi-generational, and have representation from many churches. They will expose deeds of darkness, right wrongs, rebuild old foundations in righteousness that have crumbled under corruption. The Reformation Army of the Lord is arising in these days; infiltrating the gates and mountains of influence, climbing to the top, as gates are vigilantly kept secure. God through His Bride, the Church will be given preeminence in America and across the world once again.

As for you, watchtower of the flock,
stronghold of Daughter Zion,
the former dominion will be restored to you;
kingship will come to Daughter Jerusalem." (Micah 4:8)

Prayer is ...

- the incense of the saints before His throne.
- the most sacred and important communication between God and man.
- bearing our hearts, burdens, joys, thoughts and questions with Him.
- listening as God shares His heart, thoughts, strategies, and divine keys with us.
- our heart beating as one with the Father.
- divine partakers in ruling and reigning with Him, decreeing and declaring His will on earth as it is in heaven.
- the single most obvious and essential means of securing our gates.
- our first line of defense. (title of a book by Janice Mixon)

> "Prayer our words, mixed with His power!!!" – Deborah Cattafi Martone

Prayer is essential if we are to secure the gates *and prevail.*

CHAPTER 4

SECURING THE GATE OF SELF

You will say, "I will invade a land of unwalled villages; I will attack a peaceful and unsuspecting people—all of them living without walls and without gates and bars. *(Ezekiel 38:11)*

SECURING OUR PERSONAL GATES IS vital before securing external gates. If our own gate is compromised the enemy will find legal, legitimate access points to attack us in. We would be an 'unsuspecting people and a land of unwalled cities'. The choices we make determine the condition of our gates and lives.

Jesus overwhelmingly conquered, why? Because he had no allegiance to the prince of this world. Jesus declared, "for the prince of this world is coming. He has no hold over me, but he comes so that the world may learn that I love the Father and do exactly what my Father has commanded me." (John 14:30-31)

If we're serious about taking back our land, begin with our selves: self-image, self-governance, self-doubt, self-discipline, self-confidence, etc.

The better we know who He is, the better we will know *who we are* in Him. Identity matters – Christ in you the hope of glory.

Satan is our enemy. His mission is to rob, steal, lie, and destroy the call of God upon your life. He the devil) wants to undermine those birthing and walking in kingdom purposes, but fears what you carry – Christ in you.

If he can't destroy you, wear you down, or snatch you from your divine purpose and destiny then he'll work to get *you* to do that for him. What do I mean by that? Jesus said, "many are called but few are chosen" (Luke 19:44) We can miss open doors and kairos moments, because we are out of alignment or don't recognize divine appointments. This is a day of strategic, godly alignment for Kingdom assignment.

> *Be very careful, then, how you live—not as unwise but as wise, making the most of every opportunity, because the days are evil. (Ephesians 5:15-16)*

If part of us is given to the flesh instead of the spirit then our very purpose is compromised and conflicted with God's. His Word says, "Following the ways of this world [influenced by this present age], in accordance with the prince of the power of the air (Satan), the spirit who is now at work in *the disobedient, the unbelieving, who fight against the purposes of God.*" (Ephesians 2:2, AMP) Imagine that! The disobedient, some of whom are Christians, fighting the very purposes of God.

In her book *Higher Living Leaders,* Dr. Melodye Hilton said, "Powerful positioning is an internal posturing."[1] God wants to powerfully position each of us. We have grace to discipline ourselves for the purposes of godliness. Internal posturing places demands on us to, "Deny yourself, pick up your cross daily, and follow Him." (Luke 9:23) There is a direct connect with the ability to deny yourself with maturity and success.

Social exchange theory suggests that we make relational decisions based upon getting the greatest amount of rewards with the least amount of cost. We all like rewards. Studies indicate that **successful people have a greater capacity to choose short term loss, or withholding of rewards, for long term gain.** "Neural pathways are like superhighways of nerve cells that transmit messages. You travel over the superhighway many times, and the pathway becomes more and more solid." [3] The brain is always changing (neuroplasticity) and we can create new habits and neural pathways based upon the choices we make. **We have the God-given ability to re-map our brains based upon the choices we make, repetitively, over time**.

IDENTITY – The Master Key

> *"As a man thinks in his heart, so he is..." Proverbs 23:7, KJV)*

> *"Whether you think you can, or you think you can't—you're right."*
> *– Henry Ford*

Every commercial building, regardless of how many doors within it, has a master key. The head custodian or care-taker holds the master key; one key, that locks and unlocks <u>*all*</u> the doors. The master key for our temple, is our *identity* – who we are in Christ Jesus and who He is in us.

The enemy will lie to disqualify you. He'd like to shake your confidence in yourself and in God, and cause you to fear; so that you won't move in who you were called to be. **When you *know* who you are in Christ – you are a threat to Satan**. That's right, the enemy fears *you*! Knowing who you are comes out of relationship with God. You can read books, hear inspirational messages, listen to music, but those are all substitutes – *you must have your own personal relationship with Him*. That comes through asking Him into your heart, prayer, and the Word (the Bible).

Prayer: "Lord Jesus, I want YOU! I open my heart to You, I want to be completely Yours! Come into every area of my heart, mind and being – even the areas I've held back on. Forgive me for my sins and where I've been messing up. I lay down my ways for Your ways. I want and need You and Your Presence in my life. Wash me, fill me and re-fill me with the Holy Spirit. My life is Yours. Reveal to me my true identity in You!"

MORE than ADEQUATE – ABLE & AWESOME

Sometimes our thoughts are backed by so much insecurity that they create lies that we believe. For too long many people of God have felt disqualified or inadequate.

We declare war on the spirit of 'not enough'; breaking mindsets of inferiority, that became a false reality and identity, like a cave that we lived in and saw out of.

David fled king Saul and went to the Cave of Adullam. Those who were, distressed, in debt, and discontented came to him there. He became their leader and the cave his stronghold. Under David's leadership they were transformed and became known as 'David's Mighty Men'. The prophet Gad visited David saying, "Do not stay in the stronghold. Go into the land of Judah.", the land of praise and worship. There's a time to heal and rebuild your strength, but don't make the cave your dwelling place. David left the cave ... (2 Samuel 22:5) He wouldn't settle for a lifestyle of hiding with inadequacy. Face the fear and move forward.

Keith Johnson said it well, "Your power to breakthrough lies within your ability to confess. Secrecy is often a gate keeper to strongholds." [4] We dwell in strongholds when we are vulnerable or weak. The strong don't need a stronghold, their strength is resident within them. A stronghold can become a comfort zone. Some of us need to outgrow our stronghold. **If we do not move out of the stronghold at the appropriate time, it becomes the place of our limitation, rather than a source of strength**.

For, "In just a little while,
he who is coming will come

and will not delay."
And, "But my righteous one will live by faith.
And I take no pleasure
in the one who shrinks back."

> *But we do not belong to those who shrink back and are destroyed, but to those who have faith and are saved.* (Hebrews 10:37-39)

Sometimes our thoughts are backed by so much insecurity they create lies that we believe. Haunting whispers of, "You don't have what it takes." Unseen, inaudible, the thoughts reverberate within us, shaking our confidence. **Where have you disqualified yourself, *but Jesus hasn't*?**

In the division play-offs for the 2017 World Series, the Yankees were the wild-card team. They were not favored to win against Cleveland, but they did! Yanks team member, Todd Frazier, said afterward, "No one expected us to make it, especially this season. We didn't give up believing in ourselves though. Sometimes you just have to ignore the noise."

We are nullifying the lies, and taking every thought captive to the obedience of Christ. (1 Corinthians 10:5) If you haven't read *Battlefield of the Mind*! by Joyce Meyers you need to. So much of what we deal with is within our own self, in a labyrinth of thoughts. What are the lie(s) you have believed? Break your agreement with them. Ignore the noise.

One of the biggest lies out there is the lie of 'not enough'. The enemy is constantly at work to rob God's people of their confidence with disqualifying statements of you're:

- not good enough
- not spiritual enough
- not talented enough
- not smart enough
- not pretty enough
- not strong enough
- not rich enough" (Romans 14:4)
- not old enough
- not young enough
- not enough

ENOUGH! It's time to deal that spirit a fatal blow! For every bullet there turn it into a statement that reverses the curse. Drop the 'not' from each bullet, go through the list out loud declaring:

"In Christ Jesus I am ___________ enough! I can do all things through Christ who strengthens me." (Philippians 4:13)

I reject the mindset of 'not enough'. I break witchcraft prayers, spells and word curses. Others said I would never amount to anything. That's a lie. God doesn't say that about me. I am whole in Christ, His image bearer, (Genesis 1:26), His son/ daughter (Romans 8:19) more than conqueror (Romans 8:31)!

Because of Your greatness I am strong, even in my weakness. Where I am lacking You are more than enough!"

Cancel lies with truth. You will know the truth and the truth shall set you free! You are made in the image of God, created to rule, reign and have dominion with Him. You can do ALL things through Christ who strengthens you!

If Satan can get you to believe his lies of inadequacy, then he can stop you in your tracks. When confidence and identity is shaken it renders us impotent to fulfill God's-ordained destiny and call. In Him you are more than able.

I was on a prayer-line with about 20 intercessors nationwide. We had an awesome time in prayer. One intercessor was particularly sincere, passionate and on target. At the end of prayer she timidly, yet bravely asked, "May I share something? I almost didn't participate on the prayer-line tonight. I don't feel adequate, and I always ask myself, Who am I? I really struggle with these feelings that I'm not good enough." Wow! The enemy wanted to silence her, a key watchman on the wall. One who God is using mightily to bind the strong man and advance the kingdom! Thank God she didn't let feelings of inadequacy stop her.

> "So do not throw away your confidence; it will be richly rewarded." (Hebrews 10:35)

"*Wherever you've been bitten you'll be afraid. Wherever you're called the devil will bite you.*" – Dale Mast

Gideon dealt with feelings of inadequacy. An angel of the Lord appeared to him saying, "The LORD is with you, O valiant warrior." (Judges 6:12) Gideon was in a wine press beating wheat, hiding from potential enemies; hardly an image of valor.

3 things negatively impacted Gideon's self-image and confidence:

- being the 'least in his family' (Which indicates he was looked down upon within his family and probably the youngest child.)
- the family's position or station in society was not affluent or influential, it was the weakest.
- A lengthy season of oppression from the enemy.

> "Pardon me, my lord," Gideon replied, "but if the LORD is with us, why has all this happened to us? Where are all his wonders that our ancestors told us about when they said, 'Did not the Lord bring us up out of Egypt?' But now the Lord has abandoned us and given us into the hand of Midian."
> The LORD turned to him and said, "***Go in the strength you have and save Israel out of Midian's hand. Am I not sending you?***"
> "Pardon me, my lord," Gideon replied, "but how can I save Israel? My clan is the weakest in Manasseh, and I am the least in my family." (Judges 6:16)

I'm so thankful that your ability and mine doesn't rely on our strength, how we feel, or our limitations. **Our ability is dependent upon our availability to Him.**

> The LORD answered, "***I will be with you,*** and you will strike down all the Midianites, leaving none alive." (Judges 6:16)

Initially 32,000 fighting men stood with Gideon. God whittled them down to just 300; so that all glory would go to God, not man. Gideon with 300 men against approximately 135,000 Midianites. What was the secret of Gideon's 'ability'? The Presence of God. He promised, "I will be with you."

Moses understood the importance of His Presence also; he knew that was all that was needed. "If your Presence does not go with us, do not send us up from here. How will anyone know that you are pleased with me and with your people unless you go with us? What else will distinguish me and your people from all the other people on the face of the earth?" (Exodus 33:15) The promise of His Presence is still with you and I today, "For lo I am with you always, even to the very end of the age." (Matthew 28:20)

God doesn't call the qualified; He qualifies the called. *He delights in calling the least likely.* God doesn't call according appearance, how others view us, or how we see ourselves. Moses had a speech impediment, he stuttered; yet was made the mouthpiece of God to Pharaoh. David was a shepherd boy, whose earthly Father didn't even call him in from the fields when Samuel came to visit; yet he was the one God chose and anointed. Deborah was a woman, not even seated amongst the elders of the land; yet she was judge over all Israel. Esther was an orphan, a woman; chosen to save the Jews from annihilation. Rahab, went from whore to heroine in one day and is named in the genealogy of Christ. Countless others qualified by His favor, Presence, and say-so. **He speaks and His Word causes us to become. Just as He spoke in Creation and that which was not, became that which was.**

And now let the weak say I am strong! I pray that every lie of inadequacy is broken and replaced with the confidence of Christ. Declare, out loud:

"In the name of Jesus Christ – I break the intimidation and power of the lie of inadequacy. I am complete in Christ, He has equipped me with every good thing, for godliness. I am fearfully and wonderfully made, in the image of God. His Presence is with me always."

Once we realize who we are and move in that revelation and anointing watch out! For the creation waits in eager expectation for the children of God to be revealed. (Romans 8:19) He in you and you in Him, one with Him; His power will flow through you.

We have value and are loved because Jesus came, and there isn't anything that can separate you or I from that reality. Are you more focused on where you've failed, what others think? Or are on His love and forgiveness? How deep has His love penetrated and saturated you? "I pray that you, being rooted and established in love, may have power, together with all the Lord's holy people, to grasp how wide and long and high and deep is the love of Christ, and to know this love that surpasses knowledge—*that you may be filled to the measure of all the fullness of God*." (Ephesians 3:17-19)

Paul Lackie says it this way, "**One of the hardest things you will ever do is believe what God says about you. At some point, you have to shift the way you see yourself and ask God what he has to say.** He will speak to not just who you are, but who He is shaping you to be. When you hear and see who is he molding and shaping you to be, it can feel overwhelming but He stays close to you no matter where you go. You must receive and become all He desires you to be!" [5]

It does not honor the cross to live in shame. Just come, enter into the truth of who you are. We cannot enter the intimacy of love with shame. You are washed by the blood of the Lamb. You are free to love.

Dale Mast said, "If our identity is defined by our assignment instead of who we are to Father God, the shift into our next season will be very difficult. Our activity has morphed from an assignment into our identity. **Even though assignments can reveal identity, they can't be the source of our identity.** Security in who we are gives us the strength and flexibility to take necessary risks in strategic moments." [6]

When our identity is firmly established and rooted within us, then a genuine unity (not the rhetoric of unity) becomes a 'natural' by-product of our growing relationship with our heavenly Father.

No Longer Slaves to Fear

"There is no fear in love. But perfect love drives out fear, because fear has to do with punishment. The one who fears is not made perfect in love.

We love because he first loved us." 1 John 4:18-19

Sometimes I just can't hear God because my circumstances are crushing me, or so it feels. To hear His voice I need to first silence fear. When the winds of adversity become like a raging, howling wind, then I only hear the storm and my voice of anxiety amplified.

Fear is an enemy of the soul that gives birth to: Insecurity, Doubt, Lack of Confidence, and Paralysis. One thing these children have in common is self. Their focus emanates on and from self. At no point does fear magnify God, but it makes it harder to quiet our own spirit to hear His.

It amazes me that in the middle of a storm He speaks in a quiet voice, even in a whisper. Jesus was grace under fire. In Matthew 8:23-27 He and the disciples where in a boat as a furious storm came up. The disciples were afraid as Jesus slept peacefully. When they woke Him, He spoke, not yelled, spoke to the winds and the waves and they became still. He turned to the disciples saying, "You of little faith, why are you so afraid?" Faith is spelled r-i-s-k. Face the fear and do it anyway!

I taught school for many years. When a class is loud and unruly speak in a quiet, calm voice. Usually the class quiets down to hear what you are saying. Teaching in an inner-city school whenever I had laryngitis I was always amazed at how quiet, respectful and well-behaved my students were. Speaking in a quiet voice places demands on the listener to be quiet, quieting our spirit to hear His still, quiet whisper.

'Greats' of the faith wrestled with fear. Faith and fear can go hand in hand. Those who operate with great faith have faced and overcame great fear. Faith, fear or discouragement are choices. Every time you "level up" there is a new mountain and a new depth to conquer. Often overwhelming circumstances and attacks of fear come before or as we move through open doors, or after great miracles. (Almost always when fasting there will be attacks of one sort or another.)

As we moved out in ministry planting and pioneering a new work, His Kingdom Ministries, my husband and I were hit with wave after wave of attack. Financial trials, an unparalleled attack on health, and more assaulted us. We almost lost our home, and my husband almost died at the hands of the enemy, several times. Phew! there were times we were tempted to throw in the towel. But God's grace and strength came through everything. The area(s) that we were tried in are the very areas that He is giving us a breakers' anointing in; not just for our own lives, but to lead and bring breakthrough to others lives as well. It's not always easy to hear the voice of the Lord during the storm.

Elijah experienced personal fear and anxiety after a great triumph with the prophets of Baal on Mt. Carmel (1 Kings 18:16-45) Jezebel & Ahab threatened him and a raw, cold, chilling, fear gripped him. He even had a hard time hearing the Lord. One of the greatest prophets ever known, was struggling to hear the voice of the Lord, because his own voice of fear was drowning out his ability to hear the Lord's.

> "Go out and stand on the mountain in the presence of the LORD, for the LORD is about to pass by."
>
> Then a great and powerful wind tore the mountains apart and shattered the rocks before the LORD, but the LORD was not in the wind. After the wind there was an earthquake, but the LORD was not in the earthquake. After the earthquake came a fire, but the LORD was not in the fire. And after the fire came a gentle whisper. When Elijah heard it, he pulled his cloak over his face and went out and stood at the mouth of the cave." (1 Kings 19:11-13)

Hearing His voice and obeying; usually requires being still.

The Struggle is Real

Securing the gate of Self will cut across the very fiber of your being. It requires a lifestyle of self-denial and self-governance. It is the most difficult as well as the most important of all gates to secure. Outside gates than are easier than mastering your own. Each of us is constantly in danger of choosing what feels good over what is right.

> *Each of us is constantly in danger of choosing what feels good over what is right.*

"For I have the desire to do what is good, but I cannot carry it out. For I do not do the good I want to do, but the evil I do not want to do—this I keep on doing. ... Who will rescue me from this body that is subject to death? ... but I see another law at work in me, waging war against the law of my mind and making me a prisoner of the law of sin at work within me. Thanks be to God, who delivers me through Jesus Christ our Lord! (Romans 7:18-19, 23-25)

Strengthening personal gates with self-governance is essential or we will become a land of 'unwalled villages, an unsuspecting people ripe for plunder by the enemy'. People tend to be lovers of themselves. Christians love Him more than their own lives. "For to me, to live is Christ and to die is gain. ... I count all things to be loss in view of the surpassing value of knowing Christ Jesus my Lord, for whom I have suffered the loss of all things, and count them but rubbish so that I may gain Christ. I do not regard myself as having laid hold of *it* yet; but one thing *I do*: forgetting what *lies* behind and reaching forward to what *lies* ahead, I press on toward the goal for the prize of the upward call of God in Christ Jesus." (Philippians 1:21; 3:8-10, 13-14)

Are you all-in?

When not guarding our gates and borders we are vulnerable and exposed. Without God's standards and boundaries in our lives we invite attack. The obvious must be secured and guarded; our eyes, ears, mouth, hands, and feet, loins (areas of our sexual being), and our very heart. These are processed through our mind. **There is a battle for our thought life, our heart, our very allegiances and affections.**

The most noble characters in the Bible were flawed. They struggled with the same arch nemesis that we do; Me, Myself, and I. The struggle is real!

Abraham was a friend of God (James 2:23) the father of a multitude of nations. Yet he spinelessly, did not man-up and bowed to the fear of man. On more than one occasion he handed his wife over to other, powerful men. (Genesis 12:10-19; Genesis 20:1-3). Abraham also tried to make the supernatural promise of God for a son come to pass by fleshly, illegitimate means – having sex with his wife's slave girl, Hagar. (Genesis 16:1-10) Poor Hagar, she was the loser in that triangle, taking quite the beating from Sarah. Again, Abraham was spineless, he turned his back and walked away during the beat down, not wanting to get in the middle of the whole dysfunctional mess. Abraham still became the father of multitudes through *both* Isaac and Ishmael. However, it was through the legitimate, covenant union of Abraham & Sarah – the miraculous God-seed that brought forth Isaac, that His chosen people, the Jews were birthed and descended from.

Moses, was a friend of God (Exodus 33:11), deliverer of Israel (Exodus 3:7-10; Acts 7:35) He had serious anger management issues, murdering an Egyptian (Exodus 2:11-14) and striking the Rock that represented God, instead of talking to it. (Numbers 20:8-13) Yet, Moses the most humble man in all the earth (Numbers 12:3), knew God personally, His ways and mannerisms.

David, brought down Goliath, the giant that defied the army of the Living God, as a small shepherd boy. He captured, defeated, and subdued kingdoms that rose against Israel, but never mastered dominion over himself. Women were his vice. David, had an affair (2 Samuel 11:2-4), sent her husband to the front lines to be killed (2 Samuel 11:14-15) and looked to the strength of man rather than God by numbering the fighting men, bringing a curse on all of Israel (1 Chronicles 21:2, 8). He was still a man after God's own heart, and God's heart was for him as well.

A person is considered righteous because of the atonement of Christ. God looks at the heart; and the blood of Christ that grafts us in as sons and daughters of God.

Faith in Christ, backed by a surrendered life yields fruit. (James 2:24) Actions speak louder than words. Action indicates where Self and one's faith is really at. **A tree is known by its fruits, but what defines us is the blood propitiation of Christ Jesus.** I am known as an educator, but what defines me is a living faith of salvation in Jesus Christ. His blood makes me a blood relative of the King of Kings and Lord of Lords, his daughter in Him – *in* Jesus' name! His love is in His blood, and it is *for* us! "For in Christ all the fullness of the Deity lives in bodily form, and in Christ you have been brought to fullness." (Colossians 2:9)

Only one Champion successfully conquered self, that is our Lord Jesus Christ. I'm so thankful, "Mercy triumphs over judgment." (James 2:13) that we, the righteous, live by faith; being continually built up so we don't compromise our promise, purpose, integrity. When our walls and boundaries are broken down our God-filter is compromised. We become desensitized to the Spirit, living out of self-will and desires.

When our walls and boundaries are broken down our God-filter is compromised.

Filters are important. Back in the day, I did survival camping. We had to find water, preferably via a moving stream or babbling brook. First we'd boil it to kill bacteria, then run it through a cloth as a filter. Without the filter micro-organisms and bacteria can slip through undetected. If our boundaries and God-filters are compromised we're exposed to bacteria and at risk for deception and manipulation.

Filters and character make a difference. When they're in place we can self-sabotage without realizing it. As Keith Johnson said, "Don't let your undeveloped character dismantle your favor... Pull yourself together, and carry yourself well!" [7]

If desensitized to the Spirit, one can easily yield to self-will and desires. There's a constant war between the desires of our flesh and the spirit. "Thanks be to God who leads us in His triumph!" (2 Corinthians 2:14)

The Gospel According to Self

> *Beware that your hearts are not deceived, and that you do not turn away and serve other gods and worship them. (Deuteronomy 11:16)*

Self has never been more elevated than in these end times. God fore-warned us, that we'd create our own difficulties as lovers of ourselves!

> "Realize this, that in the last days difficult times will come. For men will be ***lovers of self***, lovers of money, boastful, arrogant, revilers, disobedient to parents, ungrateful, unholy, unloving, irreconcilable, malicious gossips, *without self-control*, brutal, haters of good, treacherous, reckless, conceited, *lovers of pleasure rather than lovers of God.*" (2 Timothy 3:1-4)

The solution:

> *"walk by the Spirit, and you will not gratify the desires of the flesh. For the flesh desires what is contrary to the Spirit, and the Spirit what is contrary to the flesh. They are in conflict with each other, so that you are not to do whatever you want." (Galatians 5:16-17)*

> My friend, Lisa Palieri-Perna, of *Touched by Prayer*, put it like this, "Change starts when your mind, will and emotions agree!"

For if you live according to the flesh, you will die; but if by the Spirit you put to death the misdeeds of the body, you will live.

For those who are led by the Spirit of God are the children of God. (Romans 8:13-14)

Now the deeds of the flesh are evident, which are: immorality, impurity, sensuality, idolatry, sorcery, enmities, strife, jealousy, outbursts of anger, disputes, dissensions, factions, envying, drunkenness, carousing, and things like these. – Galatians 5:18

Securing the 'Gate of Self' is difficult, on-going and full-time job. Many hire life coaches for help in; decision making, personal interactions, relationship building, establishing healthy habits, and more. A plethora of books have been written on this. This chapter is just a quick overview on the topic of taking dominion over oneself. All other gates are affected by the gate of Me, Myself & I. **Individuals, corporate bodies, and societies hinge upon the strength of individual self-governance**. As we rule and reign *by the Spirit* we ensure that we are not ruled by our fleshly: thought-life, lusts, moods, etc.

If personal gates are not secured our outlook and perspective will not be pure, it will be tainted. Our ability to discern according to the mind of the Holy Spirit will be skewed. As my spiritual Mom, Apostle, Dr. Melodye Hilton says, "One of the greatest things you can do for others is to enjoy a well-ordered and healthy personal life." [8]

We have family and friends that have struggled with addictions. When they were in sobriety, their families flourished, and they were the absolute nicest, smartest, kindest, most gifted individuals you had ever met – at work, church and home. But when they were actively using, phew! It was Dr. Jekyll and Mr. Hyde! During active addiction their life-style was not well-ordered and healthy. Their families and all those around them suffered during active addiction. It cost some their marriage, career, etc. They were hurt, but their deepest regret was how their actions hurt those who were closest to them.

Self-Sabotage & Fear of Success

> *"But my people would not listen to me;*
> *Israel would not submit to me.*
> *So I gave them over to their stubborn hearts*
> *to follow their own devices. (Psalm 81:11-12)*

Me, Myself, and I can be our worst enemy! Sometimes we give Satan way too much credit. If the enemy went on vacation, we could do a lethal job all by ourselves.

Some fear failure, but fear of success can be just as real, and just as damaging, causing self-sabotage without realizing it. Fear of success is more common than we realize.

"Our deepest fear is not that we are inadequate. Our deepest fear is that we are powerful beyond measure. It is our light, not our darkness that most frightens us. We ask ourselves, Who am I to be brilliant, gorgeous, talented, fabulous? Actually, who are you *not* to be? You are a child of God. Your playing small does not serve the world. There is nothing enlightened about shrinking so that other people won't feel insecure around you. We are all meant to shine, as children do. We were born to make manifest the glory of God that is within us. It's not just in some of us; it's in everyone. And as we let our own light shine, we unconsciously give other people permission to do the same. As we are liberated from our own fear, our presence automatically liberates others." [9]

I have watched people repeatedly get out of a hole, then just as opportunity and success are before them, they begin to self-destruct. Missing appointments, not calling to cancel, fault finding, becoming argumentative with the one opening doors for them, go back to addictions, etc. Many, don't take responsibility for these behaviors, instead they blame and scapegoat others, rationalizing why its someone else's fault. Then often, they cut off supportive relationships out of their own inner shame, that they don't want to acknowledge. It's too painful to take responsibility for their self-sabotage and remain in healthy relationships.

People afraid of success often don't realize they have this fear. Frequently it's a subconscious fear so it is hard to deal with. You can't deal with something you won't admit to or acknowledge. Beneath the fear are several layers of lies emanating from self-image, personal histories and experiences. These lies hide under fear of success (in parenthesis are Scriptures of truth to counter each lie):

- The idea of being in the spotlight is scary (1 Peter 2:9)
- Fear you don't have what it takes, lack the necessary skill(s) – even after proven capability (Ephesians 3:20; Philippians 4:13)
- Think of yourself as an imposter, that your success is just a charade (Genesis 1:27; Ephesians 2:10; 2 Corinthians 1:20)
- Fear that success will corrupt you (James 4:10; 2 Peter 1:3)
- Fear that success will place more demands on you and you don't want added responsibilities or change (2 Corinthians 8:12; 1 Timothy6:18)

Warning signs of behaviors that may indicate a fear of success:

- Procrastination
- Distraction – you're known for it
- Working on many things feverishly at once, without focusing deeply on any of them
- Your personal vision and goals remain the same, not changing within 5 years
- Feeling as though your work is not good enough, that you don't 'measure up'
- The big give away – you're on the verge of success and things start going really wrong

About now you may be recognizing yourself or someone you love with having a fear of success. To combat the fear of success first, recognize it. Then, answer every lie with the anecdote of truth! Ask the Lord to give you fresh revelation of who you really are in Him. Then live, think and act from that identity.

Lord, I ask for fresh revelation, like the aroma of fresh bread, to fill each one reading this, of who they really are, who You have created them to be, Your image bearer.

Emotionalism

The enemy creates, fabricates and manipulates perception through lies. A half-truth is still a lie. The more perception is twisted by half-truths, *especially those that elicit strong emotion*, the less inclined and capable one is to hear and recognize pure truth when it is spoken. One may be more inclined to embrace the half-truth because of the passion of emotion, and/or the frenzy of 'group think' that has been provoked by a half truth. Jesus brought this to light as he exclaimed to the Jews, "Why is my language not clear to you? Because you are unable to hear what I say. The devil was a murderer from the beginning, not holding to the truth, for there is no truth in him. When he lies, he speaks his native language, for he is a liar and the father of lies. Yet because I tell the truth, you do not believe me!" (John 8:43-45)

Many, live by their emotions, standing on emotional reasoning—if one *feels* something to be true, then it's true. Not. What God says is true, despite our logical reasoning or our feelings.

The more perception is twisted by half-truths, especially those that elicit strong emotion, the less inclined and capable one is to hear and recognize pure truth when it is spoken.

A former pastor of mine, Pastor Vinnie Manzo, gave me wise counsel many years ago as I faced significant decision making that had deep emotions attached to it. Basically, he told me that I needed to get into God's presence, grab hold of the horns of the altar, get still before Him and hear what He was saying amidst it all. "You may still come to the same decision, but you will make your decision from the confidence of God, not from the heat of your changing, conflicted emotions. You don't want to be out in the middle of the ocean, unable to return, and then second guess yourself or be filled with regret. You need to be certain you have heard from God."

Millennials are very experiential, and feel things deeply. Hence the expression, "Please don't confuse me with the facts.". Previous generation(s) tended to be ruled by facts and scientific evidence. **God's truth, must shape us more than the trends of our generation**. Intimacy with Him in prayer and the Word, transcends the flaws of every generation. "Forever oh Lord Your word is settled in heaven!" (Psalm 119:89) His standard and His ways will keep us from the error of being ruled by our emotions or 'just the facts' void of feelings.

As James Goll pointed out, "**We have had Purpose Driven Lives and now we have Presence Motivated People. But what we need for the days that are ahead are Values Anchored Believers.**" [10] What are the non-negotiables, the bedrock that is at your very core? Lord help us to know Your Word, rule and reign by Your Spirit, not our emotions. We shouldn't be void of emotion, but if they're in the driver's seat life will be a tumultuous roller coaster ride.

Deindividuation

We must guard our hearts. Emotionalism if unchecked can lead into deindividuation, a term used in social psychology. **Deindividuation can be explained as having a crowd mentality, whereby individual personalities become dominated by the collective *mindset* of the *crowd*.** (Its even been used as a legal defense in trials.) It can occur when one is so immersed in a group, that one loses a sense of self-awareness, and feels less responsible for their actions. Examples: Groups of rioting sports fans celebrating a big win can end up committing acts they would never do alone, such as vandalism or arson. Political oppression, mass violence, riots, and bullying can all stem from deindividuation. As a person moves into a group there is a loss of individual identity and a gaining of the social identity of the group. Deindividuation can lead to a mob mentality as critical thinking is deterred, as the group becomes their identity.

> You were running a good race. Who cut in on you to keep you from obeying the truth? That kind of persuasion does not come from the one who calls you. "A little yeast works through the whole batch of dough." (Galatians 5:7-9)

Do not believe everything you hear and see. What we think and believe is the lens through which we see our lives, circumstances, and opportunities. Be especially wary of groups, news and imagery that evoke and stir up emotion. "The heart is deceitful above all things and beyond cure. Who can understand it? (Jeremiah 17:9) Are you 'going along with the crowd' question and think. Before accepting information (whether news or social media) as true do the following:

1. Choose not to be a reactionary. Its fine to respond to things, but don't be like a jack-hammer. Let your response be weighed, measured, researched and informed. Take a breather and give yourself cool down time. Be quick to listen, slow to speak, and slow to anger. (James 1:19)
2. Take every thought captive. (2 Corinthians 10:5) Cover your mind, put on the helmet of salvation. (Ephesians 6:17)
3. Ask God for wisdom and discernment. (James 1:5; Pr. 10:13
4. *Look at, listen to differing, search different sources and perspectives on a topic.*
5. Pray (*at all times*, without ceasing). (1 Thessalonians 5:16)

Know the Word of God – it's an unchanging standard and will keep you anchored. Be men and women of prayer. Hold steady and run the race.

> "Above all else, guard your heart, for everything you do flows from it." (Proverbs4:23)

Beware – Guard Against Deception

If you're confident that you can't be deceived watch out! That makes you a prime target for deception! The hardest person to warn and correct is the one who insists there is no error with them. Jesus told Simon Peter that he would deny him 3x Peter was incredulous! Peter had a combination of pride and ignorance going on; proud because he didn't believe he would ever deny Jesus, ignorant because he didn't know what was in him. But Jesus did.

We had a friend who was warned prophetically that Satan had targeted to remove them from leadership and even from our ministry. Immediately the person looked at me and said, "That will never happen." For a while all was well. Then, immense trials pummeled this leader non-stop. We covered him in prayer. Eventually he left.

Keep humble and be quick to agree with God – even when, especially when, it isn't how you *feel*. Feelings are fickle. It will take more than passion (eros) or brotherly love (phileo), it will take His agape (godly, unconditional love) and great grace to run the race and finish the course.

The depth of our character guards our personal gates against deception.

No one wakes up saying, "I'd like to be deceived today!" Deception can come in subtly. The depth of our character guards our personal gates against deception. Go deep!

Five doorways can open to deception. Forewarned is fore-armed. Knowing this will keep us more vigilant. These 5 doorways are:

1. Rationalizing our desires. *(A longing fulfilled is sweet to the soul, but fools detest turning from evil. – Proverbs 13:19)*
2. Pride *(Pride goes* before destruction, And a haughty spirit before stumbling. *– Proverbs 16:18)*
3. Ignorance, is not always bliss! *(He will die for lack of instruction, And in the greatness of his folly he will go astray. – Proverbs 5:23; He is on* the path of life who heeds instruction, *But he who ignores reproof goes astray. – Proverbs 10:17)*

4. Idolatry *(We can put people on a pedestal to the point where we worship them. It could be a boyfriend, spouse, minister, etc. When we idolize someone, we can't see the trees from the forest, and may blindly follow them into error.)*
5. Rebellion and/or a deep abiding anger

I can deceive myself with rationalizing. For instance, the moment I begin dieting cheesecake becomes very appealing to me. I'll tell myself, "Just a little taste won't hurt." Then more self-thinking follows, "Just go for the whole slice, one time won't matter." Before the day is out my mission to diet is derailed due to succumbing to temptation and rationalizing.

Warning: "A longing fulfilled is sweet to the soul, but fools detest turning from evil." (Proverbs 13:19) A man hears what he wants to hear and disregards the rest. The flesh wants what it wants. It's easy to compromise and that leads into enemy territory. Keep submitted to the Spirit.

Adam and Eve desired fruit, especially appealing because it was forbidden. They bought into the lie, "Surely you won't die!" (Genesis 1:27) taking hold of a half-truth and walked into sin. (Genesis 3:1-11) Spirit-filled believers can manipulate the 'scripture of the half-truth' to support whatever they'd like, validating homosexuality and more. Homosexuality is sin in the eyes of God. He hates the sin but loves the sinner. God said, "'Do not have sexual relations with a man as one does with a woman; that is detestable." (Leviticus 18:22) This same principle applies to women having sexual relations with other women. We can't rationalize and manipulate the Word, regarding any sin.

> *Do not deceive yourselves. If any of you think you are wise by the standards of this age, you should become "fools" so that you may become wise. For the wisdom of this world is foolishness in God's sight. As it is written: "He catches the wise in their craftiness"; and again, "The Lord knows that the thoughts of the wise are futile."* (1 Corinthians 3:18-20)

Pride goes before a fall. Those who walk in pride won't receive correction. They'd rather argue than repent. There's one correct perspective and its theirs. (The last one to recognize pride is Me, Myself and I.) I've learned, the hard way, when I'm irked by someone else's pride to first take inventory of myself! What is it within me that is reacting to them?

Rebellion mixed with Pride is a stunning, 'steam-roller' combination. "For rebellion is as the sin of witchcraft, and stubbornness (or arrogance/pride) is as iniquity and idolatry. Because thou hast rejected the word of the LORD, he hath also rejected thee from being king." (1 Samuel 15:23) If these areas are in action simultaneously it pretty much guarantees falling into deception, error, sin, and defiling others along with you. (Hebrews 12:15)

We've all witnessed someone lose their patience or become judgmental with others that they perceived weren't as spiritual as they were, in the Word, prayer, worship, etc.. Whenever I see that I know that they are in a danger zone of slipping or falling headlong.

One young man, had just returned from a drug rehab program. He was doing quite well. One prayer meeting he scoffed at how another member wasn't praying and in the Word like he was, etc., going on about their lack of zeal and basic inferiority to him in the spirit. Unfortunately, he hasn't been back to prayer meeting since. He's regressed, and is walking in rebellion. We continue to pray for him, believing he'll be back stronger than before.

We all have unhealthy doses of 'stumbling pride' with or without an addictive past. PRAYER: "Lord help me to, do nothing from selfishness or empty conceit, but with humility of mind regard others as more important than myself. (Philippians 2:3) Lord give me grace to remain submitted to godly authority."

Made a Searching and Fearless Moral Inventory

Let us examine our ways and test them, and let us return to the Lord. (Lamentations 3:40)

Taking a moral inventory is designed to:

- Help us better understand ourselves
- Bring us to dependency on God for true transformation

"If you know the enemy and know yourself, you need not fear the result of a hundred battles. If you know yourself but not the enemy, for every victory gained you will also suffer a defeat. If you know neither the enemy nor yourself, you will succumb in every battle." (Sun Tzu, *The Art of War*) **Facing our own demons can be more difficult than facing an army. Being honest with ourselves takes courage**. Surrendering our will to His, isn't a sign of weakness, it is an act of confident faith and strength. It's in my weakness that I come to know His strength. (1 Corinthians 12:9)

"But everything exposed by the light becomes visible—and everything that is illuminated becomes light.

> "Wake up, sleeper,
> rise from the dead,

> and Christ will shine on you."
>
> Be very careful, then, how you live—not as unwise but as wise, making the most of every opportunity, because the days are evil." (Ephesians 5:13-16)

Taking a moral inventory is to help us, NOT disqualify us. Don't get so down on yourself that you can't get up. Most people that do a 'searching and fearless moral inventory' do so with the support of a sponsor, mentor or spiritual Mother or Father.

Be committed to forgiving yourself before you begin. We all have 'stuff' that wasn't anyone else's fault but our own. The hardest person to forgive can be yourself. Christ died for each of us, to not only forgive our sins, but to remove the residue of shame that sin leaves behind. His will for us is to "have life and have it abundantly." **Not forgiving yourself is to say that Christ's blood reaches everyone but you. His blood is for you.**

> *Instead of your shame*
> *you will receive a double portion,*
> *and instead of disgrace*
> *you will rejoice in your inheritance.*
> *And so you will inherit a double portion in your land,*
> *and everlasting joy will be yours.* (Isaiah 61:7)

Some prisoners who are in jail live with more abundance in Christ than those on the outside. Persons on the outside can live as captives in man-made prisons of unforgiveness, anger, shame, etc. It was for freedom that Christ set you free. Stand firm in your freedom! (Galatians 5:1)

Moral inventories are for everyone, daily, keeping a spirit of honesty and humility. Repentance is a kingdom life-style, just like bathing is a necessary part of daily living. If we don't bathe spiritually, with repentance, we'll have an offensive odor, in the nostrils of God and those around us.

Forgiveness

Forgiveness isn't a feeling, it is not deserved or earned, it's a choice. Forgiveness is not a natural response to injustice, pain, sorrow, offense, loss and injury. The ones we forgive may reject us and our forgiveness. 'To err is human, to forgive is divine." Only through great grace, and His Spirit can one forgive – deep calls to deep.

In my weakness, I am strong. (2 Corinthians 12:9) In forgiveness I am humbled. **We win by surrender, are strong through weakness, gain when we give, and are elevated in humility**. Walking out our faith is contrary to our flesh. We are perpetually working out our salvation with fear and trembling, denying ourselves, picking up our cross daily to follow Him. (Philippians 2:12; Luke 9:23)

I went back into education after a long sabbatical. (I had taken time off to be a full-time Mom of 5 children). As a full-time substitute I went the extra mile. Students showed great gains in learning, and I was well-loved by students, parents, teachers and administrators. A full-time teaching position opened. Everyone thought I'd be a shoe-in for it, but I didn't get it. A girl who had never taught, with no experience got it. She was the police-chief's daughter and next-door neighbor to the superintendent of schools. They waited until mid-August to tell me. (In education that's equivalent to being unemployed for the next school year.) I was hurt and angry, I felt robbed, it was unfair, unjust, and there wasn't a thing I could do about it.

I whined and cried to God about it. He spoke clearly, "**You can stay in this chapter for as long as you'd like, or you can forgive it and move on**." I've learned the hard way to be quick to obey Him. Immediately I *chose* to forgive and let it go. I prayed, I didn't want to be stuck there! Within 48 hours I had a full-time teaching contract with another district, that I hadn't even applied to, made me an offer. That's unheard of in the field of education to be contracted that quickly. The details were miraculous. It was a far better opportunity, it also opened many other wonderful doors for me. If I hadn't chosen to forgive I'd still be stuck in a cesspool of my own bitterness. **Often, right before promotion, a political spirit comes against you. Trust Him, He's got you**.

When you are moving in the power and strength of God's spirit Satan will leave you alone, but he'll return at your dry or low point. When the devil had finished tempting Jesus in the wilderness, *he left him until an opportune time*. (Luke 4:13) If he tried it with Jesus, he'll try it with you and I too! How strong are you in your weakest moment? "My flesh and my heart may fail, but God is the strength of my heart and my portion forever." (Psalm 73:26) **God's strength begins where ours ends**. (2 Corinthians 12:10) If only we would humbly cry out in our weakness.

Especially when we are unfairly offended we need to forgive. Unforgiveness opens a toe-hold for the enemy. A young woman I knew, Andrea (fictitious name), was incredibly bright, talented and pretty. She had been through a lot of difficulties. Someone had even attempted to kill her at one point. Her mother had also been through many unfair life struggles. Andrea, was showing signs of mental and emotional instability, becoming defensive fault finding with almost everyone that got remotely close to her over trivial matters. She read innuendo into communications that didn't exist. Andrea felt accused by others; she became defensive, withdrawn, obsessing over things. People asked me if Andrea was ok, behaviors became more pronounced, and she looked disturbed. Several were concerned for her. She had so much bottled up, stuffed down unforgiveness. **Unforgiveness is a breeding ground for the activity of the enemy.**

Those who hurt and offended her unjustly may not have *deserved* forgiveness. (At least no more or no less than any of us deserve forgiveness.) But SHE deserves to live a life of freedom and abundance, that would only come if she forgave them.

You can't run a race if you're carrying a suitcase. **To forgive others, frees yourself. YOU deserve to be free. Forgiveness, is the road to freedom.**

Note: forgiveness is NOT synonymous with trust. They are two entirely different things. Forgiveness you give freely, trust is earned, or not. *Forgiveness brings us closer to His nature when we forgive, and frankly we can't do it without Him.* As Dr. Martin Luther King, Jr. said, "I have decided to stick with love. Hate is too great a burden to bear."

Unforgiveness, due to unhealed hurt, can open a door to brokenness and demonic activity. Forgiveness demolishes strongholds while building and strengthening our own personal walls and gates.

Forgiveness demolishes strongholds while building and strengthening our own personal walls and gates.

Shut the front door!

This is a season of open doors. Closed doors can be as important as open doors. I thank God for the closed doors or I might have chosen the wrong door.

We lock our front doors during the daytime and at night. If we don't know you and you're not for me and my family then you're not crossing my threshold! (**If someone has stabbed you in the back, stop inviting them in!** Set up boundaries and hold the line. If someone is not for you they're against you don't give them access or a place in your home.) Some things need to go!

God says, "The ball is in your court! I'll drive them out, but *you* need to dis-invite and uproot them! Go slay your Goliath"

The battle is real. Often it originates or is played out in our mind. The enemy of your soul wants to prophesy doom and gloom to you. Hear what the Spirit is saying. Stand and fight. **How you fight, or not, will be affected by what you really believe.**

> "Finally, brothers and sisters, whatever is true, whatever is noble, whatever is right, whatever is pure, whatever is lovely, whatever is admirable—if anything is excellent or praiseworthy—think about such things." (Philippians 4:8)

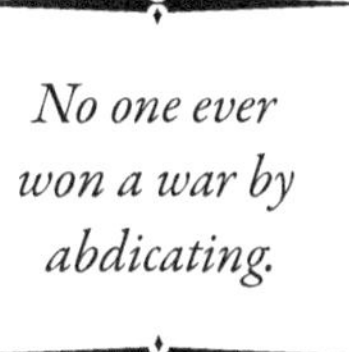

No one ever won a war by abdicating.

Not thinking is thinking. Don't be passive about your thought life. **If you don't choose to direct your thought life then you have abdicated your authority over yourself!** Not choosing is choosing. **No one ever won a war by abdicating.** David ran to the battle lines where Goliath was taunting and mocking the army of the living God. (1 Samuel 17:48) Take every thought captive to the obedience of Christ! **Maintain victory; choose and direct thoughts and actions by the spirit.** You were created to be more than a conqueror, it's in your God-given DNA.

> *"If God is for us, who can be against us? In all these things we are more than conquerors through him who loved us. For I am convinced that neither death nor life, neither angels nor demons, neither the present nor the future, nor any powers, neither height nor depth, nor anything else in all creation, will be able to separate us from the love of God that is in Christ Jesus our Lord." (Romans 8:31, 37-39)*

CHAPTER 5

FREEDOM

The eternal God is your refuge,
and underneath are the everlasting arms.
He will drive out your enemies before you,
saying, 'Destroy them!'.
(Deuteronomy 33:27)

VITAL TO SECURING OUR GATES is walking in freedom. We must break unholy ties and alliances that have bound us. Satan enjoys binding people up, and having a hook or a line in that he can pull on keeping one trapped in a cycle of guilt, fear and shame. A sense of failure limits your confidence and effectiveness. **Christians whose identity is anchored in Christ are, unstoppable, walking in freedom and purpose, causing hell to tremble.**

BREAKING WORD CURSES: GIDEON – Kill the bull!

Dismantle, crush and uproot word curses spoken against you! Negative speech comes at us from everywhere: family, work, school, neighbors, witches, even in the Church, etc. Toxic words become curses, witchcraft chatter in the atmosphere.

Alex's father belittled him, swore at him and called him names. One day at school he and I talked. He shared how much it hurt his heart to be talked to like that and how much he loved his father despite the verbal tirades. I listened, empathized and affirmed Alex as best as I knew how. We prayed and rejected the negative words and loosed words of affirmation. We prayed for his father also. I asked Alex to promise me that he would believe who God said he was, the real him, not those negative things. Prayerfully we placed a shield around his heart to not allow those negative words to penetrate. Sometimes we need to take our father's bull, kill it, and put it on the altar, just as Gideon did:

> "The LORD said to him, "Take the second bull from your father's herd, the one seven years old. Tear down your father's altar to Baal and cut down the Asherah pole beside it. Then build a proper kind of altar to the Lord your God on the top of this height. Using the wood of the Asherah pole that you cut down, offer the second bull as a burnt offering." (Judges 6:25-26)

BREAKING GENERATIONAL CURSES

Most of us have generational curses to break. What is a generational curse? Simply they are negative, oppressive things that you see recurring throughout the generations in your bloodline. The secular world uses the term hereditary or 'genetic predisposition'. Various health issues (heart disease, diabetes, sickle cell anemia, etc.), infertility, psychological (mental and emotional) issues such as bi-polar disorder, depression, anger, rage, etc.), being accident prone, premature death, and financial issues, and more, are often generational curses that have been passed down in families. Don't accept them – break them, and reverse the curse!

You shall know the truth and the truth will set you free! (John 8:32) **When we know the truth of who we are in Christ, we have the freedom and authority to walk in it.** Walking in our authority in Christ we break unholy ancestral ties, alliances and curses. **We proclaim and invoke the truth of who we are in Christ as it is greater than whatever the facts of our history in our natural bloodlines may be.** You have authority in Christ, to renounce, nullify and void any deals with the devil your ancestors may have made in Christ.

Declare your blood bought inheritance of sonship, in Christ Jesus over your life:

"Father, thank you for the blood of Jesus Christ that makes me Your son/daughter. I am free from generational curses that were in my bloodline. (*Name them: health concerns, addictions, mental/emotional issues, occult practices, poverty, etc.*) I am a new creation in Christ Jesus. **I decree and declare that the DNA of heaven is my portion!** I have been freed from the sin of my forefathers, from the law of sin and death."

If you're adopted and don't know the history in your bloodline if you know your nationality it may reveal information on your heritage, do some research. Break known potential strongholds or stereotypes associated with certain ethnicities. For example, the Irish are known for excessive drinking and fighting, Germans are known for stubbornness, the French are known for romantic love affairs, etc. (I'm Irish, German and French.) Some ethnicities and races are known for a pre-disposition toward specific diseases, ie; sickle-cell anemia, high blood pressure, etc.

Break any residue of rejection or abandonment that may be lingering from birth. You are chosen and beloved!

A friend of mine asked me once, "Why do generational curses seem to be so resilient? They don't seem to leave! Even after binding and loosing." The answer is five-fold:

1. Our DNA has been altered by generational sin repeatedly committed over time through the generations and passed down. (The world calls this heredity.) It needs to be restored. Things occurring over several generations can actually alter DNA. You've heard of people having a genetic predisposition to things, for example, diabetes, alcoholism, etc. There are family diseases that were handed down. (But healing is the children's bread!) *Decree the DNA of heaven over your life*!
2. Our mindsets (thinking) became compromised. Things that are 'familiar' in our bloodlines we accept as normal, or rationalize away, making excuses for them. **It takes a minimum of 3 weeks, or longer, to break a habit and about 1 nano-second to reinstate it.** *Be intentional about your thought life. Arrest old ways of thinking with God thoughts* (Phil. 4:18) Temptation and going back to old ways usually begins in the battle of the mind.
3. Stand firm. Satan is a liar. Often after times of deliverance and prayers for healing things manifest that are contradictory. Standfast, God may bring us into 'progressive' breakthroughs. Our faith is stretched in the waiting. Watch, pray and persevere.
4. Some generational curses were invoked by witches and covens under evil alliances, they are broken with a corporate anointing. Seek corporate prayer and ministry.
5. We like our sin. *You won't cast out and keep out what you still enjoy playing with.*

More come into breakthrough and deliverance than maintain it.

There was a gentleman, Stanley, who struggled with a spirit of infirmity. In his bloodline many had died tragically and prematurely. He had out-lived others in his family, but was afflicted with one crazy illness after another – strange, obscure things. Stanley received miraculous healing, documented in his medical records, only to have another thing afflict him. (That's one sure sign you're dealing with a spirit of infirmity; if the pain or ailment travels from one area to another.) He had several miracles in his life, one right after the other! I've never seen anyone as unexcited about miraculous healing and deliverance as Stanley. He'd get healed and then wouldn't say much about it. He did not want to draw attention to himself. I wanted to scream, "Stanley, it's not about you, it's about

Him! Don't be backward about it. Boldly declare His goodness!!" Do NOT be shy about God's blessings in your life. Magnify, glorify and boast about His goodness!! (Psalm 34:3)

Regarding healing, physically, mentally, and emotionally often God performs 'progressive miracles'. Sometimes it appears things get worse before they get better. Satan is a liar. One of the devil's favorite tactics is to wear down the saints with discouragement. Don't let him! My husband received a prophetic word of healing over his lungs. Then things got worse, via several hospitalizations and grim diagnosis. He had to be on portable oxygen 24/7. Our families thought we were nuts believing for healing. Next doctors detected a growth in his lungs requiring surgery. However, they couldn't operate, he was too weak. They couldn't do anything for him medically. Almost a year later, the doctor called, they couldn't explain it, but the CT scan showed NO growth in his lungs! We believe for complete healing in every part of his body. He will also have a gift in healing. **God is granting him authority in the area he was attacked in. The Lord is reversing the curse!**

Hard to Break

When a curse has been invoked by a satanic coven, stand in a corporate anointing, breaking that curse. "A three-fold cord is not easily broken." (Ecclesiastes 4:12) "But you will chase your enemies and they will fall before you by the sword; five of you will chase a hundred, and a hundred of you will chase ten thousand, and your enemies will fall before you by the sword. I will turn toward you and make you fruitful and multiply you, and I will confirm My covenant with you." (Leviticus 26:7-9)

One of our members, Luwanda (fictitious name), had been designated by a coven at birth for satanic purposes. The opposition she encountered, especially once she dedicated her life to Christ, was immense. The demons were infuriated that she was serving the Lord. But like Stanley, Luwanda was very quiet about her battles, victories, and struggles, even defensive about attention brought to it. She tended to hold people at arm's length, she'd start to get close with people and then retreat. Whether you are a Stanley (with multiple infirmities) or a Luwanda (with witchcraft spells & curses set against you), don't allow the enemy to keep you isolated. ***Isolation is a snare of the enemy***. The enemy wants to cut you off from corporate anointing and relationship because he knows that would terminate his lease or hold on you.

You were called for freedom (Galatians 5:1) and to inherit a blessing! (1 Peter 3:9) **You will be more than a conqueror; you will have victory, *with dominion and***

authority to minister to others in that area you were tested in. The anointing comes through the life.

If we don't cut the ties and lies they establish themselves in our life; creating a false sense of identity and dependency that we become tethered to. Ties such as: addictions, sexual promiscuity, homosexuality, transgenderism, cutting, etc. If not dealt with a false identity and appetites take root spiritually and are passed down generationally.

To maintain liberty and freedom in Christ, Chuck Pierce exhorts, "**Cut ties with immorality that have been in your bloodline or the land where you are** the steward.

This issue is one that we must take seriously. Immorality has become a vague term, and a non-issue for those in power. Our society has come to believe that anyone can do whatever is right in their own sight. But Satan knows that every immoral act opens up a greater legal right for him to infiltrate land and homes. With the advent of the internet, there is even greater access to things like pornography and adult chat rooms. None of these things is benign. **What is done in secret can bring serious consequences through defilement** – not only of those involved, but upon the land on which their sin occurred." [1]

We've got to stop playing with our demons; learn to hate what He hates and love what He loves. Decree and declare the DNA of heaven to be re-established in our bloodlines, retrain our thought life, as we "deny ourselves, pick up our cross and follow Him." (Luke 9:23)

Too often people are set free and then go back into old bondages. **Maintaining our freedom is vital to securing our gates.** I loose great grace for victorious living and establishing kingdom authority over our own lives! New mindsets obedience and desires aligned with His with a washing in His love, forgiveness and acceptance.

> For if you live according to the flesh, you will die; but if by the Spirit you put to death the misdeeds of the body, you will live. (Romans 8:13)

> ***"Submit yourselves, then, to God. Resist the devil, and he will flee from you.*** *Come near to God and he will come near to you. Wash your hands, you sinners, and purify your hearts, you double-minded." (James 4:7-8)*

ESTABLISHING GENERATIONAL BLESSING
Contend in the Gates for the Generations

To identify and break curses is good and needed, but that's not enough. **We must bind *and* loose – you can't have one without the other**, they go together like salt and pepper, bread and butter. After Jesus told His disciples that He was giving them the keys of the kingdom and that the gates of hell would not prevail He said:

> "I will give you the keys of the kingdom of heaven; whatever you bind on earth will be bound in heaven, *and whatever you loose on earth will be loosed in heaven*." (Matthew 16:19)

The blessing is greater than the curse! Curses may extend for 3-4 generations, but the blessing may extend to 1,000 generations. **Beloved it's up to each of us to decree and declare His blessing over our bloodline; loosing and establishing a perpetual, generational blessing.** We stand in a double portion of authority as two covenants bind together in alignment and agreement: our God-authority, under the new covenant in the blood of Christ and the authority of our natural birthright come into alignment: (1) as a child of God and heir of salvation (2) the priestly authority of our natural, family covenantal birthright specifically designated and called over our bloodline by God. We decree as Joshua did, **"As for me and my household, we will serve the Lord!"** (Joshua 24:15)

> "for I, the LORD your God, am a jealous God, punishing the children for the sin of the parents to the third and fourth generation of those who hate me, but showing love to a thousand generations of those who love me and keep my commandments." (Exodus 20:5-6)

Many come from a long lineage of faith. Some, like myself, are the first in their family to be born again in Jesus Christ. Whether you are the first or part of a long line of believers, establish and activate blessing over your bloodline as you pray, decree and declare blessing – to 1,000 generations.

Live a life of faith, sow seeds of blessing and kindness, pray, decree and declare salvation and blessing over your family. This powerfully secures gates, transcending our lives to future generations in covenant, familial blessing – on earth as it is in heaven.

> "He commanded our ancestors to teach their children, **so the next generation would know them**, ***even the children yet to be born***, and they in turn would tell their children. Then they would put their trust in God and would not forget his deeds but would keep his commands. They would not be like their

> ancestors— a stubborn and rebellious generation, whose hearts were not loyal to God," (Psalm 78:5-8)

BREAKING SOUL TIES

"We have met the enemy and he is us." We blame the devil for so many things, giving him far more credit than he deserves. Sometimes it's as simple as uprooting ungodliness in our lives. **God sovereignly brings us into freedom and deliverance, then we walk it out and maintain it.** "Work out your own salvation with fear and trembling." (Philippians 2:12) Walking the walk is a little like dieting, we need to maintain a *lifestyle* of healthy eating, quick fix fad diets usually don't keep the weight off. We want breakthrough and then go back to business as usual.

Before we look at Satan and the world, we need to examine ourselves. **You won't cast out or keep out what you still enjoy playing with.** As Bishop Bill Hamon says, "The devil can't take anything from us that we have not given to him."

This is a generation of motivate me but leave my demons alone. (Kevin Powell) Or, as rock star Bono put it, "Stop asking God to bless what you're doing. Find out what God's doing." What He has blessed will be blessed.

It's time to 'unfriend' soul-ties. On social media when we unfriend someone they no longer have access to communicate with us and we stop communicating with them. That's what needs to happen when we break soul-ties. *Stop holding on and re-opening doors*!

We're big on blaming Satan, but we need to look at the man in the mirror! Remove Satan's legitimate gate access. If soul-ties have our heart, they hold a key. Let's examine ourselves. Some things need to be driven out of our personal gates.

Breaking soul ties and pulling out of toxic relationships can be difficult and painful. It may possibly be one of the hardest things you walk through; as well as one of the most life-giving and necessary for your well-being in Christ.

<u>Suggestion</u>: When breaking soul ties saturate your spirit with worship and the word. I have a garden that requires weeding. The best time to pull weeds is after a long soaking rain. The ground is softened and weeds come up, from the root, much more easily than they do when the ground is dry and hard. Our hearts are His garden. The more intimate we are in prayer and worship, the greater our love saturation with Him.

> "*When you fall deeper in love with Jesus, you fall out of love with the things of the world.*" – Elizabeth Estes

SOUL v. SPIRIT:

Our soul is the area of self, our humanity, that encompasses: thoughts, emotions, feelings. The spirit-man within us is that part of us that connects with God or other spirit beings. Without a personal relationship with Jesus Christ, most feel like there must be something more in life. Once Christ lives within them they sense such completeness, love and joy. Conversely those who have been involved with dark spirits, witchcraft and the occult sense a presence in their being also. 'Son of Sam' serial killer, David Berkowitz, expressed regretfully, "I thought I was appeasing the devil. At the time, I was serving him. I feel that he took over my mind and body, and I just surrendered over to those very dark forces. I regret that with all my heart."[2]

"Thanks be to God who leads us in His triumph!" (2 Corinthians 2:14) We are not marionettes, we have been given a free-will and volition to choose. "Choose this day who you will serve, as for me and my household we will serve the Lord." (Joshua 24:15)

The soul and the spirit closely relate and intertwine, but they are separable. "*For the word of God is alive and active. Sharper than any double-edged sword, it penetrates even to dividing soul and spirit, joints and marrow; it judges the thoughts and attitudes of the heart.*" (Hebrews 4:12)

Soul ties are the things and relationships that our soul desires and craves; they have become attached to our heart and/or mind. Soul ties are often, but not always, formed through sexual relationships. Because soul ties carry deep-seated feelings and emotions, some people can never bring themselves to cut the ties. If we are not careful our soul ties become idols – things that we love more than God.

> *When tempted, no one should say, "God is tempting me." For God cannot be tempted by evil, nor does he tempt anyone; but each person is tempted when they are dragged away by their own evil desire and enticed. Then, after desire has conceived, it gives birth to sin; and sin, when it is full-grown, gives birth to death. (James 1:13-15)*

Picture a hot air balloon tethered to the ground by several ropes. You're in the basket waiting to rise and can't wait for the ride to begin. It doesn't rise and you sit waiting. You realize that unless *you* remove the ropes you'll never soar, but to remove the ropes will cause you temporary pain. You may even get rope-burn, because it's so hard to let go.

> *And the God of all grace, who called you to his eternal glory in Christ, after you have suffered a little while, will himself restore you and make you strong, firm and steadfast." (1 Peter 5:8-10)*

What soul ties are holding you back? Mindsets, relationships, detrimental habits, pornography, promiscuity, orgies, homosexual relationships, drugs, prejudice, etc. Anything prioritized over God are idols, ie; sports, television, food, etc. Whatever has preeminence over God in your life has a hold on you. Judge yourself and act, so that God doesn't have to. A gentleman in our church couldn't fast from food due to medical reasons. I suggested he consider fasting from tv instead. He looked stunned. LOL! I think fasting from food would have been far easier for him.

> *For it is time for judgment to begin with God's household; and if it begins with us, what will the outcome be for those who do not obey the gospel of God? (1 Peter 4:17)*

The way of the cross wasn't only for Jesus.

> *"Then he said to them all: "Whoever wants to be my disciple must deny themselves and take up their cross daily and follow me. For whoever wants to save their life will lose it, but whoever loses their life for me will save it. What good is it for someone to gain the whole world, and yet lose or forfeit their very self?"* (Luke 9:23-25)

> *Woe to the world because of the things that cause people to stumble! Such things must come, but woe to the person through whom they come! If your hand or your foot causes you to stumble, cut it off and throw it away. It is better for you to enter life maimed or crippled than to have two hands or two feet and be thrown into eternal fire. And if your eye causes you to stumble, gouge it out and throw it away. It is better for you to enter life with one eye than to have two eyes and be thrown into the fire of hell.* (Matthew 18:7-9; Matthew 5:28-29)

Simple steps and prayer in breaking soul ties:

1. Identify it and Repent if any sins were committed in forming the soul-tie.
2. Get rid of tokens of the tie or ungodly aspects of the relationship. (rings, gifts, cards, pictures)
3. Renounce and repent of any vows that were made with one another in Jesus name. ("I could never love anyone else like I do you.";

4. Renounce the actual soul-tie: "In Jesus' name, I now renounce any ungodly soul ties formed between myself and ____*name*_____ as a result of ____*action*______."
5. Break the soul-tie, standing in your God-given authority in Christ. "I now break and sever any ungodly soul ties formed between myself and __*name*____ because of _____*action*______ in Jesus' name."

Breaking soul-ties, is freeing, but can be painful, temporarily. There may be a relational tearing in our hearts. God will restore 100-fold anything that we sacrifice. I'm so proud of those who choose God's ways over their own soul-ish ways.

One of our young men, Raul (fictitious name) had a rough past. He'd been a street-fighter and drug dealer. Raul didn't just accept Jesus as his Savior while he was in prison, he enthroned Him as Lord of his life! Raul got out of prison and went immediately to church (that is how we met). One Sunday Raul came to church carrying a gym bag. He told me, "Pastor, please don't open it in the sanctuary. What's inside is from my old life. I want to lay it on the altar and never pick it up again." Together we prayed at the altar, renouncing the soul-ties, while decreeing and declaring his identity in Christ. Raul stomped on the bag 7 times, as a prophetic act akin to striking the ground with arrows for victory based upon this passage:

> "Then he said, "Take the arrows," and the king took them. Elisha told him, "Strike the ground." He struck it three times and stopped. The man of God was angry with him and said, "You should have struck the ground five or six times; then you would have defeated Aram and completely destroyed it. But now you will defeat it only three times." (2 Kings 13:17-19)

After prayer, crushing the gym bag and its contents, we threw it out. That was over 5 years ago. Raul never looked back, or picked up any of those things again. He broke all soul-ties thoroughly. He is now leading, moving in healing, the prophetic, signs and wonders.

Another couple, John and Maria (fictitious names) came to me, they were pregnant, out of wedlock. They asked me what they should do. They were committed to having the baby, but not sure about their relationship. John and Maria didn't want to stop living together, but weren't sure they wanted to marry either. I encouraged them not to over-complicate things. One of 2 things needed to take place either: a.) commit to marriage b.) separate and stop living together. Bottomline, in Christ there just isn't a scriptural precedent for living together outside of a covenant relationship. God designed the beauty of sex, children, and family to be within the context and sacredness of covenant; a holy bond, agreement and secure commitment to one another with God's partnership. If your partner is not the one to have a lifetime commitment to in marriage, then why are you still living together? They chose marriage. John and Maria have been through hard times and good times together. They and their family are growing. Their children are secure in their love and union as a family. They move prophetically and are growing as a kingdom couple and family!

Maturity and obedience brings growth in dominion over our own spirit and in kingdom authority.

> *'Well done, good and faithful servant! You have been faithful with a few things; I will put you in charge of many things. Come and share your master's happiness!'* (Matthew 25:21)

Samuel when he anointed David as king, used anointing oil from a ram's horn. It didn't come out of a glass bottle or vial. It came from the life and strength of the animal.

SHIFTING Brings Hidden Areas to Light

This is a time of shifting and clashing of kingdoms! Naturally and spiritually tremendous shifts are taking place. Have you ever moved a major appliance (stove or refrigerator) for repair or replacement? Mercy! The dust and dirt that's behind it gets uncovered!!

The Church thought she was doing so well. Then came rumbling and shifting at home and abroad. God divinely moved some of the 'furniture and appliances'. Our hidden dust and dirt, such as; prejudice, discord, unforgiveness, control, manipulation, fear, insecurity, religiosity, and more has been uncovered. He loves His Bride and is cleansing her. A lifestyle of on-going Repentance and prayer will align us and bring forth revival.

RECOGNIZING WITCHCRAFT in the ATMOSPHERE

Because of Satanic activity, anti-Christ mindsets, and sin some areas have become bastions or havens for witchcraft. It can permeate the atmosphere of a region. The gates of an area need to be taken back and secured or destruction comes. Possessing the gates is the equivalent to possessing the city. (Genesis 22:17; 24:60)

In regions with witchcraft strongholds there's an increase in crime, drunkenness, addictions, backbiting, fighting, sexual promiscuity, homosexuality, etc. We live in a region where there is a high concentration of witchcraft and sorcery practiced and a corresponding high crime rate.

Lifestyle choices and habits determine the ties of our hearts. There is a small town in NJ, only about 1 square mile, yet it has 13 bars. You don't have to be Einstein or move in word of knowledge to figure out they had problems with alcoholism, fights, and family issues. That town had a high percentage of an ethnicity known for drinking.

Alcohol and drug abuse use can be a gateway for demonic activity. A Greek word for sorcery and witchcraft is *pharmakeia*, found in Galatians 5:20 and Revelation 9:21. The origin of our modern-day word 'pharmacy' comes from *pharmakeia*. Alcohol and drugs alter one's state of consciousness.

The following are signs that a witchcraft spirit may be at work:

- confusion,
- inability to focus
- depression
- unexplained tiredness and fatigue
- a general feeling of fear and anxiety
- anger and/ or fits of rage
- pain and/or chronic illness – you get better from one thing and another comes upon you or you have a pain that shifts and moves to different areas of your body

These things are normal, however, when they come upon you 'out of no-where' for no apparent reason, clinging to and oppressing you, it's a spiritual matter. Take authority over it or reach out, seek deliverance ministry.

IMPACT of our HISTORY UPON the LAND:

The actions, or lack thereof of past generations effect the land in which we live today. The ground can carry a curse. This biblical principal is evident in Genesis 4 when Cain killed Abel, "The LORD said, "What have you done? Listen! Your brother's blood cries out to me from the ground. Now you are under a curse and driven from the ground, which opened its mouth to receive your brother's blood from your hand. When you work the ground, it will no longer yield its crops for you." (Genesis 4:10-12) Just as Abel's blood cried out from the ground, there is blood that cries out from the ground today.

We are a land whose motto is "In God We Trust" yet we removed prayer and the reading of the Word, the Bible, from our public schools. Madeline Murray O'Hair led a hell-bent crusade to have prayer and the reading of the Bible removed from public schools in the 1960's. She was a tool in the hand of Satan. Madeline Murray O'Hair's American Atheists Organization were key in the Supreme

Court decision changing the face of American education, banning prayer from public schools. I was in first grade when prayer was removed. I have memories from kindergarten in public school and part of first grade of morning prayer, the reading of Psalm 23 and the Lord's Prayer, with the pledge of allegiance as part of our daily morning exercises. And then they disappeared, removed, from our schools.

Ms. O'Hair along with many others, was also in support of legalized abortion. The blood of our nation cries out from the ground. Between 1970 to 2013 over 51,883,303 babies were aborted. [Norma McCorvey is the woman that was behind Roe vs. Wade, the 1973 Supreme Court decision that legalized abortion. Roe was a pseudonym. Which by the way, McCorvey *did* have her baby and subsequently became born-again, as well as became an advocate for pro-life.]

> "*If anyone causes one of these little ones—those who believe in me—to stumble, it would be better for them to have a large millstone hung around their neck and to be drowned in the depths of the sea. Woe to the world because of the things that cause people to stumble!*" (Matthew 18:6)

> "*Make sure there is no man or woman, clan or tribe as in among you today whose heart turns away from the* Lord *our God to go and worship the gods of those nations; make sure there is no root among you that produces such bitter poison.*
>
> *The* Lord *will never be willing to forgive them; his wrath and zeal will burn against them. All the curses written in this book will fall on them, and the* Lord *will blot out their names from under heaven. The* Lord *will single them out from all the tribes of Israel for disaster, according to all the curses of the covenant written in this Book of the Law.*" (Deuteronomy 29:19-21)

Ms. O'Hair, her son, Jon Garth and granddaughter Robin disappeared in 1995. Six years later in 2001, their bodies were found in a storage locker in Austin, Texas. It wasn't until 2006 that they were conclusively identified. They had been dismembered (hands and feet removed, for no one to trace their identity). They were murdered in cold blood by one of her former employees of the American Atheist Organization. He first held them captive for a year, extorting over $610,000 from them. It was a brutal and tragic demise. Even in judgement the Lord is merciful and a remnant remains. She had one surviving child, William, who became a Christian evangelist.[3]

[*Many want to see prayer re-instated in public schools. Think twice. If prayer were to be reinstated in public schools, with America in its current state, it would no longer be in a Judeo-Christian context. Every religion would have to be given 'equal time'. Children would be praying to Vishnu, Buddha, etc. If prayer were reinstated it wouldn't be like it was in the early '60's. We are no longer a Judeo-Christian society. Reform and a major revival are needed first.*]

Know the history and events of the geographic area where you live and the land(s) that God has given you to minister in. Knowledge of territorial spirits in regions will yield a correlating increase in effective praying.

In the USA our history is deep and wide; in addition to slavery and injustice against African-Americans, anti-Semitism, Native Americans experienced extreme injustices, Chinese-Americans were enslaved in order to build the trans-continental railroad, Japanese-Americans went through deep prejudice in 'determent camps' during WWII, women were treated as 2nd class citizens (1920's won the right to vote, 1930's secured the right to an education), racism against Mexican and Latino-Americans, and the list goes on. We repent prayerfully of the wrongs that have taken place.

As Chuck Pierce said, "Declare an end to covenant breaking. During the reign of King David, a great famine came on the land. When David inquired of the Lord concerning this famine, God said to him, *"It is because of Saul and his bloodthirsty house, because he killed the Gibeonites"* (*2 Samuel 21:1*). The Gibeonites entered covenant with Israel in the days of Joshua. This covenant guaranteed their safety. Yet Saul broke covenant by murdering many of them and planning to massacre the rest. As a result, famine came on the land as God removed His blessing and Satan was allowed access. The famine did not strike immediately, but came when the new king came to power. Many of our homes in the United States have been built on land which was taken through broken treaties with Native Americans. Those broken treaties from years ago can defile and give the enemy a foothold on the land where we live today!"[4]

Let's listen for the voice and strategy of God in how to unseat the defilement of broken covenant, the offense of injustices and uproot territorial spirits that have taken false claim in the land. He will reveal prophetic intercessory strategies to us. Just as the Jews commemorate Purim with fasting and celebration, there will be times to be set aside and observed as a memorial from our own histories.

COMMUNION as PRIESTS_
Standing in the Gap – the Blood of the New Covenant & Repentance

The following is a true story regarding 'The Devil's Triangle' in the Bahamas. This is an area of ocean in the Bahamas where there have been countless mysterious disappearances of ships and planes. Historically the Devil's Triangle is an area where atrocities at sea occurred; slaves were thrown overboard by sea captains on their journey to the States. There have been reports by some of a continuous haunted sound (like mournful singing) that could be heard while they were sailing in the waters of the Bermuda Triangle.

Between 1650 and 1860 as many as 15 million enslaved people were transported from West Africa to the Americas. And from the 9th to the 19th century millions more were dispersed throughout Asia and the Middle East. The African Diaspora refers to the movements of these people and their descendants throughout the world.[5]

In situations where water was running out, or there was an outbreak of disease some captains, reasoning that the slaves were going to die anyway, would throw slaves, thought to be too sick to recover, overboard. (They would recoup their financial losses on their 'cargo' through insurance.)

This abhorrent practice brought with it the judgement of God, as slavery has upon our land and with Cain and Abel the blood cries from the ground and sea.

During the 1990's, a convocation of ministers, representing various races, ethnicities, and denominations held communion, with the express intent to repent for the sin and atrocities of the past in the Devil's Triangle. This diverse group of ministers knelt in the unity of covenant, faith, worship and intercession, repenting – weeping, for the blood of those murdered, they grieved at the guilt of the abusers. These ministers stood in the gap partaking of the Lord's supper; appropriating the elements of the body and blood of Christ. Therefore, only a blood sacrifice would do. As the Word says, He saves to the uttermost.

They believed God repented, prophetically appropriating the sacrament of communion, which activated a divine outpouring that healed the land:

Since then, the mysterious disappearances of ships has ceased. Bishop Joseph Garlington shared this with me, as he was one of the ministers who participated in this sacred time of repentance and communion in the Bahamas.

The God who was, who is and who is to come; time is relative to Him. **The power of the blood of Christ transcends time and place.** Moving in revelation and faith men moved by the Holy Spirit could stand in the 1990's and cleanse the stain of the blood that cried from the grave from 1650 to 1860. There is nothing that He can't do! The blood that Jesus shed 2,000 years ago on Calvary, will never lose its power!

- Romans 3:25 (NASB) "God displayed publicly as a propitiation in His blood through faith. *This was* to demonstrate His righteousness, because in the forbearance of God He passed over the sins previously committed;"
- Hebrews 2:17 (NASB) "so that He might become a merciful and faithful high priest in things pertaining to God, to make propitiation for the sins of the people.
- 1 John 2:2 (NASB) He Himself is the propitiation for our sins; and not for ours only, but also for *those of* the whole world.

Uganda:

I shared this with pastors and friends Pastor Nelson Abaliwano and Pastor Saul Ashabah in Busoga, Uganda. They have been burdened by dysfunction within families in Uganda. As we prayed and looked at the history of the land God gave us insight. In the 1970's ('71 to '79) Uganda was ruled by an evil dictator named Idi Amin. During his reign Idi Amin ordered the brutal murder and genocide of approximately 300,000 people, men, women and children. Families were left parentless or fatherless. Fear and terror were a way of life. Although the ruthless regime has ended, the blood still cries, the land and its families are healing. We will be traveling there to join them for a time of prophetic intercession, ministry and communion over the land.

The blood of Jesus Christ cleanses, heals, brings reconciliation, and restoration. The blood of Christ is alive and active today and it is for the nations.

Face the fear and do it anyway!

Sometimes the only way out is through. "Dress for success and fake it 'til you make it!" Just do it! We are finding our voice and using it.

God is calling His people to deal fatal blows to insecurity and fear that have retarded our progress of kingdom advancement. As former President George W. Bush once stated, "I think it's very hard to fight the war on terrorism if we're in retreat. ... The enemy is very good about exploiting weakness, ... It's going to be very important ... that we project strength."[6] We're arising to face the fear and 'do it anyway'! Truth will no longer stumble in the streets.

> *Do not bow down before their gods or worship them or follow their practices. You must demolish them and break their sacred stones to pieces. Worship the LORD* your God, and his blessing will be on you. *(Exodus 23:24-25)*

"Lord, even the demons submit to us in your name." He replied, "I saw Satan fall like lightning from heaven. I have given you authority to trample on snakes and scorpions and to overcome all the power of the enemy; nothing will harm you. However, do not rejoice that the spirits submit to you, but rejoice that your names are written in heaven."" (Luke 10:17-20)

Deliverance and Freedom
Jezebel, Ahab, and Athaliah

Much has been said about the demonic influence of: Jezebel, her daughter Athaliah, Leviathan and Belial in the world and the Church today. Whole books have been written on each of them. (If you're not informed about these spirits I highly recommend you learn about them. Forewarned is fore-armed. See the *Recommended Reading List*.) Some demons love to hang out in casinos & bars and some love to hang out in church! The ones named here are partial to churches, but will go wherever they're granted access.

Witchcraft infiltrating the Church in America is different than in places, such as Africa, there witchcraft is overt and in your face. **In America witches often astro-project and you may not realize you're being influenced by witchcraft.** It comes cleverly disguised as wolves in sheep's clothing. I've seen witches sit in the back row of churches quietly placing incantations over a body.

I was in a church where a woman had a blank expression on her face sitting in the back. At first I felt a wave of sympathy for her. The Holy Spirit told me, "Rebuke the spirit that is operating within her, bind it and mute it." So I did. Then I watched as we worshipped. She still sat, with a blank expression, her lips were moving, but she was not participating in worship. The worship was so intense, the presence of God so profound that she left before the meeting was over. Worship is warfare. God inhabits the praises of His people. No witch can stand in the throne room of the Presence of the true and living God. Our God is a Warrior *and* King of Kings.

A tree is known by its fruit. Witchcraft spirits in the church produce: rebellion, stubbornness, deception, control, manipulation, jealousy, gossip, backbiting, seduction, an attack on finances, health and more.

Saints are rising to expel witchcraft and religious spirits from the Church! If not dealt with it gets worse vying for domination. We must first recognize them. **Growing in discernment and have our spiritual senses trained to discern good from evil is increasingly important!** Things are not always what they appear to be. Salt can look like sugar.

JEZEBEL

The spirit of Jezebel is rampant in American churches. I've only given a summary here. (Learn more about this spirit if you're not familiar with it. See 'Recommended Reading' at the back of this book.)

Jezebel's name means "chaste, free from carnal connection". She was the opposite of what her name stood for. **Jezebel was a seductive, deceptive, manipulating woman** who would go so far as murder, she put a hit out on the prophets, worshiped idols, and is Biblically linked to witchcraft and sorcery. This same spirit is at work today to seduce the saints into sin, control, and bring apostasy. **Jezebel bewitches and blinds people with flattery as she deceives, manipulates and gains control.** Often people are not aware that a spirit of Jezebel is at work until it is too late. This spirit is subtly deceptive and rampant in churches.

The evil Jezebel committed came out of a hurt and broken spirit. She was the daughter of king Ethbaal of Zidonia (Tyre and Sidon), a region that worshipped Baal & Ashtoreth. Jezebel was fervently devoted to Baal worship. Crude and lewd sexual rituals and orgies were routine aspects of Baal & Ashtoreth worship. (Ashtoreth was the mother of Baal and said to be his mistress.) The ritual, sexual abuse of daily 'worship' produced a brokenness within Jezebel. Add to this her father brokered her in marriage for political gain. Both kings Ahab and Ethbaal) wanted to strengthen their alliance and power base in the region. Thus, Jezebel moved to a foreign land, as men arranged her marriage to Ahab, Israel's king.

Today, the spirit of Jezebel attempts to take control, often bringing great confusion amidst deception and manipulation. I have witnessed the spirit of Jezebel attempt 'takeovers' of godly leadership from within church governments. **The Jezebel spirit purposes to stop the flow of God's spirit in the Church as godly leadership is undermined.**

AHAB

So much time is focused on Jezebel that we almost overlook the fact that **you can't have a Jezebel without an Ahab. He was a milk-toast of a man, who hated confrontation. He abdicated his authority and position, by not taking a stand.** He was content to let Jezebel run the show; placating her and trying to keep her happy. As he tried to appease and please her **he compromised his own core beliefs and values.** He allowed her to bring into Israel about 450 priests of Baal and 400 of Ashtoreth, 850 pagan priests, from Tyre & Sidon. Then he erected a temple in Israel to Baal for his wife and her priests to worship in. This brought a curse upon the land. Moreover, Jezebel put a hit out on the prophet

Elijah, Ahab did nothing to stop her. Scripture has recorded him as one of the wickedest kings ever. It is worth noting that the authority of America's men in the home and in church has waned – in large part through abdication.

America needs godly, manly men, who won't abdicate, but will firmly, lovingly, take up their authority, as the Father does – on earth as it is in heaven.

ATHALIAH

Some have said watch out for Athaliah, Jezebel's daughter, she will be on the rise soon following after her mother Jezebel. She's already in motion! Athaliah's been on the move for several years now. She, like her Mom, Jezebel, are thriving within the Church in America. Athaliah is more seducing, and more treacherous than Jezebel was! **Athaliah was going to murder her grandchildren because of her lust for power.** (2 Kings 11:2)

Many ministers have shared with me their stories – called by God to plant and pioneer churches, as they ventured out they were ill-treated by the ministry that they were initially birthed from. Some have jokingly referred to it as being given the 'left foot of fellowship', but this phenomenon is more than that. These pioneers left the initial ministry submitted, with a right spirit, and were ostensibly blessed both publicly and privately. That is how it appeared (deception) – they were cut off, spoken about behind their backs, and literally mocked and cursed.

Still others, who have been in ministry for several years, as they began to thrive, grow, expand and become 'known' came under attack. As one minister said to me, "Oh everyone blesses you to your face – even prays public blessing over you, praising you when you're small. But succeed and then see how they act toward you." That Athaliah-like spirit of jealousy came against them.

There are ministries coming to the forefront that have His anointing upon them, at the threshold of a mighty release of His glory. Jezebel, Ahab, and Athaliah are at work to thwart destiny and glory at the gateways. **When we cheer one another on, fanning the flames of the Spirit not trying to extinguish them, speaking highly of one another we suffocate Athaliah and glorify God.**

Sadly, like Athaliah, the Church in America has tried to kill her own children and grandchildren. Just like Saul tried to remove his successor, David, who rose by anointing into position. Like the brothers of Joseph, who threw him into a pit – the spirit of Athaliah casts doubt and stigma on the personhood and ministries of her offspring and grandchildren. This is an offense that rises before God.

Church REPENT!

Cut soul ties and all personal 'in-roads' with these spirits.

As Sandie Freed says, "Ask the Lord to show you the Jezebels and Athaliah's in your life, the ones who are coming against your destiny. Its best to cut all soul ties with them so they can no longer intrude into your calling and rob you of your destiny. When you cut the soul ties, do it all the way .... Cut deep! Get rid of their e-mails, pictures .... Anywhere you are connected to them! Ask the Holy Spirit to lead you to where the open gates are to their poisonous venom!"[7]

We pioneered a new planting, coming out of a Jezebellian/ Athaliah-like setting. We left Believers' Church (fictitious name) with a right heart, submitted, honoring the other ministry and leadership. They blessed us to our face in a public meeting, but spoke negatively about us behind our backs. (When Christians speak against other Christians their words become as witchcraft words and prayers.) In addition, Believers' Church members literally visited our members, at their place of business, and continued to call them for over 2 years, urging them to come back to them. Our members were told by Believers' Church that they'd never amount to anything or enter their personal purpose or destiny because they had left them. That is controlling, manipulative and deceptive behavior.

If you have laughed, scoffed or belittled another ministry, REPENT – quickly!

We renewed our ordination afresh, as our initial ordination as ministers was through Believers' Church. However, we never spoke negatively regarding them. We blessed Believers' Church and moved on. It wasn't easy, it seemed wherever we went, someone from there followed us, literally, in an oppressive fashion. Father forgive them, they didn't know what they were doing.

The Church must reject jealousy and in-fighting. **The one who invests in his brother and sister is the one the Lord's favor will rest upon.**

Family Comparison Chart: Jezebel, Ahab, & Athaliah

Attributes	**Jezebel**	**Ahab**	**Athaliah**
Relationship & origins	Daughter of king of Tyre (Baal worshippers, married his daughter off for political & economic gain & alliances) Queen, Mother – in Israel	Husband – king of Israel married Jezebel	Daughter of Ahab & Jezebel
Known for/ characteristics of	Deception, manipulation, control through seduction, willing to murder prophets of God	Abdicated, placates, easily vacillates & compromises convictions	Jealousy, controls through power, willing to murder – even her grandchildren, causes delay of destiny, attempts to steal anointing
Appears today:	Hurt that hasn't healed properly. Desires control. Takes over and subversively usurps another's authority, often without them realizing it, until it's too late.	Men who abdicate their authority due to fear, leaving the spiritual upbringing of children to the wife. Convictions are selfish. Appease the one they're joined to, compromise godly principles out of fear, hoping for tranquility.	Born out of an unholy, unhealthy union, there is an unquenchable thirst for power at all costs. Motivated by jealously. Speaks negatively about others.

Scriptures	1 Kings 18-21; 2 Kings 9; Rev. 2:20	1 Kings 16-21	2 Kings 8:26; 2 Kings 11; 2 Chronicles 22-23; 24:7

God may or may not unseat those who came against your destiny. But one thing is for certain, He will lift you above, to be the head and not the tail, just as He did with Joseph before his brothers.

Through the struggle, 'Did you learn to love?' We are in the end times. There are several things that are clear about the end times: there will be wars and rumors of wars, earthquakes and natural disasters, apostasy, brothers turning against brothers, children against their parents, wickedness and lawlessness of all types. Where lawlessness and wickedness increase the love of many will grow cold. When love grows cold faith and faithfulness falter. There is only one question that He asks us, that is, 'DID YOU LEARN TO LOVE?' Joseph's brothers did bow before him. However, God did a deep work within his heart first. Joseph wept several times once reunited with his family (Genesis 43-50) And, eventually wept openly before them all. (Genesis 50:17)

The former glory will be greater than the latter. However, it must come forth in love or it will be tainted, void of His love. **God is love. We must reflect Him**. If you've been affected by Jezebel or Athaliah you have known hurt; forgive fully, move forward, healed and cleansed.

Prayer: "Thank you Father, You have given us authority to break every witchcraft prayer of Jezebel and Athaliah in the name of Your Son, Jesus. Others said that I would never amount to anything. But You have said otherwise. Your Word is established. You are breaking the teeth of the devourer. You have called me to be the head and not the tail. Fill the void that the abdication from the spirit of Ahab created. Let the fullness of Christ arise in my life, in my family, and in Your Church today!"

LEVIATHAN

The original Hebrew word for Leviathan means, "twisted," or "coiled." It is thought to have been a crocodile-like creature that lived in the Nile, with curved and piercing teeth. Like a crocodile, its teeth grab its live prey, submerging it into a death roll, before devouring it. The Nile is the main river running through Egypt, symbolic of a land of bondage. Leviathan is a monster-like creature always found by water – looking to attack ships, which are symbolic of ministries, business, and government. He wants to devour kingdom and get us to devour one another. Leviathan is not just a spirit, but a principality.

Recognizing 5 key attributes of how Leviathan attacks:

1. Lies: He lies with, gossip, accusation, criticism, faultfinding and slander the character and name of another.
2. Miscommunication: Miscommunication is rampant in the world as well as within the body of Christ, just look at today's headlines. Often people disagree over something, only to find that they are not in disagreement, but hear one another incorrectly, OR don't truly listen to what another is really saying and stumble over semantics. Leviathan seeks to hide true revelation from you.
3. Sowing discord: When lies and miscommunication flourish then so does misunderstanding, which is a breeding ground for discord.
4. Suggest lies and negative suspicions to us about another.
5. Promote a spirit of pride: Pride in self-righteousness and SELF is especially evident.

Put a gag order on negative talk, not only on what you say, but what you listen to. Be discerning without being demeaning. Satan is the accuser of the brethren, have nothing to do with anything akin to that. Be quick to forgive and quick to bless. "Do not repay anyone evil for evil. Be careful to do what is right in the eyes of everyone. If it is possible, as far as it depends on you, live at peace with everyone." (Romans 12:17-18)

There can be a great deal of 'white noise', like a spiritual haze or fuzziness many have experienced in their ability to hear the voice of God. The atmosphere can be filled with a great deal of witchcraft chatter. (Witchcraft chatter occurs when many are speaking toxic negative words against you. There is a heightened amount of this in areas with anti-Christ and occult activity.) It's like trying to listen to music that is filled with constant, loud static. It interferes with the ability of Christians to properly hear and discern the Father. God is releasing a new level of revelation through dreams to His people that will be off limits to witchcraft chatter. His proceeding rhema goes forth. Lord gives us ears to hear You accurately.

A spirit of pride opens the door to the spirit of Leviathan.

> *Who may ascend the mountain of the LORD?*
> *Who may stand in his holy place?*
> *The one who has clean hands and a pure heart,*
> *who does not trust in an idol*
> *or swear by a false god.* (Psalm 24:3-4)

Walk in love, obedience in a spirit of humility. An ounce of prevention is worth a pound of cure. Do not entertain an accusation of one of your brothers against another, instead by love serve one another.

> *Love is patient, love is kind. It does not envy, it does not boast, it is not proud. It does not dishonor others, it is not self-seeking, it is not easily angered, it keeps no record of wrongs. Love does not delight in evil but rejoices with the truth. It always protects, always trusts, always hopes, always perseveres.*
>
> *Love never fails.* (1 Corinthians 13:4-8)

I've received many prophetic words, but the most significant one was this one: "The attack of the enemy has been great. You've had many offenses, but with each offense, each time, you responded with love – and each time because of that you have put (God has put) a hedge of protection round about you that the enemy has tried to grab you, but he can't because of that love. You've liked slipped through the hands of the enemy because of that love. You've known His love, but now it will be even greater ...

And your family – because of your love, because of all the things, there's been a hedge of protection placed around them of His love as well. The enemy can't have them. God has them corralled in by His love. And God says – He's bringing them in!" [8]

Press into Him for His love. Love deeply, especially amidst offenses – and offenses will come. (BTW – love does NOT mean being a doormat, it does mean forgiving and dealing with yourself. I have a friend that can't say "No" to anyone and is taken advantage of a lot. Once you recognize that you're being manipulated it's up to *you* to draw the line and say NO. If you don't then that's not manipulation anymore, its self-appointed victimization – get help!) **The enemy cannot have a grip or a hold on you when you choose the way of love**. It is costly, but anything less won't stand.

BELIAL

Belial was worshipped as the god Baal. He is part human, part angelic being; ruler over demon spirits and powers. He's also referred to as Beelzebub. Belial is more of a principality than a demon spirit, he was known as an opponent of Christ.

> "*...there shall rise unto you from the tribe of Judah and of Levi, the salvation (Yeshua) of the Lord, and He shall make war against Belial*" (Daniel 5:10-11)

One of the main things evident when Belial is operating is rebellion. Often a self-proclaimed leader emerges, with illegitimate authority. Once again, this spirit flourishes where hurts fester, aren't forgiven or do not heal properly.

This last season was one that Belial battered many in the body of Christ with one crisis, heartbreak, trial and setback after another, to wear out the saints.

> "*He will speak out against the Most High and wear down the saints of the Highest One, and he will intend to make alterations in times and in law; and they will be given into his hand for a time, times, and half a time. But the court will sit for judgment, and his dominion will be taken away, annihilated and destroyed forever. Then the sovereignty, the dominion and the greatness of all* the kingdoms under the whole heaven will be given to the people of the saints of the Highest One; His kingdom *will be* an everlasting kingdom, and all the dominions will serve and obey Him.'" (Daniel 7:25-27)

Warning signs of Belial at work:

1. Physical attacks and weakness, worn out
2. Generational spiritual wickedness
3. Overwhelming shame and hopelessness
4. Lies, uncontrollable feelings of failure
5. Thoughts of suicide
6. Recognizing a thief in finances or losing inheritance
7. False accusations
8. Selfishness, greed, self-centeredness,
9. Lust, perversion, unclean thoughts

As with fighting any spirit, you must be a warrior, engaging in spiritual warfare. Fighting by the spirit, not the flesh.

If you are up against a stronghold or a principality do not go after it until you have ample prayer support and covering. Do not be unwise, or fearful, be strategic, the warfare is real. The Army doesn't send 1 soldier in to war against a nation – many troops are sent in. The larger the opposition, the greater the need for an army of intercessors. **Get prayer covering and prevail!**

Spirit or stronghold 'test':

a. When the faces and names change, but the situational circumstances remain the same you're dealing with a spirit, not a one-time event, person or personality.

b. When something continually comes against you and/or your ministry that seems to be resilient, unrelenting and doesn't seem to go, and attacks on every front, you may be dealing with a principality that either has established or is attempting to establish a stronghold, not just a spirit.

God is positioning you to recognize, expose, fight and overcome, bringing down those spirits in your region and sphere of influence.

These spirits: Jezebel, Ahab, Athaliah, Leviathan, and Belial had to be mentioned and called out by name as they are so prevalent in the Church. I've been extremely brief in talking about these anti-Christ spirits because:

1. The purpose of this book isn't to go in-depth into deliverance and spirits. (However, many have written excellent books and manuals on the subject. See the Recommended Reading List.)
2. There are many spirits in operation that are anti-Christ. These aren't the only ones
3. Focus on Jesus and having the Father's heart. Cultivate repentance, love and humility. Keep yourself pure, everything else will fall into place.

I had a friend who worked in a bank. Do you know how bank tellers are taught to spot counterfeit bills? By handling the real – a LOT! Tellers become so familiar with the look and feel of the real that they're able to intuitively spot a counterfeit even with their eyes closed, by touch. Safeguard yourself against bondage and deception through intimacy with Jesus.

> *He that dwelleth in the secret place of the most High shall abide under the shadow of the Almighty. ... He shall cover thee with his feathers, and under his wings shalt thou trust: his truth shall be thy shield and buckler.* (Psalm 91:1, 4)

As Jesus said,

> *"his sheep follow him because they know his voice. But they will never follow a stranger; in fact, they will run away from him because they do not recognize a stranger's voice."*
>
> *"I am the good shepherd; I know my sheep and my sheep know me—just as the Father knows me and I know the Father—and I lay down my life for the sheep.*
>
> *My sheep listen to my voice; I know them, and they follow me."* (John 10:14-15, 27)

He whom the Son sets free is free indeed! (John 8:36) Remain free!

Keep in relationship with the Father, through the Word, worship & prayer

- Walk in forgiveness
- Walk in love
- Walk in obedience
- Stay in fellowship

Walking in fellowship will stretch you, sharpen you, and keep you in balance. If you feel that any of these spirits and/or generational curses, soul ties have a hold on you, that you can't shake, reach out to your pastor for counsel, prayer and help.

It is for freedom that Christ has set us free. Stand firm, then, and do not let yourselves be burdened again by a yoke of slavery.

> *You, my brothers and sisters, were called to be free. But do not use your freedom to indulge the flesh; rather, serve one another humbly in love.*
>
> *Those who belong to Christ Jesus have crucified the flesh with its passions and desires. Since we live by the Spirit, let us keep in step with the Spirit.* (Galatians 5:1,13,24-25)

CHAPTER 6

Family & Relationships

"For this reason I kneel before the Father, from whom every family in heaven and on earth derives its name. I pray that out of his glorious riches he may strengthen you with power through his Spirit in your inner being, so that Christ may dwell in your hearts through faith. And I pray that you, will be rooted and established in love" *(Ephesians 3:14-17)*

FAMILY, IS SO DEAR TO the Father's heart, that He puts His name on each one, 'every family in heaven and on earth derives its name from Him. (Ephesians 3:14) Family is the bedrock and framework that all cultures rest upon. Healthy societies have healthy families. Family is the context that we come to know God in, 'our Father, who art in heaven, hallowed be Your name'. The framework for the gateway of Family is love, the 'hardware' is communication and connection – fundamentals to healthy relationships.

God's essence is of family and fellowship, the Trinity, 3 in 1; Father, Son and Holy Spirit. He said, "Let Us make man in Our image." (Genesis 1:26) "It is not good for man to be alone." (Genesis 2:18) We are made in His image, to be His image bearers. Setting the lonely in families. (Psalm 68:6) He made iron to sharpen iron; as we rub each other, we sharpen one another, care for and minister one to one another.

Our first call to ministry is family. Priesthood begins at home. Men are called to be the priest of their home. Women if you are single step up and take your place. Do so without resentment and bitterness, or you will hinder your own prayers.

The nail that holds it all together, the under-pinning of society, is family. The health, or not, of family has a domino effect that influences every stratosphere of culture. "The hand that rocks the cradle, rules the world."

"For want of a nail ..." is a proverb reminding us that seemingly unimportant acts or omissions can have grave and unforeseen consequences.

"For the want of a nail the shoe was lost,
For the want of a shoe the horse was lost,
For the want of a horse the rider was lost,
For the want of a rider the battle was lost,
For the want of a battle the kingdom was lost,
And all for the want of a horseshoe-nail."
- Benjamin Franklin

Dysfunction in Family has a far reaching, ripple effect, globally.

> Note: This chapter contains many facts and statistics on the status of Family, at home and abroad. Perhaps you are easily bored with statistics and tend to blow past them. Look with new eyes! Statistics may appear as numbers, but they represent people, individuals, in vast numbers across America and the world. I urge you to read with your heart, not just your mind. Embrace the peoples that these facts represent. The statistics allow me to paint a picture that speaks volumes, in just a few short pages.

A first step to problem-solving is identifying the problem. Lord, open our eyes that we would see from Your perspective. Fill us with the heartbeat of heaven and break our heart with what breaks Yours.

Moral, societal lines have blurred. Morality is laced with shades of gray in areas that were once black and white. Norms and standards of society have undergone major change, in the last 30-40+ years. Same sex marriage, premarital sex, out of wedlock pregnancies, abortion, gender identity confusion, single parent families. The standard of the Word of God has remained constant, it hasn't changed in ages; the Word of God 5,000+ years vs. current, continually changing, societal mores.

Polls and research on the family in modern society reveal truths. They provide snapshots of the current state of family in America, like taking the temperature of a child.

<u>Stats & fast facts on the USA Divorce Rate</u> [1]:

- The divorce rate peaked in the 1970s and early 1980s at about 40%, according to the US census in 1980, and has been declining since then.

In fact, if current marriage and divorce rate continues, only about one-third of American marriages will end in divorce.

- The probability of a first marriage lasting at least a decade was 68% for women and 70% for men between 2006 and 2010.
- The probability that they would make it 20 years was 52% for women and 56% for men, so that percentage is *closer* to the frequently-cited «half,» but still not there.

During the 1980's reports predicted that at least half of the couples married 1976-1977 would end in divorce and the divorce rate would continue to increase from there. But it's clear that things haven't exactly played out that way. Today, our picture of divorce is much more complicated — it's one that changes based on your education level, income, location, and a whole bunch of other factors. Plus, of course, the decision to get married in the first place, is no longer a presumed societal expectation for having sex or starting a family. The decision to marry or not, as one magazine article put it, "is an incredibly complex and personal one." By the standard of the Bible it's not complex, it's quite simple, marriage is a covenant bond that God has given for sexual union. "Not my will, but Thy will be done on earth as it is in heaven." (Matthew 6:10)

Stats & Facts (as of 2016) of the American Family [2]:

- During the 1960-2016 period, the percentage of children living with only their mother nearly tripled from 8 to 23 percent
- the percentage of children living with only their father increased from 1 to 4 percent. The percentage of children not living with any parent increased slightly from 3 to 4 percent.
- The 1st most common living arrangement are 2 parent households
- 2nd most common living arrangements are households with single Moms
- About 38 percent of opposite-sex unmarried couples have a child under age 18 living with them.

Family Growth:

- Households have grown smaller over time, reflecting the decrease in family size and the rise of living alone. The average number of people living in each household has declined from 3.3 people in 1960 to 2.5 today.
- Today 28 percent of households have just one parent living in them — an increase from 13 percent in 1960.

Basically, the above is saying that the traditional family: father, mother and children is still the majority norm, followed by households run by single Moms.

Internationally the structure of Family is in transition. Adults are most likely to be married in Asia and the Middle East, and are least likely to be married in Central/South America, with Africa, Europe, North America, and the islands falling somewhere in between. Cohabitation (living together without marriage) is more prevalent among couples in Europe, North America, the islands, and, to an especially high degree, Central/South America. [3]

The USA is *not* the only country where family is hurting. On every continent family is under attack. Perhaps for different reasons, but under fire nonetheless. In some countries family has 'unraveled' due to: poverty, war, fatherlessness, an increase in violent abusive behavior. News from around the world underscores this, for example:

- Colombia & Venezuela (South America) – border wars have separated families and prompted smuggling. 1,000's of Colombians are staying in shelters after leaving Venezuela. Colombia has been attempting to reunite Venezuelan families.
- Syria (Central Asia) – due to war many Syrian men have died. It is estimated that 25% or 1 in 4 Syrian households are without their father, being run by women.
- North Korea (Asia) – Family structure from all accounts seems strong. However, child indoctrination to communism and the deification of its ruler begins at an early age. The government offers free nursery care called *t'agaso* for babies over 3 months old (usually grandparents care for babies birth to 3 mos. while the parents work). The t'agaso provides infants and small children with the 'foundations of a thorough ideological, political education'. When meals are given to infants, they are expected to give thanks to a portrait of "Father Kim Il Sung" (Kim Jong-Un's grandfather).
- Uganda (Africa) – had an arduous recovery from the brutal regime of Idi Amin back in the 70's. He ordered mass killings of civilians in the hundreds of thousands which tore families apart and brought the country into economic collapse and poverty, the impact of which lasted decades. (He is a classic example of hurt people hurting people. As a child Idi Amin's father abandoned his family and his mother practiced witchcraft.) Uganda's current president publicly proclaims and honors Jesus Christ as Lord.
- Sudan (Africa) – is in constant violence, conflict and poverty the people live in fear. Because of ongoing conflict, many children live under the threat of violence, as well as the possibility of exploitation and abuse. They have food and water shortages, inadequate or non-existent healthcare and little hope for an education.

- Honduras (Central America) – fatherlessness has increased along with a serious rise in gangs. In Honduras, 50% of the population is 15 years old and younger (as of January 2006). The average woman in Honduras is only 15 years old when she gives birth to her first child. In 2006, 80% of all birth certificates issued did not name a father.
- Central America – Rampant gang violence in parts of Mexico, El Salvador, Honduras and Guatemala, is rising, causing many families to flee. It is estimated that 66,000 children in 2014 alone fled these countries with their family.
- Croatia, Bosnia & Kosova (Europe) – The effects of war (1998-1999) and extreme poverty brought about an increase of mental illness in post-war Kosovo. Mental illness radically effects families and can become a generational cycle.

The health of family directly reflects in relationships of every kind, impacting nations. The well-being of every society is largely dependent upon the moral health of its individual members. Moral health is developed at a young age in the context of family. Parents intentionally or unintentionally impart values that are internalized by their children, a moral sense of right and wrong. Recent Gallup polls reveal that, "Americans' views about the declining state of moral affairs largely reflect a belief that there is a deteriorating collective moral character. That is, their views have less to do with greater acceptance of same-sex marriage or having babies out of wedlock and other hot-button issues, and more to do with matters of basic civility and respect for each other." [4]

It's not easy for a Christian to walk the walk amidst conflicting values between the world and the Word. This anonymous social media post underscores the dichotomy of two kingdoms, "Dear Virgin, while the world mocks you for your inexperience, God is smiling at you for your strength." We need to be voices of encouragement and cheer on those who are all-in following Jesus, in nitty-gritty, real-life, relational settings.

Abortion

From 1973 to 2015, more than 57 million lives have been lost to abortion. There's some good news! The abortion rate is decreasing and more women are choosing life increasingly over the last several years. We pray this trend continues. Even though this is good news the blood still cries out from the lives that have been taken while they were being formed. Ministers, servants, prophets, anointed ones of God, whose destinies were cut short before they ever breathed their first breath.

Stats & Facts on Abortion [5]:

Fertility and Abortion

- 21% of all pregnancies in the US end in abortion
- 60% of women who report their pregnancy as unintended choose life (up from 53% in 2001). About half (51%) of all pregnancies are reported as unintended by American women

Rate

- In 2013, 664,435 legal induced abortions were reported to the CDC, a number that has been decreasing dramatically since 1990, when there were 1,429,577 abortions.
- The abortion rate, as of 2013, has dropped to 12.5 abortions per 1000 women aged 15-44.
- Between 2004 and 2013, abortion rates decreased in all age groups except in women 40 and older, where it remained stable. The greatest decrease was among adolescents 15-19, where the rate decreased 46%, meaning that the percent of abortions accounted for adolescents has decreased 31%.

Millennials [6]

- Millennials have had an average of 8 sexual partners—which is less than any generation since the 1960s
- boomers had an average of 11 and
- Generation X an average of 10
- 53 percent of Millennials (individuals between 18 and 31) think that abortion should be either illegal or legal only in cases of rape, incest, or to save the life of the mother.
- The percentage of high school students who are currently sexually active (meaning they had sex during the past three months) dropped from 38% in 1991 to 30% in 2015

The Church and Abortion [7]

- Only 48% of self-identified evangelicals who attend church once or twice per month strongly agree with the statement "Abortion is a Sin."
- 70% of women who have had an abortion indicate their religious preference is Christian.

- 35% of Christian women who have had an abortion indicate they currently attend church once a week or more.
- As women considered their abortion decision, the most typical reactions/expectations from a local church were "judgmental" (33%) or "condemning" (26%.)
- 51% of women agree that churches do not have a ministry prepared to discuss options during an unplanned pregnancy.

Perhaps the most effective 'activism' to reverse the Roe vs. Wade, legislation legalizing abortion in our country, was 4 days of intensive worship night and day during Sukkot (the Jewish Feast of Tabernacles) in Washington, DC. This was during Awaken the Dawn, October 2017. It culminated in prayer as over 1,000 believers under an open sky, faced the capitol building in a moral outcry, declaring and decreeing an end to this law and a shift in mindsets.

FATHERLESSNESS –

Our identity comes from the Father. Jesus' identity came from His Father. Every family in heaven and earth derives their name from our heavenly Father. (Ephesians 3:14). Children, get their identity from their father. Nurturing comes from the Mother, identity through the Father.

Strike the shepherd and the sheep will scatter. (Mark 14:27) The Father is the Great Shepherd, whereas earthly fathers shepherd and oversee the 'pasture' of their family. **The enemy is in the gates attacking Family by attacking fatherhood**.

Fatherlessness has reached epidemic proportion in America and many countries abroad. The fact that the divorce rate declined in America could mislead you into thinking that things are improving for Family. While the divorce rate and abortion rate have declined the percentage of single Moms, and children without fathers has increased.

Stats on Consequences of Fatherlessness in America [8] (*These stats are based on research conducted in America, but the consequences and impact of fatherlessness can be applied to most cultures and countries.*)

- 63% of youth suicides are from fatherless homes (US Dept. Of Health/ Census) – 5 times the average.
- 90% of all homeless and runaway children are from fatherless homes – 32 times the average.
- 85% of all children who show behavior disorders come from fatherless homes – 20 times the average. (Center for Disease Control)

- 80% of rapists with anger problems come from fatherless homes –14 times the average. (Justice & Behavior, Vol 14, p. 403-26)
- 71% of all high school dropouts come from fatherless homes – 9 times the average. (National Principals Association Report)

Daughters of single parents without a Father involved are 53% more likely to marry as teenagers, 711% more likely to have children as teenagers, 164% more likely to have a pre-marital birth and 92% more likely to get divorced themselves.

- Adolescent girls raised in a 2 parent home with involved Fathers are significantly less likely to be sexually active than girls raised without involved Fathers.

THE FATHER ABSENCE CRISIS IN AMERICA

There is a crisis in America. According to the U.S. Census Bureau, 24 million children in America—one out of three—live without their biological father in the home. Consequently, there is a "father factor" in nearly all of the societal ills facing America today. Research shows when a child is raised in a father-absent home, he or she is affected in the following ways...

POVERTY

4X GREATER RISK OF POVERTY

BEHAVIORAL PROBLEMS

MORE LIKELY To Have BEHAVIORAL PROBLEMS

MOM-CHILD HEALTH

2X GREATER RISK OF INFANT MORTALITY

INCARCERATION

MORE LIKELY TO GO TO PRISON

CRIME

MORE LIKELY TO COMMIT CRIME

TEEN PREGNANCY

7X MORE LIKELY TO BECOME PREGNANT AS TEEN

CHILD ABUSE

MORE LIKELY TO FACE ABUSE AND NEGLECT

SUBSTANCE ABUSE

MORE LIKELY TO ABUSE DRUGS AND ALCOHOL

CHILD OBESITY

2X MORE LIKELY TO SUFFER OBESITY

EDUCATION

2X MORE LIKELY TO DROP OUT OF HIGH SCHOOL

The Father Absence Crisis in America [9]

These stats only scratch the surface of the effects of fatherlessness that is a reality, bearing down on America. The percentages aren't just numbers; they have names and faces, they're OUR children, the next generation that is rising.

Dad's your role in your family is more important than anything else you'll ever do in your life. Whatever you do, don't abdicate it! We've all seen the saying, "To the world you may be one person, but to one person you are the world." You are the world to your child(ren). The greatest gift you can give them is your love.

Some of our families, even the ones that are together, are so broken and hurting. Reconciliation is worth fighting for. Albert Eisntein, a genius, that brought brainiac solutions to the world and a social advocate for justice, had an estranged relationship with his son for most of his life. His house servant had the word of wisdom for him. She said to him, "You fight for the world and others but why won't you fight to reconcile with your own son? Don't you understand!? Your family is your legacy! You're so concerned with the world; when will you realize that the world begins and ends with your family?" After that Albert Einstein worked to heal the relationship with his son. Before he passed he had reconciled with him. Fight for your family, put on humility and forgiveness and be reconciled with one another.

Often, in ministry we meet moms with three or more children: each one from a different father, each father no longer in their lives. For some the father was in her life just long enough to get her pregnant, some of the men disappeared or had minimal involvement once they learned of pregnancy. In some situations the single Mom never told the father she was pregnant, and he never had the opportunity to step up to be a father.

The latter almost happened to a member of our family. One day when I was home alone, I answered a knock at the door, a woman I'd never met (we'll call her Amanda) stood there, asking if my son (we'll call him Bobby) was home. Amanda became agitated and annoyed when I told her that Bobby wasn't home. She abruptly told me, "See him!?" Amanda pointed to a small toddler (we'll call him Joel) he was about 2 years old. "Well that's your grandson!" Amanda let loose, in a loud and agitated voice she exclaimed, "You have no idea how much courage it took for me to come here! And now you tell me he's not home! Are you yanking my chain??!!!" She was hurting and afraid and I was stunned and wary – she was a stranger to me. This wasn't the way I had dreamed of finding out I would be a grandmother! Her approach made me uneasy.

Praying silently, I invited her to come back later when I knew Bobby would be home. First, once he got home, I made sure that I had a couple of hours to talk with Bobby. I knew he might need time to process the magnitude of this news.

Although he'd graduated high school he was still young. (Amanda initially had been a bit emotional and we weren't sure what the facts were. We needed to proceed with caution and not add gasoline to a potential fire.) He was shocked and said that it was impossible. I reminded him that it only takes once, and she seemed pretty certain. Bobby asked, "What should I do? I don't think I could live with myself if I'm the father and I did nothing." My advice was to be nice and friendly, get a paternity test done ASAP, and proceed accordingly based upon results.

Amanda returned with Joel later, thankfully their visit with Bobby went positively. Joel was adorable. In our spirit we sensed that yes, Joel was his. It was somewhat surreal meeting a child that was your flesh and blood, for the first time at the age of two.

A few weeks later Bobby sat with the unopened mail in his hand, a bit nervous. The results of the paternity test were in his hand. He opened it and then shared it with me. The outcome showed a 99.8% likelihood that Bobby was Joel's biological father.

Sadly, Amanda never really allowed any of us to be involved in Joel's life in any meaningful way. She tried, but a 'normal' relationship, we never came close to. We were never allowed to have him over for visits, or to go places with him. She usually didn't answer or reply to Bobby's calls to visit with Joel. When she did allow Bobby to visit she and a friend were present and gave an endless monologue of fault finding and putting Bobby down. I would go with Bobby for visits to provide a buffer zone to the insults. I'd take the insults, giving him time to play with Joel. Bobby only sees Joel about once or twice a year now. The Christmas gifts he bought and wrapped still sit in the corner (in June) as Amanda hasn't returned any of Bobby's calls. He tried to be more involved, but Amanda didn't want that. Joel is amazing and is growing into a remarkable young man. He's an overcomer. Amanda has done a super job raising him. And Bobby is doing well. He now has another child that he pours himself into and he is a fabulous father. I'm proud of him.

Along the way Amanda confided in me that before Joel she had wanted a baby and intentionally tried to get pregnant. She didn't want a relationship, just a baby. She contacted Bobby when Joel was 2 years old, because friends kept telling her it was the right thing to do. I also have a cousin, Brenda (fictitious name) who did likewise. I say this because we hear a lot about 'dead-beat' fathers; and while that does exist, not every absentee father is a dead-beat. Some have been denied the knowledge that they have a child(ren), while others are denied the privilege of access to their children and are therefore unable to be true fathers. *In fairness to your child, let their earthly father be a father to them.* (And Dad's show the same respect for your child's Mom as you would want shown to you.)

Mom, if Dad is a 'dead-beat' make sure you introduce your children to their heavenly Father. And connect them with a godly, male mentor. Many churches have mentorship programs, there's also Big Brothers & Big Sisters and more. People have asked if their child's mentor should be the same race as the child. Some feel that it is important for the mentor to look like them in terms of identity. If a mentor is available that is of the same race great. The most important qualities to look for are; character, maturity, and that they are loving, caring and pure. After genuine care for your child, their character is most important. (Some of the fathers that provided the seed may be of a different background.) If a quality, sincere mentor doesn't look like your child, but loves and invests into them then that's a win-win!

Dad's your role in your family is more important than anything else you'll ever do in your life. Whatever you do, don't abdicate!

Guard your time! Be intentional. **You have time for the things that you value most.**

Finding time for family is paramount. Ministry begins with family. Dad's be the priest of your home. Find time to have fun and enjoy one another.

> He will restore the hearts of the fathers to *their* children and the hearts of the children to their fathers, so that I will not come and smite the land with a curse. (Malachi 4:6)

I learned a whole lot as I raised my family. Two things I want to pass on:

1. Respect one another – even when respect isn't deserved or earned.
2. Don't judge others – you haven't walked in their shoes. Mercy triumphs over judgement!

1. **Respect**: <u>Mom's no matter how rough its been speak well of your child's father to them; *even if he's not in the picture*</u>. Do so for your child(rens) well-being. If you need to vent do so with a trusted friend, minister, support group, or counselor. Your child(ren) only have one mother and one father in life. THEY deserve to love and respect them. They want to be proud of each of you. For their benefit let them have that. Their identity is attached to their father, don't injure it. (The one who puts the other down is the one that children see as the villain.)

   Things were less than ideal for me as I raised my 5 children. My spouse was an active alcoholic, with all the craziness that goes along with it. It was like being a single Mom, but perhaps even harder, because my children witnessed unacceptable behavior, often, ie; irrational outbursts of temper, verbal tirades and abuse, etc. I did my best to create an atmosphere of respect for their father, while I explicitly taught them right from wrong. (I never respected the behavior, but I respected the person. There is a clear difference. Jesus hated sin, but loved the sinner.)

Some may say I was a weak fool for attempting to maintain an atmosphere of respect amidst craziness. No! It took great strength of character to choose to build up and speak life. I wasn't always successful, but I tried. Honor what God honors, and He will honor you. His command, the first one with a promise, is for children to obey and honor their Father and Mother that it will be well with them and that they may enjoy long life. If they were to honor their Father an environment of respect needed to be established. Its easy thing to put down and belittle. *The wise woman builds her house, but with her own hands the foolish one tears hers down.* (Proverbs 14:1)

Honor what God honors, and He will honor you

Even after the divorce I refrained from negative talk about him, to anyone. If you are divorced and want to move on with your life, then move on, exercising forgiveness. **You can't run a race if you're carrying a suitcase!** Carrying past offense is too a heavy burden, it will weigh you down. Get rid of it! When I hear someone talking negatively about their ex, I know that there is unforgiveness and open hurt that needs healing. You owe it to yourself and your children to get help and get healing. If you need a support group or counseling then search it out.

I am so incredibly blessed! Each of my adult children, despite a very difficult childhood, have grown into incredibly awesome, responsible young men and women. Watching them interact with and care for one another is one of my greatest blessings. They are loving, fabulous parents, aunts and uncles. Watching them raise their children and care for one another, I don't have sufficient words to express the joy and fullness of my heart. I love and am so proud of each of them! They are overcomers. We are a tight family and there for one another. We're not perfect, far from it! But love overflows among us. And yes, they each have a positive relationship with their father also.

Hatred stirs up conflict,
but love covers over all wrongs. (Proverbs 10:12)

> *Beyond all these things put on* love, which is the perfect bond of unity. *Let the peace of Christ rule in your hearts, to which indeed you were called in one body; and be thankful. (Colossians 3:14-15)*
>
> *Above all, love each other deeply, because love covers over a multitude of sins. (1 Peter 4:8)*

2. **Don't judge others**. Be part of the solution, not the problem. Mercy triumphs over judgement! I was judged because my kids acted out as if I 'allowed these problems', judged because I had problems, judged for not divorcing, judged for getting divorced. No one walked my walk, only Jesus was qualified or had the right to judge me. And He didn't/doesn't judge me!

Prior to my divorce things were very difficult as my spouse was actively alcoholic. And quite frankly the Church didn't make it any easier on me. My pastor was phenomenal, but not so much the members.

Don't judge what you don't understand. You may think you know, but you don't. I wasn't one to share our family drama, in the name of prayer requests in corporate church prayer meetings. (Which is a bad habit many Christians have, using prayer requests as an excuse for gossip and to air grievances. Stop doing that!) Share with your pastor or a counselor. Cover one another's nakedness among your loved ones. Not all family business is for public consumption – in the Church, or Facebook, etc.

When we went on family retreats with our church, I had five small kids to take care of by myself. If my spouse came with us he didn't help out too much. He was overwhelmed with his own personal battles. Often, I'd go on vacation by myself with the kids. (I had learned that if I wanted to have a life then I had to live it. Blame shifting wasn't going to allow my kids or I to have a full life – it was only going to make me bitter. I wanted better not bitter!) I would have so appreciated someone stepping up offering to help me or giving me a little 'time off'.

Now, my kids tended to act out or fight with each other due to the daily tension and stresses they were fielding. We were less than a perfect family by a long shot. Church, when you see someone with unruly kids, don't judge them, help them! You don't know what you don't know. People need love, help and support. Covey in his book "7 Habits of Highly Effective People" talks about paradigm shifts. One example he gave was of unruly children on a bus. Everyone on the bus was highly annoyed as the father seemed to be ignoring their behavior, letting them run buck wild. A woman leaned over and asked the father why he didn't reprimand them. The father answered that they'd just come from the hospital where their mother was dying and he didn't know how to tell them, what to do, or say to them. *Shift*

– people's paradigm shifted from judgment and annoyance to compassion. **Err on the side of compassion. It will do far more to draw people to Him.**

People looked down their nose and judged me as if I was a bad Mother, I was judged because I 'allowed' these problems in my marriage, judged because I had problems with my children, judged for not divorcing, judged for getting divorced. (For the record, I am not an advocate of divorce. I had been married 27 years before I divorced. I exhausted every avenue I knew of for reconciliation. Aside from the magnitude of hurt and trauma I went through, the most important thing was that I wanted to hear God. Don't make your decisions from the seat of your emotions. Make them seated in His presence, in stillness and quietness. Until I heard from Him I was holding steady.) No one had walked my walk, precious few even knew the hell that I was going through, only Jesus. The only One qualified to judge me – didn't judge me! Nor does He judge my ex. "Who are you to judge the servant of another? To his own master he stands or falls; and he will stand, for the Lord is able to make him stand." (Romans 14:4)

People can feel it when they're being judged, even if you don't say a word what's in your heart is felt. We all have excellent crap detectors. Judgement doesn't help people. It doesn't bring others closer to God. It tends to push them away. Flip side, if you have been judged, fairly or unfairly by others, don't judge them, forgive them. "Therefore, rid yourselves of all malice and all deceit, hypocrisy, envy, and slander of every kind." (1 Peter 2:1)

> *"Love your neighbor as yourself." Love does no harm to a neighbor. Therefore, love is the fulfillment of the law." (Romans 13:10)*

To those of you going through difficult times in your family. *Peace be to your house*. I pray for you and encourage you. Keep on keeping on. Sometimes the only way out is through. We pressed through as a family and He made something beautiful out of us. He can for you too! May His love rest upon you and guide you. I pray when you have times of weariness that He brings you joy and infuses you with His strength.

For those who are enjoying a tranquil and strong family environment, continue to nurture your family and love those around you. **Share the love of your family with others, without judging them for their lack. Your example is needed at the gateway of Family**.

The Cry for Spiritual Fathers and Mothers

> *A father of the fatherless and a judge for the widows,*
> *Is God in His holy habitation.*
> *God makes a home for the lonely;*

> *He leads out the prisoners into prosperity,*
> *Only the rebellious dwell in a parched land. (Psalm 68:5-6)*

Fatherhood, Motherhood, a sense of family belonging is in the nature of God.

Gang membership and violence is on the rise. Why? Many do not feel a sense of belonging within their own family. One can be in a home with a Mother, Father and siblings and still feel estranged. Some parents are so busy with their jobs or overwhelmed with life's struggles that they neglect their family. Some parents are addicts and/or emotionally and mentally troubled ignoring their children. Other parents fight so much that the children avoid being at home because it's a warzone. **Having a sense of belonging is a basic human need.** When that is lacking people will seek it elsewhere. Many carry open wounds from abuse, neglect, rejection, and hurts from negative family environments. They are filled with anger and rebellion. Gangs offer a sense of belonging, a pseudo type of family; gangs such as the Bloods, Crypts, MS-13, Latin Kings, Neo-Nazi groups, and more. They are all fallen false images of family, that come with a heavy price. Once initiated in its VERY difficult to get out, it's possible but not easy.

The Church was intended to be a family, welcoming others into an atmosphere of love, and refuge. Look at the vernacular of how He addresses relationships the Church is called His Bride. Words regarding Church relationships are: father, mother, son, daughter, brother, sister, my dear children, newborn babes needing milk, etc. God designed the body of Christ to be one body, a family, "fitted and held together by what every joint supplies, according to the proper working of each individual part, causes the growth of the body for the building up of itself in love.". (Ephesians 4:16)

> *Just as a nursing mother cares for her children, so we (apostles) cared for you. Because we loved you so much, we were delighted to share with you not only the gospel of God but our lives as well. (1 Thessalonians 2:7-8)*

There is such a deep need for spiritual Mothers and Fathers to step forward, to be reproduced and multiplied. You do NOT need to be an apostle or full-time minister to be a spiritual Mother or Father. You simply need to be mature in Christ and have a heart of love. The title of Larry Kreider's book says it, "The Cry For Spiritual Mothers & Fathers: The Next Generation Needs You to Be a Spiritual Mentor". We at His Kingdom Ministries use that text and workbook to intentionally train and reproduce spiritual mothers and fathers. We don't simply hope that will happen and leave it to chance.

New believers need spiritual parenting. Healthy families are not about control or manipulation, they're about love, support and nurturing. Parents love, encourage and expect growth. They provide a safe, nurturing environment, and model accountability. Parents affirm their children, help them 'find themselves' and assure them of their worth and significance. Parents build up, restore, provide relational security, counsel with, pray for their children. Spiritual parents or mentors do likewise. Why call someone a spiritual parent and not simply a mentor? Because parenting emulates from a familial, love relationship.

Tom Hamon said it so well, **"The fathers in our government, in family, in business and in the Church can lead our land into healing or Hell. Restoring back and setting in those with the true father's heart in our generation will bring sorely needed security, stability, true identity, courage and healing to our land."** [10]

"It takes a village to raise a child." (African Proverb) Church we ARE that village. **The Church itself is a prototype of family established in heaven**.

Rebecca Francis said it well, "It will take no convincing to activate the next generation into their positions of influence, but will require care from Church leadership to steer that influence in line with Biblical principles." [11]

Stay relationally connected to others – Who do you go to when you get weary? Who are you connected to? As Bishop Bill Hamon would say, "It's the banana that gets separated from the bunch that gets peeled and eaten." You can't walk this walk by yourself, you're not supposed to be a solo act. God Himself said, "It is not good for man to be alone." (Genesis 2:18)

Belonging to, being grafted into a healthy Church family is Scriptural and important for your spiritual development.

> Let us hold fast the confession of our hope without wavering, for He who promised is faithful; and let us consider how to stimulate one another to love and good deeds, not forsaking our own assembling together, as is the habit of some, but encouraging *one another*; and all the more as you see the day drawing near. (Hebrews 10:23-25)

> but speaking the truth in love, we are to grow up in all *aspects* into Him who is the head, *even* Christ, from whom the whole body, being fitted and held together by what every joint supplies, according to the proper working of each individual part, causes the growth of the body for the building up of itself in love. (Ephesians 4:15-17)

God's Word instructs us not to forsake "the assembling of ourselves together" (Hebrews 10:25). Several logs burn brightly together, but put one aside on the cold hearth and the fire goes out. It's like that with your relationship in Christ with other Christians.

If you do not belong to a church prayerfully consider seeking a good church to grow in near you as soon as possible.

What to look for in a church:

- The Lord Jesus Christ is at the center of their belief, vision & mission
- Preaching that is Christ-centered and based on the Word of God
- There is an environment of caring & fellowship
- They have a regular prayer meeting

COMMUNICATION –

No relationship can continue to exist without communication. How would you rate the quality of communication in your relationships: Shallow or Deep? Shallow communication = shallow relationships. Deeper relationships stand the tests of time, turbulence and hardship better than shallow ones. The deeper and more personally vested one is, the more one is willing to commit and sacrifice to working it through – in good times as well as bad. Depth comes, in large part, from communication. No relationship can survive without communication, it's the mortar that holds the bricks of relationship together.

As my husband and I were watching news on tv one of the featured stories was "The Death of the Dinner Date". My first thought was, well it must be a good day in the world that this is the news story tonight. My second thought was, how sad. What have we done to this next generation? They are more relationally handicapped than I realized.

The reporter went on to explain that going out to dinner was too much of an investment in time than people want to make. It was said, "Why spend time or money, when grabbing drinks or a quick coffee will do? It's more casual — you know, less of a commitment." [12] Dating relationships have become shallow 'hook-ups' void of relationship. Women and men give themselves away sexually, not only outside of commitment and marital bonds, but without even knowing who their partner is. What a sad commentary on the disrepair of our gates!

T-i-m-e is a four letter word that spells *LOVE.* Investing time in establishing *and* maintaining relationships isn't an option. My husband is a very quiet kind of a guy. It takes time to get to know him. We had many dinner

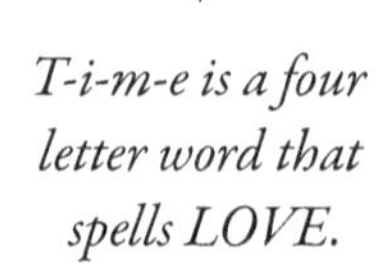

dates before I really got to know him. If the investment of time wasn't made I never would have gotten to truly know him, and the awesome person he is. He has a bull dog exterior and a teddy-bear interior. He is funny and the most caring, insightful, sensitive person. Back in the day a coffee date alone would have been the beginning and the end of our relationship. Shallow relationships don't have a long life expectancy, deeper relationships do.

Common sense isn't so common. And that is abundantly apparent relationally. **Relationship IQ has hit an all-time low**. Courses are emerging for people to learn the *basics* of how to function in healthy relationships. One example is Danny Silk's, "Loving On Purpose Academy". As Danny Silk puts it, "We spend thousands of dollars on schooling throughout our life, yet the skills to live well or to build and protect relationships feel all too elusive."[13] The courses are offered online. **Successful relationships are the result of intentional decisions.**

ADDICTION, CYBER ADDICTION & VIRTUAL RELATIONSHIPS

Addictions, of all types, are the destroyer of intimacy, self-confidence, esteem, dreams, and, most of all, relationships. Support groups, conferences and volumes of books are out there on drug, alcohol, and sexual addictions. Newer on the scene is cyber addiction. Addiction is addiction, the same principles apply. **Cyber addiction and virtual relationships are insidious, more common and pervasive than we realize.**

The bulletin board in front of a church read: "Honk if you love Jesus. Text while driving if you want to meet Him!"

Today's generation lives with a glaring dichotomy: they are more connected (digitally) than preceding generations, yet more disconnected than any other in history. The technology that brings us close to people that are far away, is the same technology that brings us further away from those we are close to. Intellectually our IQ's are fed at a veracious rate, while emotional IQ's languish. Social media has created false images, fictitious personas, and an overall skewed perception of relationships. **We live in a perennial dichotomy – constant connectivity yet the most profound void of healthy, relationship**. Connected yet simultaneously disconnected most of the time.

The technology that brings us close to people that are far away, is the same technology brings us further away from those we are close to.

Your greatest strength is often your greatest enemy. Silas Titus says it plainly, "The unique privilege of this generation is the power of information and access it enjoys compared to the past generations. It is a blessing and curse at the same time."[14] It is said that awareness is half of the battle. Set boundaries. **Only an aware and self-disciplined individual can escape the subtle yet powerful psychological manipulation of this addiction to know the boundaries and where to draw the line.**

Virtual relationships formed over the internet are just that – virtual. Often people create a fantasy online persona, and they fall in love with a false image. Do true romances come from people finding themselves on the Internet? Yes, but test the relationship in real face to face time. Frequently there is a huge gap between virtual relationship vs. real life relationships, since the latter is more challenging and lacks the idealism that the former appears to have.

Cell phone and Internet addiction is rampant and is interfering with what use to be considered 'normal' living. Activities such as the family dinner, children's school functions, dinner dates, the movies, and more used to be 'quality time' in families and relationships. These have been sabotaged by excessive cell phone usage, but not with the one that you are sitting with.

Here are more stats: The percentage of smartphone users who would be classified as **addicted** is estimated between 10-12%, according to the director of the Center for Internet and Technology Addiction, Dr. David Greenfield. However, in a survey of cell phone users, Dr. Greenfield found that around 90% of Americans fall in the category of overusing, misusing or abusing their devices. A recent study also found that 50% of teens feel that they are addicted to their devices. [15]

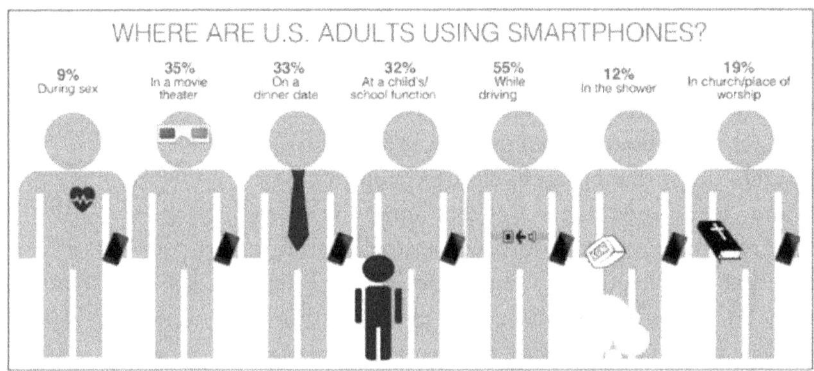

Where are Americans using cell phones? [16]

Virtual love-relationships over the internet may be fantasy-land, based upon false images that one or both parties choose to project. They lack the element of non-verbal communication i.e. tone, facial expression, gesture and touch. Hence, it is easy to use one's imagination to perceive assumed behaviors of the other person in favor of your own desire and fantasies.

This becomes extremely problematic when someone is married and becomes involved in an online, virtual relationship(s). The spouse who engages in online relationships find themselves more interested in their online friends rather than their spouses, because they have created that person in their own heads, not having the imperfect facts seen in their spouses. In such a scenario the imperfection of their partner is amplified to such an extent that it has potential to break down the need for communication and intimacy with one's real-life partner. It's a recipe for the perfect storm – creating distance and a real-life problem.

A word of caution: **You can be physically, sexually 'faithful' to your spouse, but emotionally abandon them.** That is not true marital faithfulness. When you notice that occurring get help – you're on thin ice and about to fall through.

Internet relationships and social media often presents false realities. People fall for the pretense of utopia and false images. The ease with which we can edit and manipulate our social media accounts proves that any of these sites allow us to create a false reality, a version of ourselves as we want to be seen, a false self to increase the feeling of self-worth, reflected by the number of likes and followers. Social media can thwart and diminish the development of long lasting, meaningful relationships. There may be a lack of true, transparent emotional connections being made.

True friendships do occur on the Internet as well. I have also met men and women of God, divine connections, via Facebook, from different countries on different continents. We each have given our friendships the test of time to mature, leading to cultural exchange, ministry enrichment, and short-term mission trips. Our online friendship has never become a substitute for friendships of those around us in our daily lives, and proper boundaries are maintained.

Life is meant for living in the present, in truth, integrity and real-time reality.

Add 'cyber-sex', an online 'fulfilling' of one's desires and fantasies. **Faithfulness and fidelity are not just about physical sex.** Many feel as though if they didn't 'do the deed' then they were faithful. By the letter of the law, that is true. But, husbands and wives – your spouse wants ALL of you. Wanting to spend more time online with someone, rather than with a person who is physically present is not only addiction, but most certainly deceitful.

Guard Against Real-Time Disengagement

Marriage is a 300% covenant. It is an 'all-in' relationship.

100% God + 100% Husband + 100% Wife = 300%

If you are physically faithful to your spouse, but emotionally and mentally elsewhere then you are only putting in 50% at best. When you're only 50% there you're not a very interesting or appealing package. If you're not all-in the tendency is for your spouse to withdraw. They may begin to shut down emotionally and spiritually, perhaps even physically toward you. Physical fidelity is important, but relationship is more than that; it's about heart and soul.

100% God + 50% Husband + 50% Wife = 200%

Which yields a 100% shortfall or deficit in marital relationship. Yikes!

When you keep making withdrawals, but don't make deposits in the Bank of Relationships don't be surprised when you go bankrupt!

When you keep making withdrawals, but don't make deposits in the Bank of Relationships don't be surprised when you go bankrupt!

Even as this is being read some are coming under conviction. You're wondering if your marriage can be salvaged. Like Nehemiah and Ezekiel said, "Can these burned stones be revived?" (Nehemiah 4:2), "Can these dry bones live?" (Ezekiel 37:3), YES!!!! They can! The good news is God never stopped giving at 100%!

Repent, turn, and re-invest.

I love gardening. Sometimes, in the heat of summer I've been late in watering my plants. Recently, my basil plant looked very droopy. Its leaves were turning brown and it hung limp; it looked half dead. I quickly watered it thoroughly. Later that afternoon I went out to check on it. It had revived and looked healthy once again. Now I am careful to maintain watering it regularly.

Some of our relationships simply need to be watered. Swallow your pride, get help jump starting a relationship that's dying due to neglect. Relationships are more complex than watering a basil plant but you get the point. Nurture it until it returns to health and continue caring for it. My husband gives great fatherly advice to others. He'll say, "I know; sometimes a woman can be demanding. The good ones always are. Make sure you care for her, it's worth it." And ladies, honor your man – he's worth it!

Intentionally Making Memories – BUILDING ALTARS of REMEMBRANCE

Fun is the crazy glue of relationship. Don't forget to laugh and have fun together. Creating memories. With the bombardment of busyness in our lives: jobs, friends, church, sports, school, etc. sometimes we can be all work and no play. All work and no play, makes us boring and short-tempered people.

I concluded as I was raising my children, that creating memories was really important. They are the touch-points, cornerstones that anchor our bonds, histories, and relationships.

The mind and the heart are funny. I remember vignettes and memories from my childhood they replay like a movie in my mind; conversations, laughter, poignant moments. Often, I don't even work to remember them, a site, a smell, a situation, triggers them. What are the memories that our families will carry of us? Be intentional about it.

Holidays can become major stressors for families. Everyone wants the big family gathering at Christmas to be picture-perfect utopia. It rarely happens that way. Give space to be less than perfect, laugh at yourself, and learn the fine-art of making lemonade out of lemons.

When I became engaged, yes, I re-married, **we intentionally created family memories**. Our children (my 5 and his 3) are now adult-children, we didn't have to worry about child-rearing as they were already grown. My husband is also the family patriarch, on his side of the family. It was our heart that our families to feel a connection with us. It was our job to create that atmosphere, intentionally, on purpose. We planned a backyard engagement party at what would be our house. It was a festive, blow-out celebration; complete with food, music, dancing, and more. The party began at noon and didn't end until midnight. What fun! Dancing, singing, playing, eating – we ended the evening gathered around a campfire, recounting family memories on both sides and laughing. It was a memorable time – a touch point of the heart, marking us as a family. Together we had created a new place of welcome, celebration, and belonging.

The kingdom of God is righteousness, peace and joy. (Romans 14:17) Is the kingdom of God evident and flowing in your family? So many families are together, but miserable and don't even like each other much less enjoy one another. God wants to change that to righteousness, peace and joy.

Take a moment and pray this simple prayer, with all your heart, *out loud* :

"Lord, renew me and put a right spirit within me. Forgive me for ___*name the offense(s)*____, as I forgive ___*name the family member(s)*___ for __*name the offense(s)*___.

(Don't rush this area. If you have a lot of hurts and offenses to forgive or be forgiven of, pause go over each one and invite the Holy Spirit in to minister forgiveness and the love of God. Then continue praying.)

Restore Your kingdom in my home. I ask for Your love to dwell in me. I speak Your righteousness, peace and joy to rest over my family. Help us to laugh and love one another. Lord, restore us. Show me how and where to start. I need Your help. Transform me daily, as Your priest, faithfully ministering Your love to my family. Transform my family through Your love. Infiltrate every family in our land as our heavenly Father, in Jesus' name. Amen."

The above is not a one-time prayer. When asked how many times one should forgive their brother, Jesus replied 70 times 7. (Matthew 18:22) As many times as you're offended. I speak His love, righteousness, peace, and joy over your home and family, in Jesus' name.

CHAPTER 7

Prejudice in the Gates

"Woe to those who make unjust laws,
to those who issue oppressive decrees,
to deprive the poor of their rights
and withhold justice from the oppressed of my people"
(Isaiah 10:1-2)

WHATEVER HAPPENS IN THE CITY, will eventually be seen in the gates. Discrimination (racial, gender, socio-economic, etc.) shows itself in the gates. "There is nothing covered up that will not be revealed, and hidden that will not be known. Accordingly, whatever you have said in the dark will be heard in the light, and what you have whispered in the inner rooms will be proclaimed upon the housetops." (Luke 12:2-3) It's no surprise that the world's value system is askew, but it hurts when unjust measures are seen in the Church.

> "The Lord hates people who use dishonest weights and measures. Even children show what they are by what they do; you can tell if they are honest and good." (Proverbs 20:10-11, GNB)

> "Don't take it on yourself to repay a wrong. Trust in the Lord and He will make it right. The Lord hates people who use dishonest scales and weights." (Proverbs 20:22-23, GNB)

Racial Prejudice in Our Land

Many things have shifted, but some things, sadly, remain the same. We can't ignore the elephant in the room. Racial prejudice is alive and well in America – to our shame, even in the Church! We see divides on all sides, racism, anti-Semitism, age discrimination, socio-economic – it's there. Judgement first begins in the house of God. (1 Peter 4:17) How the Father's heart breaks as cities and lives are torn apart by hatred and racism. Lord, break our heart with what breaks Yours.

I truly don't understand racism and injustice. It is in opposition to the very nature and character of God. "The Lord is a God of justice." (Isaiah 30:18)

I was a child, away at summer camp with the Girl Scouts, in 1967, as race riots ripped through Plainfield, NJ, the town next door to us. The city of Plainfield, had been known as "The Queen City". Now a spirit of fear filled the area. No one wanted to go there to shop anymore. It was looted, ransacked, and burned. Businesses left as welfare offices moved in. Plainfield, like Newark, NJ, which had also experienced race riots, never fully recovered. They remain economically depressed cities to this day, over 50 years later.

Riots leave their mark not just on business and the economy but upon the people. Thirteen years after the riots, in 1980, I was a resident of Plainfield. Pregnant with our first child I was minding my business walking home from the library to our apartment. It was a quiet sunny day. Across the street a young adult saw me, picked up a brick and hurled it at me, for absolutely no reason, screaming, "White b—-ch!!!" The brick missed me, but came close. I was shocked and looked across at them. God told me not to do or say anything, not to run, to just keep walking. Thankfully, nothing more followed. I have been called a "white b—-ch" on several other unprovoked occasions, in like situations, where I hadn't done or said a thing, but my skin is white, in certain areas, made me a target.

On the flip side of the coin, a dear friend of mine was racially profiled and unjustly treated. She was driving, pulled over for no reason, taken out of her car, handcuffed, placed in the back of a police car threatened and verbally disrespected. She didn't even have a parking ticket in her name. It was abusive treatment, for no reason, other than her race. (Yes, she is black.) It was so upsetting to hear how wrongfully she was treated.

Another African-American family, the Wilson's (fictitious name) five year old daughter told her parents two girls at school wouldn't play with her because she's not white. At such a young age. These kinds of things send me reeling. The senseless pain and hurt!

Judging a person does not define who they are, it defines who you are. Frederick Douglas, on his way to a public speaking engagement, was shamefully treated by a train conductor and made to sit in a baggage car instead of the passenger car. A white woman apologized on behalf of such prejudicial, unacceptable treatment. He straightened himself upon the orange crate he was sitting on and said, "My dear woman, the soul that is within me is too great to be degraded on account of this behavior. I am not the one who has been demeaned, he has demeaned himself by his actions."

African-Americans have been targeted because of the color of their skin, Jews because of their religion, Arabs because people fear potential terrorists. I truly don't understand the foolishness and insanity of prejudice. Murder, assault, discrimination, hate-crimes are ugly. It's as if the world has gone crazy. As an intercessor I have cried.

It doesn't matter which side of the coin you're on, an 'ism' is still an 'ism'. Racism is not from God! It is evil and unjust.

When hurts and offenses from hatred and injustice don't heal properly, deeper offenses and fear grow. They morph into a similar monster that originally birthed them, further perpetuating the hurtful cycle. Neither side listens to the other, moving away from healing. An impasse or chasm develops that can only be bridged by an intervention of divine love.

Katie Stansfield eloquently put it, "Before you speak, stop and listen. There are beautiful, complex, and intricate beings inside of every generality, label, and broad sweeping judgement. I can either name them as a whole and set them aside or close my heart or fight against them. Or, I can stop, listen, learn, love. People are not categories, they are lives. My opinion isn't worth as much as a life. And there very well may be something that I'm missing that the person next to me sees. They may just have a story that I could never tell. So one at a time, one by one. Before you speak, listen." [1]

One of the greatest problems we have today is people making decisions out of their emotions, not being led by the Holy Spirit, but instead ruled by their flesh or human spirit. Television prime time news often has opposing crowds shouting each other down – no one listening to anyone – just hot headed, hard-hearted shout downs. Lord, give us grace to calm our spirits to first listen to You, as well as one another. Let our identity be found in Christ, not the color of our skin, our gender, or any other allegiance.

We hear about celebrating our differences, which is good; but what about celebrating what unites us? There are so many things that unite us.

> "You are a chosen people, a royal priesthood, a holy nation, God's special possession, that you may declare the praises of him who called you out of darkness into his wonderful light. Once you were not a people, but *now you are the people of God*; once you had not received mercy, but now you have received mercy." (1 Peter 2:9-10)

Over the past few years I've watched with great sadness renewed waves of race riots across the country. There is so much malcontent of unhealed hurt that a spark of angst sets ablaze a wild-fire of violence. Professional rioters, incite crowds, to murder, trashing cities, then they move on, while those who live there are left with devastation and heartbreak. Intercessory teams continue in repentance, out of the seats and into the streets; taking prayer walks, treading, trampling upon the lion and the cobra. (Psalm 91:13) We, the Body of Christ; multi-cultural, multi-generational, and multi-racial walking the streets of our cities shifting atmospheres. Literal 'boots on the ground' binding hatred and injustice, releasing His Presence, love, blessing and glory. **It's up to us to see to it that no root of bitterness remains to cause trouble and defile many**. (Hebrews 12:15)

Repentance always precedes revival. A new foundation must be laid as we rebuild our broken gates and walls. **Repentance and intercession will prepare the way for Revival. The remnant must arise, leading on their knees**. We must corporately repent for our nation and fast and pray for revival

Through our actions, not just our words we must stand for justice and unity, being intentional as we reflect Christ. It starts with us. **Don't think God is going to skip the church house to change the White House."** [2]

HISTORY MAKERS & CYCLE BREAKERS

History makers and cycle breakers pay a high price. To break a cycle one cannot respond with MOTS (more of the same). History makers and cycle breakers are intentional, understanding that sacrifice is inevitable. They are motivated by a purpose and a cause that is greater than they are. Ghandi was intentional about non-violence with fasting and prayer. Rosa Parks was intentional about where she sat and how she would respond. Dr. Martin Luther King, Jr. intentionally preached a message of non-violence, held peaceful marches and shared his dream. Susan B. Anthony and Elizabeth Cady Stanton were intentional for women's right to vote and even when imprisoned. Martin Luther King, Jr. said it best, "If a man hasn't found something he will die for, he isn't fit to live." **Are we willing to pay the price?**

Out of our simplest actions and deepest pain come our greatest triumphs, when we submit to the way of the cross.

Miraculously Charleston, SC avoided race riots – how? The way of love. "By this will all men know that you are My disciples, that you have love one for another." (John 13:35) Not because of moving in gifts of prophecy, fancy preaching, miracles, etc. but by our love for one another.

His love is in His blood. It cost Jesus everything. It can be a high price to truly follow Him.

The enemy would love us to tear down our own land and one another; necessitating marshal law to be enforced, bringing us all one step closer to a police state, leading to one-world government by those who are anti-Christ.

We have divine authority to reverse the curse and establish His legacy of love over our lives, families, cities, nation, and the world.

> "Seek good and not evil, that you may live;
> And thus may the LORD God of hosts be with you,
> Just as you have said!
> Hate evil, love good,
> And establish justice in the gate!" (Amos 5:14-15)

Forgiveness isn't a feeling, it is not deserved or earned. Trust must be earned, but forgiveness is free. Those we forgive may not receive it or us. As a matter of fact others may spit upon our forgiveness, just like they spit on Jesus carrying the cross. Forgiveness begins as a choice. It cuts across flesh, mind and soul. Forgiveness is not a natural response to injustice, pain, sorrow, offense, loss and injury. Only through the spirit of God touching the spirit of man – deep calling to deep, can one forgive.

Cities that are breaking the curse of racism and violence that desecrated their gates have done so because they made intentional choices. **Intentionally they stood in solidarity; choosing love and forgiveness over hatred and vengeance.** Leading by example, amidst their deepest pain and sorrow, they set in place a godly model, quelling riots and opening doors of true healing through unconditional love (1 Corinthians 13). Establishing the same love that cost Jesus everything as He hung on the cross and said, "Father forgive them, they don't know what they're doing."

Be intentional, not emotional. – Pastor Alton Fox

God give us grace to arise as history makers and ministers of reconciliation. It comes at a cost. "Where lawlessness increases, the love of many will grow cold." (Matthew 24:12) "But when the Son of Man returns will He find faithfulness on the earth." (Luke 18:8) How faithful are we to Him and His ways? How high a price are we willing to pay? Count the cost and follow Him.

Mark Heyer, a father who lost his daughter to racism said. "You know, I just think of what the Lord said on the cross. Lord forgive him, they don't know what they're doing." [3]

Chuck Pierce in April 2017 prophesied, "In Black America and the African nations, the expression of God will unseat a wrong movement that will vie for authority in days ahead. Only My people, in their culture, can unseat the violence and hate in their bloodline." [4] African-Americans in Charleston, SC unseated the violence. We continue to pray, being confident of this Charleston, that he who began a good work in you will carry it on to completion until the day of Christ Jesus. (Philippians 1:6) May America heal from racism, injustice and prejudice as a nation. The way of love is costly, but the way of hatred even more so. As Dr. Martin Luther King, Jr. said, "I have decided to stick with love, hate is too great a burden to bear."

If we allow any minority to lose its freedom by persecution or by prejudice then we are threatening our own freedom. Dr. Melodye Hilton says it this way, "The validation of the human soul cannot co-exist with prejudice, injustice, or discrimination of any kind." [5]

"All that is needed for evil to triumph is for good men to do nothing." – Nietze

Lord, Your love is stronger than hatred. Prevail in the clash of kingdoms, between Light and Darkness. **Unite us in Your love.**

Hank Kunneman prophetically exhorted, "There is a way and there is a day that is coming to this nation. The bickering, the back-biting, the division shall become a thing that will be settled, and there is a shift that is taking place in the United States, and I am rising up upon this land and I am healing it and it is in the process." [6]

Repent, pray and prophesy over your city – protect it! Church arise, this could be your finest hour.

Times of intensive worship open gateways and break cycles of injustice. This occurred at "Awaken the Dawn" where diverse peoples from all over the nation came for 3 days of 24/7 intensive worship. One participant, Hannah Ford, exclaimed, "*I could sense the chains of racism being broken as we gathered and prayed for racial reconciliation in our country. So many people of different ethnicities were involved both in the leadership and in the audiences. There was hardcore prayer, repenting, forgiving, loving, and praying with one another. This is what the family of God is supposed to be like! This is how we wage war on darkness—with our unified prayers!*" [7]

> "*For you are a chosen people, a royal priesthood, a holy nation, God's special possession, that you may declare the praises of him who called you out of darkness into his wonderful light. Once you were not a people, but now you are the people of God.*" (1 Peter 2:9-10)

Gender Discrimination

In 2012 a young 14 year old, Malala Yousafzai, was shot in the head by a Taliban gunman in Pakistan. Her crime? She advocated for females to receive an education. Miraculously she survived. She now lives in the UK (United Kingdom) and is the youngest Nobel-laureate recipient ever. Weeks after her murder attempt, a group of fifty leading Muslim clerics in Pakistan issued a *fatwā*, or a hit, against those who tried to kill her. The plot to assassinate Mala totally backfired on the Taliban, because after she was shot her cause for women's rights gained international notoriety and momentum.

Not all Muslims are radical jihadists. Do not be guilty of Islam-a-phobia. Some of the kindest, most gentle, devout and sincere people I have ever met are Muslim. At a time when we were struggling financially it was a devout Muslim dentist that showed me kindness by doing the dental work for me, radically adjusting his fee to my humble budget. He spoke a blessing of better times financially over me. My dear friends Sonia A. and Aliyah N. are devout Muslims, and two of the kindest and most upright women I know. One day I greeted Aliyah with, "Merry Christmas! God bless you!" Then I quickly said, "Oh my, I'm sorry. I hope I haven't offended you." She laughed, smiled and replied, "Of course not! I understand you were showing me kindness and a blessing. If everyone would learn to listen to the heart we could solve peace in the Middle East." We both laughed together and continued conversing.

Gender discrimination still exists in the Church, not as dramatic as the shooting of a young girl, but it's present in 21st century America. As a woman in ministry I experienced gender discrimination many times over the years. Recently, a friend of over 40 years severed our friendship, because I was a pastor. (It was the female part of that she had an issue with.) Without a word or explanation, she hung up on me several times. I had no idea why. I wondered if I had unknowingly offended her. She wrote me a note, "I haven't wanted to talk with you for the last few years, because of the direction you've chosen for your life. I also know you were ordained as a 'pastor'. I know you, so I know your motives are to help people in Jesus' name. However, the clear Scriptural pattern for a Christian church is, an elder (includes pastor) is to be 'the husband of one wife'. You do not qualify for this position. These things greatly disappoint and upset me, and so I have tried to distance myself from you."

I prayed before I replied. This was my response, "In Scripture some of the Apostles were women – ie; Junia. (Romans 16:7) And what about where Scripture Galatians 3:28-29 that says,

"There is neither Jew nor Gentile, neither slave nor free, nor is there male and female, for you are all one in Christ Jesus. If you belong to Christ, then you are Abraham's seed, and heirs according to the promise.'

I have not fallen away from the faith.

The law of LOVE and unity in Christ is greater than doctrinal differences."

My friend retains her viewpoint, but has asked God and I for forgiveness. Mercy triumphs over judgment. (James 2:13) I have forgiven and continue to love her. **If love does not govern us, then we have forgotten who we are.** "By this will all men know that you are My disciples, that you have love one for another." (John 13:35)

> "If your brother or sister sins, go and point out their fault, just between the two of you. If they listen to you, you have won them over. But if they will not listen, take one or two others along, so that 'every matter may be established by the testimony of two or three witnesses.'" (Matthew 18:15)

Cleansing begins in the house of God, so does healing.

A pastor's wife, asked me how I dealt with the question of being a woman and a pastor. I briefly shared some Scriptures with her. Then added, "To be honest, I'm really more focused on BEING who I'm called to be than spending my energies and efforts *defending* who I'm called to be."

I was then asked if it created tensions in my home. The answer is not at all! My husband is my biggest cheerleader, heartily supporting me. Our calls and gifting are in different areas. We don't compete, we honor one another.

I am thankful that this is a day and time where women are arising in the body of Christ as His image-bearers and mouthpieces!

Strategic Positioning – DEBORAH

The following are insights on how Deborah, handled gender discrimination.

Interestingly, Deborah, a prophetess, Judge, and Mother over all of Israel did NOT sit in the city gates, the place where the elders met. "She held court under the Palm of Deborah between Ramah and Bethel in the hill country of Ephraim, and the Israelites went up to her to have their disputes decided." Judges 4:5

Imagine that! **A prophetess, a judge, and a Mother of Israel, in a position of governance, yet not sitting in the gates where the elders sat!** It is not written, but I believe that Lapidoth, her husband, *did* sit in the gates of the city. Why? Simply because he was a man and she was a woman. Also, Deborah was a virtuous woman, therefore "Her husband was known in the gates, when he sat among the elders of the land." (Proverbs 31:23)

What a neat man Lapidoth was! His name means torch bearer; one who holds a lamp. I believe that **as he sat in the gates of the elders, he shined the light, pointing to and honoring his wife. He recognized her gifting, wasn't jealous or intimidated, but rather validated her.** How else would the people know where to find Deborah for prophetic wisdom and godly, sound judgement!?

How did Deborah feel, not holding a seat in the gates? What did she do? How did she respond to being excluded and honor withheld in the city gates? Did she: get sullen or angry, pout, rally other women, hold a demonstration, whine bitterly, wear her husband out complaining, threaten and attack men, burn the gates, or plot how she could overthrow the system of the day? No! **Instead *she positioned herself strategically*. This is a season to be strategic! Wise as serpents, yet gentle as doves.** Ask the Lord where you're to be situated, and how to launch out. Position yourself!

Deborah chose to sit upon a hillside, under the palms. *She seated herself* under a symbol of triumph (the palm) and where there was shade – overlooking the gates of the city. Deborah did not allow her spirit to become defiled with anger and frustration. Nor did she allow her self-esteem to be crushed or falter. She did not accept the limitations of societal boundaries, prejudice, yet was not rebellious. Rather, she seated herself above and not beneath! She *overlooked* the city gates, with a right spirit, and prayed for them. **Deborah allowed Christ in her to be greater than she was; therefore, she became His influence in the city and the nation.**

If you are not given access or invitation to city and territorial gate(s) that you've been assigned to, you can still *influence* that city, region, the nation, and nations – securing the gates from a strategic vantage point! Prophetically Deborah understood, biblical truths: "You have been raised up with Christ and seated with Him in the heavenly realms in Christ Jesus" (Ephesians 2:6) and "Since, then, you have been raised with Christ, set your hearts on things above, where Christ is, seated at the right hand of God. (Colossians 3:1) **Her identity, insight, and perspective in God was rock solid and therefore couldn't be undermined by man!**

Deborah understood, not only her identity, but the favor and reward of obedience. "The LORD will make you the head, not the tail. If you pay attention to the commands of the LORD your God that I give you this day and carefully follow them, you will always be at the top, never at the bottom." (Deuteronomy 28:13). **Moving closely, relationally, aligned with the Lord of Lords, grants God-given, favor and positional authority.** She didn't let the mindset of limitation become boundaries of confinement or disqualification. Where the Spirit of the Lord is there is liberty!

Her husband was her light-bearer. God bless husbands who aren't intimidated by the gift and call that is upon their wife, but cheer her on, blessing her as she moves in God. I am thankful, other than the Lord, my husband is my greatest cheerleader.

People pursued her anointing, trekking to the hillside outside of the gates and the city. She was sought out. It's the anointing that breaks the yoke! (Isaiah 10:27) It doesn't matter where you are physically or geographically. Our spiritual Mom & Dad, Apostles Steven & Dr. Melodye Hilton, have a thriving church, *Giving Light*. It is a world outreach center – located in the middle of a cornfield in Pa. – for real! They are thriving. **What matters is that you KNOW who you are in Christ, your purpose and destiny, and are aligned with Him.**

We need a fresh wind of revelation of heaven's strategy to eradicate discrimination! No matter what form discrimination comes in: gender, race, economic, education levels, etc. – fighting flesh with flesh will only exacerbate the issues. Madeline L'Engle's children's book "*A Wrinkle in Time*" sends a poignant and clear message that anger, fear and hatred only feed those demons. Love is the only force strong enough to break the cycle that kept 'Its' victims captive. Love brought down the beast.

The greatest world-changers and history makers from Jesus to Ghandi, Dr. Martin Luther King, Nelson Mandela, and a multitude of others understood this. They each were unwavering in a cause greater than themselves, willing to lay down their lives, choosing the way of love over hatred and violence.

This I know and am convinced of:

Love never fails.

Let each of us examine our heart motives, and seek Him *together*, for His strategy and solution(s). Frustration and anger won't win wars, although they may agitate them. As we move away from reactionary emotionalism and press in to hear prophetic, rhema revelation, God-breathed solution and strategies then we will move in the confidence, favor and say-so of God.

He's not a cookie-cutter God. The same Lord who spit into dirt making mud patties to heal a blind man, had people blow trumpets to break down walls, has unique strategies for us too. His ways aren't our ways, but if we mix revelation and faith with obedience, we will possess and secure the gates once again, overcoming with divine empowerment. May His unfailing love and the healing oil of the Holy Spirit be poured out over our land and into every heart.

As Nelson Mandela said, "No one is born hating another person because of the color of his skin, or his background, or his religion. People must learn to hate, and if they can learn to hate, they can be taught to love, for love comes more naturally to the human heart than its opposite." He and others have also said, education can be our greatest weapon. But truly this battle is a spiritual one. Education is important, but if not mixed with faith, hope and love then education alone isn't enough. It's a heart issue.

How we heal from our offenses and wounds will determine what we reproduce. We must choose to forgive and heal completely, *or we will become the very thing that oppressed and violated us*.

In unity is our strength. There the Lord declares the blessing. (Psalm 133). His anointing will break the yoke and grant us access to be His influence in the gates (even if we're out on a hillside). I want to be found in alignment for my kingdom assignment, and BE who I'm called to be. He'll open and close the right doors.

Passed by?

Overlooked, passed by due to discrimination, undervalued, defrauded, to those who have been hidden and are the 'best kept secret' in town, **God is about to reveal you!** This is a season where those who have been hidden, overlooked, passed by, even forgotten, God is bringing you to the forefront.

When we began His Kingdom Ministries we started with a half of a handful of people. The vision was *much* larger than we were. God called us to be an apostolic hub to establish, equip and empower. We were operating out of an old traditional wineskin of 'church', but He called us to be an apostolic center. Our perspective needed to change. We needed to come into a greater understanding of what His purpose for us was, how that impacted our structure, and how to build according to His design. **We had to break out of the mold we had put ourselves in, it was limiting who we were to become.**

> Unless the LORD builds the house,
> the builders labor in vain.

> Unless the LORD watches over the city,
> the guards stand watch in vain. (Psalm 127:1)

Lift your vision higher! Old boundaries, limitations, fears and intimidations are no longer. God is re-structuring where and how we do church and outreach, first re-shaping our perspectives. "Lift up your heads, you gates; be lifted up, you ancient doors, *that the King of glory may come in*." (Psalm 24:7)

There is an old Puerto Rican proverb. In English it translates, "The higher up the tree the monkey climbs, the more you see of its behind." When one climbs a tree in their own strength or selfish ambition, it becomes evident to all and it's not a pretty sight.

Conversely, when kingdom principles are in operation His grace flows. "The kingdom of the world has become the kingdom of our Lord and of his Messiah" (Revelation 11:15) When that happens then the standard of His kingdom, not flesh is exemplified. As Lance Wallnau said, **"***Understand that the higher up you go on the Mountain of the Lord, the closer you get to your assignment on earth. The closer you get to your assignment, the closer you get to invading that second heaven realm of demonic resistance. Your job is to show up at the Gates of Influence in your assigned sphere. It does not matter that you are not well-known on earth at these gates. What matters is that you are well-known in Heaven. When that happens, you will be respected in the gates.***"** [8]

CHAPTER 8

NOW – 21st Century Gates, Gatekeepers, the Internet & Media

Blessed are those who wash their robes, so that they may have the right to the tree of life, and may enter by the gates into the city.
(Revelation 22:14)

DEFINING TERMS – gateways, gates, gatekeepers

THE SAME, BUT DIFFERENT–GATEWAYS, GATES, and gatekeepers have taken on new context and meaning in the 21st century, in comparison to Old Testament times. Gates of both time periods still share being the main points of access.

Gateways:

Gateways are strategic geographic areas and locations. They are significant portals, key passageways, highways of influence and activity. The Gateways may be influenced by either the Kingdom of God (light) or darkness. There is constant contending for domination in gates and gateways.

Nations have gateway cities. In the northeastern USA, the Statue of Liberty is in the gateway of America. It was the first site of America for millions who have immigrated here. On our western shore the Golden Gate Bridge is the gateway icon.

Interestingly, in Scripture, one of the most significant gates of Jerusalem is the Eastern Gate. It is a very prophetic gate (see Ezekiel 10, 11, 43-46) as the glory of God entered through it. It is sealed shut and not to be opened until the glory of the Lord enters it once again. It faces the east. It is called the: Eastern Gate, Golden Gate, and Beautiful Gate. Identity, purpose, and spiritual DNA are in a name. America has very significant national and prophetic gateways on both her eastern and western coasts.

I love praying in gateways, both spiritually and geographically. There is something strategic and powerful standing in gateways interceding. One senses an open heaven and angelic presence in the winds there that is carried throughout the land.

There are also locations or gateways that are known for wickedness. They have a propensity to attract evil like magnets attracts iron. This cloud of oppression is often caused by what has been or is being done, ie; war, brutality, slavery, prejudice, strip joints, pornography, drug use, astrology, spiritism, New Age, pagan burial mounds, *wicca* and occult practices, blood sacrifices, etc. often fertilize the ground of an area or region for demonic activity.

> *If my people will humble themselves and pray, then I will hear from heaven and heal their land.* (2 Chronicles 7:14)

Five biblical cities known for their wickedness: Sodom and Gomorrah (Genesis 19), Chorazin, Bethsaida, and Capernaum (Matthew 11:20-24). Interestingly, Lot was sitting in the *gateway* of Sodom and Gomorrah when he received angelic visitation. (Genesis 19:1) **The greatest sin of each of these cities was their unwillingness to repent. Unrepentant hearts bring judgement upon a land.** Righteousness exalts a nation, but sin condemns any people. (Proverbs 14:34)

Conversely, certain cities are Holy Ghost 'hot spots' and gateways, because of past revivals, initiated by the prayers of the saints that invited heavenly hosts and angelic presence to dwell there. The DNA of heaven remains in the soil and atmosphere, ripe to be re-ignited! With earnest, intense, passionate repentance and prayer we can establish more gateways and hot spots of heaven on earth! **The concentration of focused, sustained repentance, intercession, and worship releases a nuclear fission-like explosion of the Holy Spirit. It pierces through the heavenlies, creating an open heaven, for the highway of God – a gateway connecting two realms.** That's what a gateway is, it a portal connecting two realms.

> *And a highway will be there;*
> *it will be called the Way of Holiness;*
> *it will be for those who walk on that Way.*
> *The unclean will not journey on it;*
> *wicked fools will not go about on it. (Isaiah 35:8)*

> *make straight in the desert*
> *a highway for our God.*
> *Every valley shall be raised up,*
> *every mountain and hill made low;*
> *the rough ground shall become level,*
> *the rugged places a plain.*
> *And the glory of the LORD will be revealed,*
> *and all people will see it together.*
> *For the mouth of the LORD has spoken." (ISAIAH 40:3-5)*

Gateways, spiritually speaking, are like a large ray of sun beaming through the clouds. A highway in the spirit between heaven and earth. Above is a heavenly host of worshipping, warring angels. Below are pure, faithful, passionate intercessors and worshippers.

Gateways with respect to the Internet in the 21st century are the means with which one network can connect or interface with another. Gateways communicate with other gateways, gatekeepers, and their endpoints.

Unseen, but very real and intense, spiritual warfare rages in the realm of the 2nd heaven in gateways that we have never seen with our natural eye.

> "For our struggle is not against flesh and blood, but against the rulers, against the authorities, against the powers of this dark world and against the spiritual forces of evil in the heavenly realms." (Ephesian 6:12)

Prayer acts as a catalyst. This strategic-level warfare is described in Daniel as he stood in the gap for his nation, and for an understanding of God's plan. His prayers were hindered by a principality, the prince of the Persia. Daniel's fasting and prayer was heard, the kingdom of God prevailed in the gateway. Then God sent in the 'big guns'. Angelic reinforcement – the archangel Michael was dispatched, to minister to Daniel. Angels remained stationed for spiritual battle over the empire where God's people resided. (Daniel 10:20-21) Heaven sent in special forces because of one man's humble, fasting and prayers.

The weapons we fight with are not the weapons of the world. On the contrary, they have divine power to demolish strongholds. We demolish arguments and every pretension that sets itself up against the knowledge of God, and we take captive every thought to make it obedient to Christ. (2 Corinthians 10:4-5)

Gates:

Old Testament gates were tangible, made of iron, bronze, wood, etc. 21st century gates are intangible, hard to penetrate, and challenging to even describe, much less guard. They are critical access points in our way of life.

How do millions of people around the world travel from one gate to another, daily, several times per day? Answer – the Internet. **The Internet is our 21st century gateway portal, connecting the many gates instantly.** Internet growth has been so rapid that the rule book is still being written on it. In 1984 the Internet originally linked 1,000 hosts. No one anticipated what it would become in such a short span of time. Bill Gates said in 1995, "The Internet is just another passing fad.", but by 1998 it had grown to 50 million users. By 2009 1 billion users and linked more than 440 million; by 2012 the Internet reached 2.1 billion users reaching about 39% of the world's population, with usage continually rising.[1] *(In 2000 I was a part of Seton Hall University's 1st distance learning graduate degree cohort in education.)* It is clearly not a passing fad. There is a war for communication systems and a one-world mind-set

The gates all serve to provide or deny access to what enters or leaves. They communicate, influence, interconnect and affect one another. Nehemiah recognized this as he implemented strategies of protection during rebuilding. They were spread out along the wall, but if any one gate or site came under attack, at the sound of the trumpet they would all rally together to fight for one another. Each was assigned to a distinct gate, yet their mission was the same; rebuild and restore Jerusalem. The way to kingdom reformation begins at the gates.

Gatekeepers

In the Old Testament the gatekeepers were priests from the tribe of Levi, appointed by God to be 'watchmen on the wall'. The godly attributes of the priests were highly prized and valued. Appointed by the king, they were trusted priests.

Gatekeepers of the 21st century control information. The gatekeepers of today control the flow of information to Media, which controls what information the masses receive, or not.

This modern-day understanding of a gatekeeper has made its way into contemporary dictionaries:

Gate-keep-er

1. One that is in charge of passage through a gate.

2. One <u>who</u> monitors or oversees the actions of others.
3. **One who controls access to something, such as information or services: *publishers as gatekeepers.*** [2]

Most large corporations have someone who controls the flow of information and decision making. **Information control is power.**

> *When the righteous thrive, the people rejoice; when the wicked rule, the people groan. (Proverbs 29:2)*

A Direct Connect: Gatekeepers and the Gate of MEDIA

The ability to control information carries a vast say and sway over the perception of multitudes. Today's Gatekeepers have been hand-picked, chosen and positioned by a select few who have great wealth. They appointed gatekeepers, not based upon godly attributes and criteria, but those who can be trusted to carry out *their* agenda. Corporate America's goal is to perpetuate wealth for themselves which is equated with power. Elite, corporate America has enormous control over Media. Its Gatekeepers. Government, politicians are connected in this also.

Gatekeepers control information to the masses via media. Using media government can control what the hot issue(s) will be and for how long. Those hot issues are further stirred by passions, emotionalism, creating hostilities and dogged allegiances. Information is power with the potential to deceive, manipulate, and control.

Media is a primary gate, controlling information to all the other gates. Society is usually unaware of the manipulation of information omitted or cleverly embedded within truths and half-truths. Discerning deception and manipulation accurately, the lies, from truths and half-truths is key. **Discernment will be highly sought after, as well as a highly contested gift and skill, in this 'Brave New World'.**

The game plan of the enemy:

- Commerce (also referred to as Business or the Marketplace) is the means that fuels Media, with mammon as its god. Money equals power in the world's system. (The agenda of a very elite, wealthy few hold great influence through the other gates as they all need money to survive and thrive.)
- Media is a hub gate for other gates. It is the mouthpiece of communication for the other gates. It is largely 'controlled' by mammon.

- The vehicle or gateway for communications between the gates is the Internet
- One world Government is the end game, to move people into a mind-meld of group-think, one global mindset – that will probably be intolerant to differences. (A climate ripe for rulership of anti-Christ.)
- Arts and Entertainment stir emotions and passions usually in alignment and connected with Media views and perspective. Arts & Entertainment shape pop-culture and continually strengthen and reinforce it.
- Education shapes perspective through critical thinking, or lack thereof. It develops knowledge base, values and mindsets. Education shapes future leaders and followers, thereby shaping the future.

The condition of each of the mountains and gates are related to the well-being of society. A tree is known by its fruit. The plans of the enemy are being unmasked and unpacked to us because the greatest revival ever to hit earth is about to come forth. He's raising us up as reformers, like Nehemiah.

In 2008 Chuck Pierce gave this prophetic word on global communication systems: "He (the Lord) showed me how the communication system in the United States was linked with systems internationally and how **a new form of global communications was forming in the demonic world. This communication would control financial and legal structures.**" [3]

The new form of global communications is the Internet. It can be used for good or evil.

Personnel in news organization become gatekeepers, letting some stories through the system but keeping others out. Limiting, controlling, and shaping the public's knowledge of events occurring. Gatekeeping occurs at all levels of the media structure—from a reporter deciding which sources to include in a story to editors deciding which stories are printed or covered, and includes media outlet owners and even advertisers. On a micro-level, individuals can also act as gatekeepers, deciding what information to include in an email or blog.

Boundaries are only maintained through continued, daily vigilance! The gates and gatekeepers are key in influencing boundary lines. We need godly, priestly gatekeepers to rise into key positions of influence in every gate and gateway. He who possesses the gates possesses the city.

A contemporary Israeli, internet gatekeeper has the same last name as a priestly gatekeeper of Ezra & Nehemiah's day.

Karine Barzilai-Nahon literally wrote the book on Networking Gatekeeping. She has re-defined and defined the 21st century terms/ vocabulary associated with 'gatekeeping'.

One of the priests that returned to Jerusalem, listed in Ezra, their name was Barzilai.

"And from among the priests:

> The descendants of Hobiah, Hakkoz, and **Barzillai** (a man who had married a daughter of Barzillai the Gileadite and was called by that name).

These searched for their family records, but they could not find them and so were excluded from the priesthood as unclean … not to eat any of the most sacred food until there was a priest ministering with the Urim and Thummim." (Ezra 2:61-63)

The priests were appointed as gatekeepers in the Old Testament. Now thousands of years later, an Israeli, bearing the name of one of the Israelite priests in the book of Ezra is giving new meaning and definition to the gates of today. As per her web page (www.ekarine.org) she is a "Network Gatekeeper". Ms. Barzilai-Nahon is a **21st century gatekeeper, an Israeli, whose name reflects the lineage of a priestly gatekeeper of the Old Testament, from a period of spiritual awakening and reform** (Ezra 2:61).

Our gates are now access points to and from Internet networks. Dr. Barzillai-Nahon is a researcher, scholar, and activist that focuses on information politics and policy. Her public activity is aimed towards promoting transparency and accountability. She has re-defined words and terms as they relate to our world in the 21st century.

> "Gate – entrance to or exit from a network or its sections.
>
> Gatekeeping – «the process of controlling information as it moves through a gate. Activities include among others, selection, addition, withholding, display, channeling, shaping, manipulation, repetition, timing, localization, integration, disregard, and deletion of information.»
>
> Gated – «the entity subjected to gatekeeping»
>
> Gatekeeping mechanism a tool, technology, or methodology used to carry out the process of gatekeeping

> Network gatekeeper – «an entity (people, organizations, or governments) that has the discretion to exercise gatekeeping through a gatekeeping mechanism in networks and can choose the extent to which to exercise it contingent upon the gated standing.»[4]

According to her approach, the gated can have four key attributes at different levels that determine how they can interact with the gate. These are:

1. Political power in relation to the gatekeeper,
2. Information production ability,
3. Relationship with the gatekeeper,
4. Alternatives in the context of gatekeeping [5]

Fascinatingly, the year that Karine Brazilai-Nahon's released her definitions on Gatekeeping, in 2008, was the same year that Chuck Pierce delivered the prophetic word of the Lord on global communication systems. How a new form of global communications was forming in the demonic world. This communication would control financial and legal structures." *Significant, but no coincidence, it is prophetic, kairos timing!* This 21st century understanding of gates and gate-keeping brings with it added prophetic perspective, insight, forewarning us. Forewarned is fore-armed. As the saying goes, knowing is half the battle. Revelation, Knowledge and Wisdom are keys of the kingdom that we will use to bind and to loose for prevailing in the gates!

Travelling at the speed of light, the Internet lands on 7 continents instantly, simultaneously. **Gatekeepers and media specialists craft the release and withholding of knowledge, like sculptors working with clay; forming perception, perspective, that persuades and influences multitudes daily, continuously**.

COMMUNICATIONS

At the top of the mountain is where pagan cultures of old (Druids, Native Americans, cult practices in Krakow, the Chinese along the Great Wall) would communicate one with another. They communicated by sending smoke signals and sounding trumpets. This same communication is taking place today via the Internet. We must ascend to the top of this mountain, securing our gates, 'holding the fort', and taking back global communications from corruption.

There's a war for your mind!

The end game is one world government – group think. Those voicing a differing perspective will be viewed as dissident. It's occurring in America now. The enemy doesn't have to tear down our cities, he just stirs the pot. His game plan is to get the people to do that for him. **Media manipulates information exploiting the emotions of people.** It takes aim at deep seated passions and feelings that trigger emotional responses, 'crowd think', fanning emotionally charged reactions (not allowing for rational processes, due process or objectivity). **Today's media whips discontent into a fury, creating the perfect storm for riots and anarchy.** Lance Wallnau expressed, "We are also seeing into the realm of the enemy and how the powers of darkness are working through fallen man to produce chaos and conditions ripe for Satan's manipulation of nations and counterfeit of the Kingdom. [6]

Devious, deception is a hallmark of wickedness and evil. "The thoughts of the righteous are just, *But* the counsels of the wicked are deceitful." (Proverbs 12:5) "Whoever fears the LORD walks uprightly, but those who despise him are devious in their ways." (Proverbs 14:2). Devious manipulation of media is alarming. No one knows for sure, left, right or otherwise, what percentage of it is skewed. **A new level of discernment is needed in the 21st century.**

The enemy is creating and manipulating perception, influencing the gates of politics and education through the gates and gatekeepers of media.

Perhaps that is what is meant in this passage from Isaiah:

> *So justice is driven back,*
> *and righteousness stands at a distance;*
> *truth has stumbled in the streets,*
> *honesty cannot enter.*
> *Truth is nowhere to be found,*
> *and whoever shuns evil becomes a prey. (Isaiah 59:14-15)*

I am continually amazed at how ill-informed Americans are on international affairs. The average American is ignorant in current events, especially on a global level. Our media keeps us very ill-informed of the culture and current events of Asia. We are largely ignorant about world powers such as China and India. We have a friend in Bangladesh assisting victims of the worst flooding they have had in 200 years. The flooding effected over 20 million, killing over 1,000. USA news didn't cover it at all on tv.

Even news on a national level is loaded with bias. (Please use chapters 8-11 as a prayer guide.) They contain an overview of national and global current events and shifts that have taken place, a 'status of the world'. As you pray into the things in those chapters God will give you prophetic revelation. Become one of God's eagle-eye watchmen on the wall for your city and the nations. We will be an informed people on natural level *and* spiritual levels. Praying prophetically over these areas – we will secure gates and become a world changers and kingdom shakers.

Marketplace prophet Lance Wallnau remarked, "There is a battle between high-level spiritual powers to bend the minds of the masses and you need to know what is really going on. The Leviathan spirit takes communication, twists it and distorts it to gain control of the high places." [7] God gives clarity, understanding, and guidance for the times we are in through His prophets. We must take back the mountain of Media.

How do we take back the mountain of Media? The same way you eat an elephant – one bite at a time. As Vince Lombardi put it, "The man on top of the mountain did not fall there."

1. Gain understanding. Understand the plans of the enemy to expose them and bring them down.
2. Enter by the gates (Revelation 22:14). Become entrenched in the gates, gateways, and cities of the mountain.
3. Ascend – climb and work our way to the top of the mountain.
4. As 'climbers' ascend, be vigilant to maintain and secure the gates! (Advance and secure while we secure and advance.)

As we ascend and scale the mountains of influence divine connections will be made. Instead of the Church and believers seeking connections with the world, the world will want to seek connections with us. He will cause His church to be chief among the mountains.

> *Now it will come about in the last days, the mountain of the house of the Lord will be established as the chief of the mountains. And will be raised above the hills, and the nations will stream to it.* (Isaiah 2:2)

The Business mountain (or Marketplace) controls the Media through those who fund it. All the mountains are inter-connected. **If you want to understand the why's to what's happening in the world, follow the money trail**. All are sustained by money. Targeted campaigns have aimed at advertisers/sponsors to boycott specific networks (such as Fox News, and others known for their right wing stance). If a network loses key sponsors, it loses its financial ability to continue broadcasting. The world of Finance/ Commerce has a direct tie-in with influence in all the mountains.

The facts are:

"15 Billionaires own America's news media companies. News that billionaire Peter Thiel is funding Hulk Hogan's trial against news website Gawker set the media and technology worlds on fire, sparking a conversation about the ultra-wealthy's role in controlling the news. While a billionaire secretly funding a lawsuit to take down a news outlet may be a new way of using money to influence the media business, billionaires have long exerted influence on the news simply by owning U.S. media outlets."[8]

We need to hit the heads. Here are some fast facts to shed perspective on things: [9]

- 90% of media in America is owned/ controlled by 6 corporations (GE, News-Corp, Disney, Viacom, Time Warner, and CBS).
- The big 6 control 70% of your cable.
- In 2010 the revenue for the big 6 was $275.9 billion. To keep that number in perspective, that's $36 billion more than Finland's GDP.
- 15 billionaires own America's news media companies.

As my husband, James Shuler, an adept businessman, said, "When you don't understand something that doesn't make sense, just think money." Six corporations are able to create whatever narrative they'd like for the public via their gatekeepers. As we've noted gatekeepers control what information is released, suppressed, and the tone that it comes across in. These six corporations have approximately 232 'gatekeepers', those who control information dissemination. Only 232 persons are minding the gates of public media information that is intentionally, selectively, and make no mistake about it, manipulatively, fed to a nation of over 277 million people. That is a ratio of about 1 to 1,000,000 (**1 gatekeeper controlling information to approximately 1 million people**). " [10]

[See *Follow the Money* pictogram, page 185 in chapter 10.]

Media assaults targeted at specific individuals and 'fake news' are rampant and undeniable. A mechanism, a machinery is in place with the ability to twist truth, cast negative innuendo, agitate emotionalism, shape public perception, propel 'crowd thinking', and incite a people. **Information that is NOT conveyed is as vital, or perhaps even more so, than that which is shared**. As a ruler, David experienced this as he expressed himself in psalm,

> "All day long they twist my words;
> all their schemes are for my ruin.
> They conspire, they lurk,
> they watch my steps,
> hoping to take my life." (Psalm 56:5-6)

Have you noticed how certain news is inflated? From the weather report to protests to the portrayal of certain politicians; it doesn't have to even be true if it makes news. In the northeast if you want to create havoc at the local supermarket give a news cast on an impending snowstorm. (A great time to take out stock in milk, eggs, bread and toilet paper.) News media will report on the impending storm for a minimum of 3 days prior, with increasing hype. It slays me when less than 3 inches fall. So much emotional energy spent on the big non-event. This same mania is exercised with careful orchestration by a handful of wealthy corporate gatekeepers, that have a reach and hidden agenda far beyond the scope of what we see and know.

It doesn't have to be a national, macro movement to reverse the curse. God does valiantly through small micro groups of 3 or more and individuals that PRAY fervently. It's a great season for the remnant! You and the Holy Spirit are a majority!

CAREERS in NEWS & MEDIA

Public relation positions in media news are growing the most rapidly at +23%, however editors (who verify data and facts, collaborate with others) are only growing at +1%, reporters & correspondents (who gather the news, interview, research and investigate) indicate a decreasing career growth rate of -8% [11] Given these statistics, it will be rough going becoming a news correspondent, as there just isn't an in-demand market for it. Lord knows however that **we need journalists and news correspondents that are sincere seekers of truth; that will objectively search a matter out and report on it**.

More is being invested in public relations, the selling of America, than truth in Media. The trend is set to continue to increase studying likes, dislikes, trends in culture, branding, package and design etc. More is being invested in imagery and packaging than in researching, investigating and presenting truth objectively. This effects the facts, accuracy, quality, caliber and validity of the news you receive.[12] Careers researching and analyzing facts to objectively report truth to people is growing at -8%. It is NOT valued by the big 6 corporations that are holding the purse strings. (Two things reflect what people value; how they spend their time and how they spend their money.)

This shows you where the specific gates of access and opportunity are in Media. **We need men and women of virtue in public relations.** And although it will not pay as well, Lord knows ***we need lovers of truth*** **to be investigative correspondents. It would be wonderful to have affluent Christian mogul(s) filled with integrity to form a powerful Media corporation.**

Do not accept at face value the news presented to you. Question news that you read, see, and hear. Take time to look at both sides of an issue. Often, I pause and look things up on the Internet to research and understand what the real facts are. The truth is often somewhere in between opposing sides.

An attempt is being made to 'level the playing field' of media control of the news, particularly left-wing vs. right-wing coverage and skewing of the news.

> Media Matters:
>
> The left-wing keeps a grip on the control of information in the media via www.mediamatters.org The following is the description taken from their site about them, "*Media Matters for America* **is a** web-based, not-for-profit, 501(c)(3) progressive research and information center dedicated to comprehensively monitoring, analyzing, and correcting conservative misinformation in the U.S. media.
>
> Launched in May 2004, *Media Matters for America* put in place, for the first time, the means to systematically monitor a cross section of print, broadcast, cable, radio, and Internet media outlets for conservative misinformation – news or commentary that is not accurate, reliable, or credible and that forwards the conservative agenda – every day, in real time. ... Additionally, *Media Matters, according to their site,* works daily to notify activists, journalists, pundits, and the general public about instances of misinformation, providing them with the resources to rebut false claims and to take direct action against offending media institutions.
>
> (Note: *The fact that this organization is a 501c3 is staggering and significant. Contributions from big-money are tax deductible. Remember, under Lois Lerner, conservative groups were broadly being denied tax exempt status during her tenure 2005-2013, yet Media Matters was given tax exempt status in 2004. Just saying.*)
>
> Media Equalizer:
>
> Representing the right wing, in 2017 Brian Maloney and Melanie Morgan launched in www.mediaequlaizer.com, in an attempt to 'level the playing field'. Specifically, targeted campaigns have been initiated to advertisers/sponsors of media to boycott specific conservative networks, such as Fox News. If a network loses key sponsors, it loses its financial ability to

> continue broadcasting. MediaMatters has arisen as a conservative voice to counter such attacks.

We MUST look at ALL sides of issues. Otherwise, no matter which side of the coin we are on we are ripe for deception.

Social Media

Social Media has grown exponentially in a very short period. Facebook launched in 2004, by 2009 it had grown to 200 million users; by 2010, 400 million users; and by 2012, 1 billion! In 2010 an estimated 3.5 billion pieces of content were shared on Facebook weekly; by 2011 it doubled to 7 billion. In addition, in 2012, 300 million photos were added to Facebook *daily*! [13] We often text one another in lieu of talking together. As my friend Keith Johnson said, "Social media has allowed us to know people and gain access to their lives, while simultaneously decomposing within humanity, the principal of genuine relationship."[14] I'm guilty of the same. Text messaging, Facebook, Twitter, Instagram, SnapChat, Flipogram, etc. have become obsessions and addictions of the 21st century.

In this age of the Internet a lot of 'crazies' and fanatics can have just as much 'air time' as the Secretary of State.

Here's a scary statistic in 2013, according to the Pew Research Center, 72% of adults get most news from friends and family, including social media [15]. Yikes! Even among my peers I've received false news accounts. News from family and friends, or the media for that matter, is not necessarily researched and reliable. "The people will not revolt. They will not look up from their screens long enough to notice what's happening." from a 2013 British stage play inspired by '1984' written by George Orwell in 1949. [George Orwell was not a godly prophet of his time. Rather he was a Freemason, a secret society with occult roots. Their membership is kept secret and so is their agenda. His book '1984' was considered by some to be an instruction manual for "The Destruction of the Human Race" and how to create a police state. We certainly seem to be moving closer and closer to that.]

On social media I received a prayer request from a very credible friend. The prayer request was a serious one, urgently asking for prayer for missionaries being held captive in Asia, and were about to go before a firing squad tomorrow morning. Something about it just didn't set right with me. I went to one of my favorite sources, **www.snopes.com** discovering it was a hoax and a rumor. Not all fake news is intentionally disseminated. **Take a moment to stop, question, analyze, and research things before you accept them**. You may say, but that sounds like a lot of work. ... It is, but truth is worth the investment.

Moreover, there is an unspoken belief that something read on social media must be true. The power of the pen is mighty, and the power of the click even mightier. Once appearing in print what is written can morph into something that changes one's public image and status radically. Information that is sent and shared, can spread quickly into astronomical proportion and influence, reaching an unseen multitude beyond our ability to ever know.

My friend Chris' (fictitious name) teenage daughter, Tasha (also fictitious name) a typical teen, unpredictable, immature, acted upon a dare, not thinking of the consequences. Tasha posted pictures of herself naked online, participating in 'sexting'. The images went viral. Chris was devastated for her daughter. Chris arranged for Tasha to receive counseling. The damage on her self-image and esteem was overwhelming. In her high school wherever she walked down the hall, in classrooms, etc. students stared at her, smirked, made unkind comments, etc. It was impossible to get away from the fall-out from the sexting. That year Chris moved her family. Fortunately, where they moved the images weren't known. Tasha got a fresh start at 'normal'. Now a young adult Tasha is doing well. She is fortunate, her story had a happy ending.

Perception & Validity

Mass hysteria, and a stampede occurred at a shopping mall. A loud noise, was perceived to be gunfire, someone screamed, then chaos ensued. People fled toward exits. Social media posts were made reporting gunfire plus live video of the stampede at the mall. It reached multitudes, instantly. Within minutes the police were on the scene as well as news crews. There was no gunfire; a store display fell making a loud noise. Some were injured in the stampede, due to the phantom of fear. The police chief as soon they had ascertained there was no credible threat posted on social media ASAP.[16] The power of social media, the speed at which it travels, influences and shapes public knowledge and perception.

Often before God moves you into an acceleration of your purpose and assignment a political spirit comes against you. This has happened to me both in my professional and Church life. My boss spread negative innuendo about me. We had both been promoted to different positions, he was still above me, but in another office. I caught wind of his toxic negative comments through a subordinate, Marianne (fictitious name) She told me in confidence how he'd said disparaging things about me that created a false negative image. Marianne begged me not to reveal her identity to anyone, she had confided in me. It was so unprofessional, hurtful and vindictive on his part. I confronted him privately. He said to me, "Remember, Jan, **it's all about perception. Something doesn't have to be true to be believed.** All I need to do is create the perception and illusion."

He out-ranked me and was 'in' with those in power. He then asked if I could prove he'd done and said that. I explained not without revealing the identity of Marianne, and I had promised I wouldn't do that. His reply, "That's what I figured would happen." How chillingly evil, manipulative, diabolical – arrogantly, and smugly boasting of his strategy. **A half truth is still a lie.** Lies covertly plotted, behind closed doors, outside of your hearing, are very hard to address. If you defend yourself you are still perceived as guilty, while the culprit plays dumb.

This same scenario is rampant in media, social media, and the political landscape (and unfortunately in churches too). This political spirit is so pervasive in our culture that it is dramatized on tv. In the hit tv adventure series "Blindspot", there was a scene with a government FBI nemesis who says to the 'good guys' (Weller & Naz): "I don't need a whole lot of fire, I just need a little smoke that rings true in Congress."
Weller whispers to Naz: "The charges he made are ludicrous!"
Naz: "To us yes, but it's enough for Congress to buy into."
After that Naz stepped down so as not to discredit her unit. (By the way, I did not step down, but the negative perception he created was a royal pain for me to wade through.)

That's what happened to Joseph in the Old Testament. A jealous, vindictive spirit overshadowed and followed him. First, within his own family, his own brothers tried to kill him. Then later in Potiphar's home. Joseph remained pure, while falsely accused by a woman who framed him. She was unfaithful in her heart toward her husband, hardened, uncaring of anyone but herself, void of common decency. Yet she appeared to be the poor damsel in distress. Joseph paid a high price because of a lie, that had the appearance of truth. But God deepened his character in the dungeon.

Before you accept information (whether news media or social media) as true do the following:

1. Choose not to react. Its fine to respond to things, but don't be like a jack-hammer. Let your response be weighed, measured, researched and informed. Take a breather and give yourself cool down time. Be quick to listen, slow to speak, and slow to anger. (James 1:19)
2. Take every thought captive. (2 Corinthians 10:5) Cover your mind, put on the helmet of salvation. (Ephesians 6:17)
3. Cry out for wisdom and discernment. (James 1:5; Pr. 10:13)
4. Look at, listen to differing sources and perspectives on a subject.
5. Pray (at all times, without ceasing). (1 Thessalonians 5:16)

Value and love truth with the gift of discernment.

> Trust in *and* rely confidently on the LORD with all your heart
> And do not rely on your own insight *or* understanding.
> In all your ways know *and* acknowledge *and* recognize Him,
> And He will make your paths straight *and* smooth [removing obstacles that block your way]. (Proverbs 3:5-6, AMP)

> "You shall know the truth and the truth shall set you free." (John 8:32)

CHAPTER 9

SHIFTS in Immigration and Borders

"For the mountains may be removed and the hills may shake,
But My lovingkindness will not be removed from you,
And My covenant of peace will not be shaken,"
Says the LORD who has compassion on you." (Isaiah 54:10)

<u>Note to the reader</u>: This chapter provides a summary status or an overview of global affairs. In order to secure our gates we must know and understand what is going on around us and then pray into what is taking place in the world. In the throne room God gives us an increase in authority and revelation for how to prophetically pray, and strategies to secure gates and advance.

> "Ask me, and I will make the nations your inheritance, the ends of the earth your possession." (Psalm 2:8)

KINGDOM EFFECTIVENESS DEMANDS UNDERSTANDING THIS 'brave new world' that is emerging. Americans are fairly ignorant of world events. "*My people perish from lack of knowledge.*" (Hosea 4:6) American news is sub-par in covering global events. (BBC and Al-Jazeera do a better job than USA news with international coverage.) Hearing the voice of God in the midst is paramount. Know your God and, "Know yourself, know your enemy, a thousand battles, a thousand victories." (Sun Tzu)

We strip the enemy of power when we expose his plans. Watch and pray, don't be ignorant of the enemy's devices. Knowing the problem is key to the solution. Darkness is the devil's breeding ground for chaos, confusion, and fear. In the dark children become fearful, we fumble in the dark to find our keys; in the darkness we lose our sense of direction. Jesus shatters the darkness with light! (John 1:5) This chapter shines His light on the plans of the enemy; exposing them.

> Have nothing to do with the fruitless deeds of darkness, but rather expose them. It is shameful even to mention what the disobedient do in secret. But everything exposed by the light becomes visible—and everything that is illuminated becomes a light. This is why it is said:
> "Wake up, sleeper,
> rise from the dead,
> and Christ will shine on you."
> Be very careful, then, how you live—not as unwise but as wise, making the most of every opportunity, because the days are evil. (Ephesians 5:11-16)

STATUS of the WORLD – SHIFT!
Internal Conundrums: Terrorism & Immigration – no easy solutions

Every continent is experiencing some type of border dispute, if not without than within.

The USA, Canada and many European nations have renewed concerns and scrutiny over their immigration laws and vetting processes. Europe, ie; England, France, Germany, and Belgium, have been rife with terror on their soil, bombs, car bombings, car crashes, etc. London has been nick-named 'London-istan' by some, a reflection of their changing demographics.

Trump put into place a travel ban with stricter vetting processes for 6 predominately Muslim nations known for harboring terrorists and radical jihadists (Iran, Libya, Syria, Somalia, Sudan, Yemen, and all refugees). Many in the USA were protesting discrimination over the tightened restrictions as terrorist bombings ripped through European cities – Paris, London, Brussels and Berlin. Germany, France and Great Britain have welcomed a high influx from these 6 nations reaping disastrous results. They are now fighting a very difficult battle, of ISIS infiltration and attacks from within.

In the USA there has been considerable division and tension over the travel bans and more thorough vetting process of immigrants. 'An ounce of prevention is worth a pound of cure.' is the motivation behind the tightening of regulations. Others vocalize concerns over civil rights, and rightfully so. Listening to all sides will bring balance for the direction we should go in.

There's a plethora of rhetoric surrounding building a wall between Mexico and the USA – and having Mexico pay for it! Understandably, Mexico finds that laughable. What I've been wondering is why are we focused on building a wall? Why hasn't there been any talk of investing in technology, infra-red or otherwise to detect where the tunnels are located? Notorious drug lord, Joaquin 'El Chapo' Guzman was known for building a sophisticated, labyrinth of underground tunnels between the USA and Mexico. Illegal drug and sex trafficking, etc. went, undetected via these tunnels. I haven't heard anything about them. Did we find all of them and effectively shut them all down?

I am not blindly pro-Trump, anti-Trump, right wing, left wing, etc. I want to be found under the wings of the shadow of the Almighty. Please! Let's stop throwing out the baby with the bathwater and *listen* to one another. The Church needs to be the model of the way of Love – which is not, and will never be found in the political arena. Love listens. The way of love and law of grace is in Christ Jesus and no other. Our hope and trust is in Him not man. Lord align our hearts and actions with our words.

Whether you like Trump or not, I think we can all agree upon one thing regarding him: "Stop tweeting!! Mercy! Let vice-president Mike Pence and his PR people talk on behalf of the president, but he needs to pause and be quiet. Not all of what he says is a bad thing, but people can't hear him because of how he comes across, constantly putting his foot in his mouth.

Immigration:

The Davis-Oliver Act is legislation named after two US law officers who were murdered by an illegal alien in California. [1] These efforts, along with travel bans of visitors from 6 nations, known for terrorism, have sparked deep controversy in the USA.

The media villi-fied Trump for this among many other things. One thing that is imperative to understand: Families with illegal aliens, that were law-abiding, respectful, hard-working individuals experienced separation and deportation under President Obama and prior administrations as well. (I was teaching World Geography in a Christian school during his tenure in office. I did the research. We viewed video clips of heart-rending stories that occurred under the Obama administration as well. The media did not play that up, but they have only done so with respect to Trump.) No one, not Trump, not Obama, or any president to come, will get to wear the white hat on the issue of immigration. Because we already have so many illegal immigrants in the USA it makes the situation more difficult to deal with.

The tearing apart of families, situations of young adults having lived their life in the USA being deported back to 'their country' that is foreign to them. We know of a young man (Manuel, fictitious name), born in an American hospital, the son of illegal aliens. He lived his entire natural life here in the USA, but his parents, always fearing immigration, did not stay in the hospital long enough to get his birth certificate. They also never told him the name of the hospital he was born in. His parents constantly moved throughout his childhood. Bottomline, he's unable to document or prove that he is a legal US citizen, by birthright, and lives in fear and risk of possible deportation to a country he's never set foot in.

We have several friends that are illegal aliens. (NJ ranks 5th out of 50 states in the nation for undocumented illegal aliens.) I have written character letters of reference for some of the finest, most outstanding individuals I've ever met, that are seeking USA citizenship. Whole families, friends, dear to my heart, that would be split up if the letter of the law were applied.

The flip side of the dilemma; without regulating immigration the strain on our nation's overall economy would be considerable. In this era of ISIS infiltration, terrorism, and influx of radicalized Muslims due to refugee crisis makes vetting and immigration reform an imperative to deal with. It is needed. How to reform, adjust, vet, and implement needed tightening and change is in the mix now. Hard decisions of where and how to draw the line are on the table. No matter what reforms are made someone will go through a heart-rending experience.

Stats and Facts on Illegal Aliens [2]

- Six states: California, Texas, Illinois, Florida, New York and New Jersey account for 59 percent of all illegal immigrants residing in the U.S.
- 66 percent of all illegal immigrants have lived in our nation for over ten years
- in 2014, about 13,288 violent crimes were committed by illegal aliens – about 19%
- According to research and statistics by the U.S. Departments of Justice and Homeland Security, U.S. taxpayers are footing an annual bill of nearly $19 million *per day* to house and care for an estimated 300,000 to 450,000 convicted criminal immigrants who are eligible for deportation and are currently residing in local jails and state and federal prisons across the country.
- These figures include not only those immigrants who are in the U.S. illegally, but all immigrants here who commit and have been convicted of crimes. Other accounting estimates indicate that the total cost for all corrections, medical and support services for adults and juvenile immigrant criminals nationally to be over $1.8 billion dollars.
- Estimated cost of deportation is approximately $10,500 per person give or take (This includes all costs necessary to identify, apprehend, detain, process through immigration court, and remove an alien.)

Trump promised during his campaign to deport all 11 million unauthorized immigrants in the U.S., but since becoming POTUS has narrowed his focus to immigrants with criminal histories, analysts estimate that to cost at about 2 million. [3]

There are no quick fixes or easy answers. Whatever reforms are implemented today will more likely than not be revised tomorrow. Pray for our leaders and those in authority. Before siding with any perspective listen to all sides. (I mean actively listen.) The correct course of action may not be black or white, left or right – but in somewhere in between. We'll never get there if we're not open to differing viewpoints and perspectives. Each voice holds a key, if we have ears to hear. That's what will make America great again!

Borders and Battles

I've concluded that the world truly has gone crazy. Only a divine act of God will turn it around; to that end I'm praying. It's called revival.

"You will hear of wars and rumors of wars, but see to it that you are not alarmed. Such things must happen, but the end is still to come. Nation will rise against nation, and kingdom against kingdom. There will be famines and earthquakes in various places." – Matthew 24:6-7

Naively, as a child, I looked at globes and political world maps thinking that the worst battles and wars were largely a thing of the past. I grew up during a period of relative peace on earth and projected that into my world-view. I thought that border wars were history. Not! We see through the lens of our experience. How narrow and overly-simplistic my worldview was. Lord open our eyes.

As Chuck Pierce said prophetically, **"In days ahead, we will see many changing boundaries in the earth. There will be an attempt to illegally rearrange the boundaries of nations. Governments will align to overtake lands that were never destined to be overtaken.** We must watch these wars carefully in the natural earth realm because they are linked with a quest for wealth." [4]

Here are 3 primary disputes taking place in the world:

A. Immigration laws (Europe and North America in particular are examining reforms)
B. Organized Crime territorial 'jurisdiction': Drug Wars, Sex Trafficking and more (Make no mistake about it, a significant amount of monies from organized crime trickles into politics and governmental avenues. This has a domino effect/ influence in media, policy and legislation.)

C. Turf disputes between Nations: North Korea, Cypress (Turkey/Greece), Israel-Palestine, several nations within Africa (Sudan-Kenya; Cameroon-Nigeria; and many more). There are two types of turf disputes: territorial and boundaries.

Territorial disputes – A territorial dispute is a disagreement over the possession/control of land between two or more territorial entities or over the possession or control of land, usually between a new state and the occupying power.

In history, territorial disputes are the leading cause of war.

Boundary disputes – Boundary Disputes are disagreements between neighbors over their rights and duties with respect to adjacent, or nearby, real property owners. These disagreements may take many forms. As a result, there are numerous causes of action to provide appropriate legal frameworks for resolving them. A disagreement between countries about where the border between them should be drawn.

Causes of boundary disputes:

a. Religious difference, ie; India – Pakistan, Iran
b. Cultural & racial differences, ie; Turks and Kurds
c. Distrust, un-healed hurt and offense – Turkey and Cyprus, (the 911 attack of Osama Bin Laden on the USA was born out of a son's revenge for his father)
d. Lack of clearly defined boundaries, ie; This is what the problem is in the South China Sea and it is also why there is conflict to some extent as the ice melts in the Arctic.
e. Commerce competition over oil and money – this pertains to a myriad of countries within Africa [5] and Central Asia
f. Pride and a lust for power and control. – North Korea (Kim Jong-Un)

Europe is also experiencing border tensions and conflicts, as one source said, "Forget China and the Middle East: the former Yugoslavia could yet emerge as Trump's first real foreign policy headache. Now (2017), the Balkans are once again dicing with crisis. Borders are being questioned, ethnic tensions are bubbling up, and land swaps are being mooted as a last resort to prevent a slide back towards violence." [6] Past war in the Balkans; Bosnia, Kosova, Croatia between Serbs and Bosnians, was bloody, brutal with a loss of over 100,000 lives.

It's been said that you walk before you can run. Well, you need to do the due diligence before entering physical conflict, skirmishes, and battles. Thus, governments should proceed with caution before entering physical conflict over border disputes. Prudent measures governments may take to work toward peaceful resolutions include:

- Declare an open dispute and define it
- Involve commissions on both sides for study and discussion
- Involve a neutral part(ies) or commission(s)
- Involve economic commission(s)
- Examine and educate
- Negotiate

The above list is food to pray into as well. **But nothing can compare with the wisdom of the Almighty! THE singular most important thing is to hear His voice and do what He says do!** Who can orchestrate successful negotiations like Him? And as we go to pray He will show us different things to decree and declare. We will hear His battle plan, binding and loosing accordingly; divisive voices to be silenced, ministering angels to be loosed, and more. We must contend for the borders and His triumph on the earth, so that we will rejoice saying, "The boundary lines have fallen for me in pleasant places; surely I have a delightful inheritance. I will praise the Lord, who counsels me" (Psalm 16:6-7)

Not all battles Israel fought ended in victory. **It was only when they sought, heard and obeyed the Lord, trusting in Him, that they emerged victorious.** The foolishness of God is wiser than human wisdom, and the weakness of God is stronger than human strength. (1 Corinthians 1:25) As Dale Mast has said, "God can shift our lives in a day, but it will take a journey to arrive at that day." [7] When the breath of His Spirit is on something anything can happen!

Increasingly prophetic voices are speaking by the Holy Spirit over peoples and nations, Hank Kunneman gave a prophetic warning of the London Bridge terror attack in Great Britain in 2017, just days *before* it occurred. Chuck Pierce prophesied, "The Asian Church will rise up and create a prototype we've never seen. Israel will come into its greatest conflict since 1967. You have entered a new season! Let Judah arise!"

Keep your eye on the church in Asia. It would not surprise me that Kim Jong-Un is brought down from *within* North Korea. I see a people so oppressed that they will rise up against him, even one of his own generals. We may see war break out first, but it will be short-lived. I believe you will see a re-unification between North and South Korea. This will in turn have a domino effect, causing revival to explode in China (beginning near the North Korean border areas) and in Malaysia. Malaysia has long been a radical Muslim stronghold, that has previously been intolerant toward Christianity. Revival in Malaysia will affect the world (and it is rapidly rising in e-commerce as well). My heart is stirred regarding

Malaysia. It is destined to be a hot spot for revival. As an intercessor I'm investing in Malaysia!

In the days and years to come God will be raising up prophets into governmental positions and platforms influencing legislature and governmental negotiations at home and abroad. These men and women of God will be filled with His spirit, revelation, and divine wisdom.

What a privilege, blessing, and honor it was for me to teach high school classes in US Government and World Geography in a Christian school! I was very careful to anchor them in the Word, not bias them with my viewpoints and opinions, but challenged them to research issues in light of His Word. The classes were filled with life: debates on border issues, wars, the European Union, immigration, speeches, presentations, registering as voters, writing letters to their Congressmen, and more. Wow! They were awesome! Sitting before me were future lawyers, immigration specialists, technology network gatekeepers, politicians, educators and more. Young men and women grounded in His Word, prayer, with a spirit of courage and integrity! Equipped to shape the landscape of tomorrow and secure the gates!

A new boundary issue is emerging due to climate change, global warming.

> *When you hear of wars and rumors of wars, do not be alarmed. Such things must happen, but the end is still to come. Nation will rise against nation, and kingdom against kingdom. There will be earthquakes in various places, and famines.* (Mark 13:7-8)

The borders of Antarctica have changed. Icebergs, the largest ever recorded, of 2,300 square miles, broke away (July 2017) and is drifting. To gain perspective and properly appreciate the enormity of this that is the size of a state or small country; that's roughly the same size as Puerto Rico. Meanwhile, POTUS Trump has withdrawn the USA from the Paris climate agreement. The argument for breaking away is that the USA was investing a disproportionate amount of monies compared with other nations. The argument for working with together with other countries on climate change is that any type of meaningful plan of action for the future and well-being of planet earth, necessitates a combined effort.

Earthquakes, hurricanes, tsunamis, wildfires and natural disasters of all types are occurring globally, literally changing the physical landscape and borders of regions and nations. Shorelines have been altered. These events have been historic in severity and catastrophic in damages to buildings, the landscape, the ecosystem and most importantly, human life.

Prayerfully guard our borders, securing our gates. Speak to them decreeing and declaring the word of the Lord. Be proactive not reactive.

"Whoever fears the LORD has a secure fortress, and for their children it will be a refuge." (Proverbs 14:26)

CHAPTER 10

Our GOVERNMENT

"When one person gets ahold of truth, and contends in the heavens for its manifestation on earth, it can change a nation."

– Lou Engle

WHAT HAPPENS WHEN THE CHURCH gets ahold of truth and contends for it? We can change the world, forcefully advancing His kingdom here on earth as it is in heaven – thoroughly securing our gates and taking back the mountains. "One of us can cause a thousand to flee and two of us 10,000." **Divine synergy occurs in the dynamic of unity**. In unity His majesty, authority and dominion is magnified.

Tom Hamon said, "At a time when it seems like everyone wants to focus on personalities and personal feelings, **the truth is that we are fighting principalities and powers and evil spirits that are set in high places over our nation that have an agenda to steal, kill and destroy all that is good and godly.**[1] (Ephesians 6:12)

One of the things that makes America great is our freedom – the land of the free and the home of the brave. The freedom of speech and the press – freedom to disagree and hold differing viewpoints, *while still respecting one another*.

During the 2016 presidential campaign year, if I had a nickel for the number of people who told me that they didn't care who won the presidency, because they didn't like either candidate, and they didn't think they'd vote, I would be VERY wealthy now! Many wanted "Jesus for President!" There was only one problem – Jesus wasn't running for office. He most assuredly would have been my candidate if He had! (I'm not sure if Jesus would have won. He may have been too radical and controversial for people.)

Prior to the election Christians said it didn't matter who won, that God was in control. Then, Donald Trump became the 45th President of the USA (POTUS). Lord have mercy! "The poop hit the fan!" He didn't win the popular vote, but won the electoral vote. Many felt this was unfair and rebelled. There was rioting in the streets, destruction on college campuses, demonstrations, RUDE and destructive behavior was seen across the country.

Some say POTUS Trump is uncouth. I agree! Often, he is lacking in savoir faire and makes unnecessary, un-presidential barbs at people. (Stooping to commenting negatively on a woman's looks, making disparaging remarks on another's IQ, is totally unacceptable, and I don't care how much you've been attacked by others. Two wrongs don't make it right.) Trump went into his presidency, as Lance Wallnau would put it, like a bull in a china shop, a wrecking ball. He didn't give proper honor or homage to his predecessor, quite the opposite.

On both sides of the coin – it's time to grow up and find our manners! In finding our voice learn to say what we mean, mean what we say, but don't say it mean. Common respect and decency have become uncommon. As a nation we've elevated rudeness, in the name of freedom of speech, as a virtue. "Standfast in the liberty where-with Christ has made us free, and be not entangled again to the yoke of bondage. For brethren, ye have been called unto liberty, only use not liberty for an occasion to the flesh, but by love serve one another." (Galatians 5:1) Our freedom of speech should not violate the law of love. When it does we have traded our liberty for bondage.

Our freedom of speech should not violate the law of love. When it does we have traded our liberty for bondage.

New York state universities provided free counseling for students who were upset over the outcome of the elections. People were stridently chanting, "Not my President!" Shouting over Trump associated guest speakers on college campuses, making it impossible for others to cross demonstration lines to attend. On some campuses students hurled objects, smashing glass walls and doors. There was a maelstrom of discontent. Our behavior as a nation, emphasized by media coverage, portrayed a very negative image of America to the global community. We appeared rude, violent, belligerent brats that have tantrums when we don't get our way. It was a disgrace to us as a people.

Whether intentional or not, people were fighting the democratic process set forth in the Constitution of the USA. Frankly, it gave the appearance to the rest of the world of democracy in America stumbling.

<u>Fast facts about the 2016 elections the Electoral College:</u> [2]

1. President Trump is not the first president to win the presidency by the electoral vote, not the popular. He is the 5th such president to become POTUS under those circumstances. (As a matter of fact Bill Clinton did not win the majority of the popular vote in *either* of his elections.)
2. The first purpose of the Electoral College was to create a buffer between population and the selection of a President. Particularly when there are third party candidates running. (In the 2016 elections, although Hillary Clinton won the popular vote, she only received a plurality, 48 percent - *not a majority*; third party candidates took the rest.)
3. The second purpose as part of the structure of the government that gave extra power to the smaller states to level the playing field for them so to speak.
4. The original framers of the Constitution of the USA used genius in the plan of the electoral college – they had foresight to allow for fair, orderly, democratic process, to be in place over 200 years after its drafting, with factoring third party candidates. [3]

But we're not addressing facts or rational processes. As a matter of fact, people don't want to be confused by the facts. What is taking place is the clashing of kingdoms; we are witnessing incidents in the natural, but it is spiritual in nature. Many have reacted in the flesh, but neglected fighting the good fight spiritually.

There is also a clashing of generational mindsets; the current millennial generation rules from the seat of their emotions and experiential reality, the older generation navigates based upon facts and logic. Man's perspective, from any generation is flawed. We must rule, reign and take dominion based upon God's unchanging, timeless truth, not emotionalism, experience, or scientific reasoning! **Truth is what God says.** True prophets of God are arising in this hour. There is an increase in prophetic gifting. With that comes the need for us to sharpen the gift of discerning of spirits so we don't become deceived.

Some Christians say Trump is a modern-day Cyrus (bringing needed, godly reform), others say he's a Nebuchadnezzer (whose pride led to downfall). Even those standing in support of him, such as Lance Wallnau and others, have referred to him as a wrecking ball, a bull in a china shop, 'God's Chaos Candidate', that he is in power as a judgement to America. [4] Curt Landry says, "We struggle with our views due to a lack of biblical understanding of *who exactly God uses.* We tend to come through a Western religious mind-set where we prefer our presidents to be Holy pastor-types, but that is not reality. Sometimes God will take a person who is a real mess, put them in place, change them, and then ultimately use them." [5]

What does it mean when people talk about a modern-day Cyrus? Tom Hamon is so spot on as he explains, "What did Cyrus do? His main mission from God was to free God's people from captivity and pass legislation that would authorize them and empower them to repossess their land, rebuild the temple and rebuild the city. He unlocked the money, manpower and legislative authority to go and rebuild the temple and the city.

Rebuilding the temple has everything to do with the restoration and reformation of the Church in the earth in our generation—restoring the Church to its original call to operate in the power and character of Jesus Himself, so it can rightly represent His heart and purposes in the earth. Restoring the "walls of the city" has everything to do with rebuilding the culture and addressing the ills of society in our generation. ... He issued commands that helped Israel **restore the judges, the teachers and the fathers of the land.** It was this strategy that eventually turned the tide of the nation." [6] Today key strategic positions for the Supreme Court are being filled which will effect legislative decisions for about 30 years. (The length of term for a Supreme Court justice ranges between 10-30 years, as they usually serve for the remainder of their natural life.)

Whatever your view is, one thing we can all agree upon, our problems as a nation go well beyond Republican v. Democrat and one individual over another. **Our problems are spiritual at their root**. "*If My people, who are called by My name will humble themselves and pray, then I will hear from heaven and heal their land.*" (2 Chronicles 7:14) Worship and prayer unify us. Let's get unified! *Praying in the spirit*, not according to our will but His!

Win lose or draw, Donald J. Trump is the 45th president of the USA and needs our prayers. If the Church, filled with our diversity and differences, lay down our passionate, emotional divides to be one in the Spirit, then God will be so impressed He'll make a personal visitation! (Matthew 18:19-20)

Media with Arts & Entertainment and their connection to Government has blurred and crossed the lines stirring up furor. There is no doubt that most of Media and the bulk of Hollywood favors the left. Trump is viewed as right wing. The constant tension and attacking is as if one can hear electrical crackling in the atmosphere. Media's relentless assault on POTUS Trump, much of which he's unquestionably earned, has been excessive. Truly God must have been contending for him. He certainly didn't get to be POTUS due to favorable Media coverage.

Keep in mind the role of Gatekeepers who control the flow of Media information, which intentionally, shapes national perspective, opinion, and mindsets – often without people realizing it.

LEFT vs. RIGHT/ INTOLERANCE & HYPOCRISY

Conspiracy theory aside, Whatever your political ideology is, whether conservative, liberal, or somewhere in between do not assume that you have a corner on truth. **Only God has a corner on truth**. Discern, weigh and judge everything by the spirit. The area that I live in is extremely liberal (leftist). There is a profuse intolerance and overt hostility toward conservatives (right wing). I imagine that in other areas of the country that are very conservative and those with liberal views are treated with bias by the conservatives. Stop assuming whichever side of the fence you're on is infallible and above reproach. Satan disguises himself as an angel of light (2 Corinthians 11:14) to deceive. "**The clashing of Heaven and Hell will show up in the conflict of ideologies**. The swords will collide as two incompatible spirit realms clash through vessels under their influence. *This collision of kingdoms has already started in the political mountain, but will expand to all seven*!" – Lance Wallnau[7]

Whatever your political ideology is, whether conservative, liberal, or somewhere in between do not assume that you have a corner on truth.

Let's each take the log out of our own eye. (Matthew 7:1-5)

I applaud public news commentators such as Fareed Zakaria (left-wing) and Michael Brown (right wing) they both acknowledge and expose intolerance and hypocrisy, within their own ranks. As Fareed Zakaria remarked, "**at the heart of liberty in the Western world has been freedom of speech. *From the beginning, people understood that this meant protecting and listening to speech with which you disagreed*.**

Freedom of speech and thought is not just for warm, fuzzy ideas that we find comfortable. It's for ideas that we find offensive. There is, as we all know, a kind of anti-intellectualism on the right these days. Denial of facts, of reason, of science. But there is also an anti-intellectualism on the left. An attitude of self-righteousness that says we are so pure, we are so morally superior, we cannot bear to hear an idea with which we disagree.

"Liberals think they are tolerant, but often they aren't," Zakaria concluded.[8]

I highly recommend to you Michael Brown's article, "*Left-Wing Intolerance and Right Wing Hypocrisy*". It is exceptionally well-done with piercing candor and a healthy dose of objectivity – a rare blend and precious commodity in these times. Here are salient excerpts:

"Leftwing intolerance has been on full display, from the riots against free speech at Berkeley (the home of the free speech movement), to some entertainers receiving credible death threats if they performed at the inauguration to other entertainers getting blacklisted for performing.

Making this leftwing intolerance even more galling is that it is done in the name of tolerance and enlightenment and carried out in the name of progressiveness and open-mindedness, thereby putting leftwing hypocrisy on full display.

But the leftwing does not have a monopoly on hypocrisy. Those of us on the right have our fair share of it as well. In the end, though, it's still hard to deny that hypocrisy is just as rampant (or nearly as rampant) on the right as it is on the left" [9] Michael Brown then specifically itemizes the many hypocrisies of the right wing as well as intolerances of the leftwing and provides a warning checklist to measure yourself by.

Church it's time to pray! Time to bury the hatchet and not in one another!

Donald Trump winning the presidency was a mega shift/ game-changer, leaving a rather divided nation; to the point where there is a type of civil war going on, a palpable clashing of kingdoms. What's alarming is to see a divided Church.

In talking with another pastor, the topic of praying for those in leadership came up, specifically President Trump. Pastor X's reaction became adamant, emotional and agitated in tone that they would NOT pray for him! They further categorized him as representing an anti-Christ system. (It is worth noting that I've heard right-wing believers describe Obama likewise.) Bottom line you don't have to like someone to pray for them. For that matter you don't have to like someone to love them. We are under the law of love and grace – or should be.

Everyone stop! It doesn't matter who it is. God said pray for those in leadership – period. Mercy! Can we put down the axe we're grinding long enough to pray, TOGETHER??! God has something to say to ALL of us. Sometimes we're making too much noise to hear Him. World leaders need our prayers, especially the ones we don't like. Let's be still, before Him, long enough to hear His voice over ours! God's people need to love one another, and PRAY.

Whatever your views, God didn't ask you or I for our opinions and feelings regarding any leader. He simply tells us to pray for those in authority. So, let's PRAY!

> "First of all, then, I urge that entreaties *and* prayers, petitions *and* thanksgivings, be made on behalf of all men, for kings and

> all who are in authority, so that we may lead a tranquil and quiet life in all godliness and dignity. " (1 Timothy 2:1-4)

Many have their identity wrapped up in their gender, race, political ideology, nationality, etc. They give lip service to their identity being in Christ, without realizing it became secondary in the whirlwind. Lay down anything interfering with our identity in Jesus Christ. "For all of creation is groaning in eager anticipation for the sons and daughters of God to be revealed." (Romans 8:19, paraphrased)

Whatever your views, God didn't ask you or I for our opinions and feelings regarding any leader. He simply tells us to pray for those in authority. So, let's PRAY!

"Again, truly I tell you that if two of you on earth agree about anything they ask for, it will be done for them by my Father in heaven. For where two or three gather in my name, there am I with them." (Matthew 18:19-20) It's time to put ourselves in check and PRAY! No matter who the leader is PRAY! Hear the voice of God, not the voices of men, and PRAY!

Lord may we become so focused on You that the things of earth take a backseat. "There is neither Jew nor Gentile, neither slave nor free, nor is there male and female, for you are all one in Christ Jesus. (Galatians 3:28) Lord I want to be hid with Christ in God. Help me to live the truth of Your word that we, "Set our minds on things above, not on earthly things. For I've died, and my life is now hidden with Christ in God." (Colossians 3:2-3)

For our struggle is not against flesh and blood, but against the rulers, against the powers, against the world forces of this darkness, against the spiritual *forces* of wickedness in the heavenly *places*. (Ephesians 6:12) As Tom Hamon said, "God is raising up a Joseph Generation that will know how to operate in the realms of government and commerce, yet stay pure and purposed.".[20] And the gates of hell will NOT prevail! (Matthew 16:19)

PRAY for the world leaders of today and tomorrow. They face many pressures and a myriad of voices screaming for their attention. Some of those voices are God, some Satan, some simply the flesh. Now, more than ever, we must lay down our agendas to hear His, be anchored in the Word, and pray for ALL those in leadership and authority.

> *Blessed are those who wash their robes, so that they may have the right to the tree of life, <u>and may enter by the gates into the city</u>. (Revelation 22:14)*

Corruption & Conspiracy in the Gates

Darkness is Satan's environment of choice, there he hides and thrives; it is the devil's breeding ground for chaos, confusion, and fear. In the dark children become fearful, we fumble in the dark to find our keys; in the darkness we can lose our sense of direction.

> Have nothing to do with the fruitless deeds of darkness, but rather expose them. It is shameful even to mention what the disobedient do in secret. But everything exposed by the light becomes visible—and everything that is illuminated becomes a light. As it is said:
>
> "Wake up, sleeper,
> rise from the dead,
> and Christ will shine on you."
> Be very careful, then, how you live—not as unwise but as wise, making the most of every opportunity, because the days are evil. (Ephesians 5:11-16)

Our issues as a nation go much deeper than Republican or Democrat or one candidate or politician over another. There is covert, hidden conspiracy afoot leading to one world government. The various gates are working together regarding influence in the world toward this end. Conspiracy theory is not new, it's been around for a while. In America the conspiracy theory that is widely held by many is called "Deep State".

Deep State – is a term that means what it says. It is a state within the state, or political influence operating covertly within the visible/ overt power, governmental structure. Usually the 'deep state' or state within the state is conspiratorial in nature, there are exceptions to that.

Arts & Entertainment reflect our times and culture. Three of prime time tv's hit series "*Blindspot*", "*Designated Survivor*" and "*Blacklist*" are dramas all about deep state conspiracy theory. Several presidents of the USA talked about Deep State. Some believe it is what was really behind the assassination of JFK.

In 1961 Eisenhower, in talking about 'Deep State' warned Americans about a 'military-industrial complex'. If he were present today he would undoubtedly include media in the mix.

The Deep State, eluded to by Theodore Roosevelt (1901-09) and Woodrow Wilson (1913-21), talked about by Eisenhower (1950's) and JFK (1960's), is comprised of a small group of people and their corporations/institutions. "It has been this way for many years, as so many presidential candidates, like Dr. Ron Paul and Bernie Sanders, have exposed. This organized power completely controls politics, and they do not care who you vote for.

Arjun Walia, says it plainly, "Regardless of who is elected president, this hidden power has an agenda, and they use politics to justify it.

Our perception of politicians and presidents largely comes from mainstream media, not our ability to think critically about what is going on. If mainstream media praises a candidate, that's who the masses prefer. Their power to influence the minds of the masses is tremendous." [10]

'Deep State' is what conservatives call it now, though it goes by other names, such as; the administrative state, the entrenched governing elite, Lois Lerner, the federal bureaucracy.

> [History behind the term Lois Lerner:
> She became director of the Exempt Organizations Unit of the Internal Revenue Service (IRS) in 2005, and subsequently became the central figure in the 2013 IRS controversy in the targeting of conservative groups (such as Christian Coalition, Tea Party and others), either denying them tax-exempt status outright or delaying that status until they could no longer take effective part in the 2012 election. On May10, 2013 Lerner stated that the IRS was "apologetic" for what she termed "absolutely inappropriate" actions. In 2014 the IRS conveniently lost 2 years of her emails. The investigation concluded in June 2015. Lerner resigned over the controversy.]

Whatever the term used to describe 'Deep State', what's pertinent to Washington, DC is that this cadre of federal employees, are actively working from within to thwart Donald Trump's agenda, according to Kimberly Strassel.[11]

As my husband says, "**Whenever you want to understand something, think money and follow the money trail.**" Perhaps you believe that some are simply power-hungry. Money is power.

Theodore Roosevelt observed, "Behind the ostensible government sits enthroned an invisible government owing no allegiance and acknowledging no responsibility to the people. To destroy this invisible government, to dissolve the unholy alliance between corrupt business and corrupt politics is the first task of the statesmanship of the day."

Most Americans followed the events of 9-11 in the news. But very few are aware of these startling facts that the Bush family covered the bin Ladens. (report by Cindy Rodriguez of the Denver Post in 2006):

"In 1978, Bush and Osama bin Laden's brother, Salem bin Laden, founded Arbusto Energy, an oil company based in Texas.

Several bin Laden family members invested millions in The Carlyle Group, a private global equity firm based in Washington, DC. The company's senior advisor was Bush's father, former President George H.W. Bush. After news of the bin Laden-Bush connection became public, the elder Bush stepped down from Carlyle.

Interestingly, on Sept. 11, 2001, members of the Carlyle Group – including Bush senior, and his former secretary of state, James Baker – were meeting at the Ritz Carlton Hotel in Washington, D.C., along with Shafiq bin Laden, another one of Osama bin Laden's brothers.

While all flights were halted following the terrorist attacks, there was one exception made: The White House authorized planes to pick up 140 Saudi nationals, including 24 members of the bin Laden family, living in various cities in the U.S. to bring them back to Saudi Arabia, where they would be safe. They were never interrogated." [12]

Bottomline, the Bush family had strong business ties, in the millions of dollars, with the Bin Laden family, and flew them home safe and snug to Saudi Arabia, not interrogating them. Did they even really want Bin Laden found?

While George Bush was president there were fewer than 50 ground troops surrounding the massive Tora Bora region in the mountains of Afghanistan where bin Laden was hiding, ground commanders pleaded for 800 more soldiers – that didn't happen.

How could these facts, made know 5 years *after* 9-11, not have been common knowledge? Why wasn't there a public outcry? Remember: A mere 232 media executives control the information diet of 277 million Americans (approximately 1 media exec to every 850,000 subscribers) **There is a collusion between government, or at least some government officials and mega multi-national corporations.** It's deeper than we know, hence the term 'Deep State'.

Foster Gamble heir, grandson to James Gamble of Proctor & Gamble, made a documentary on conspiracy theory, "*Thrive: What On Earth Will It Take?*". He is quoted as saying, **"I believe that an elite group of people and the corporations they run have gained control over not just our energy, food supply,**

education, and healthcare, but over virtually every aspect of our lives; and they do it by controlling the world of finance. Not by creating more value, but by controlling the source of money." [13] This pictogram, *Follow the Money* conveys a great deal.

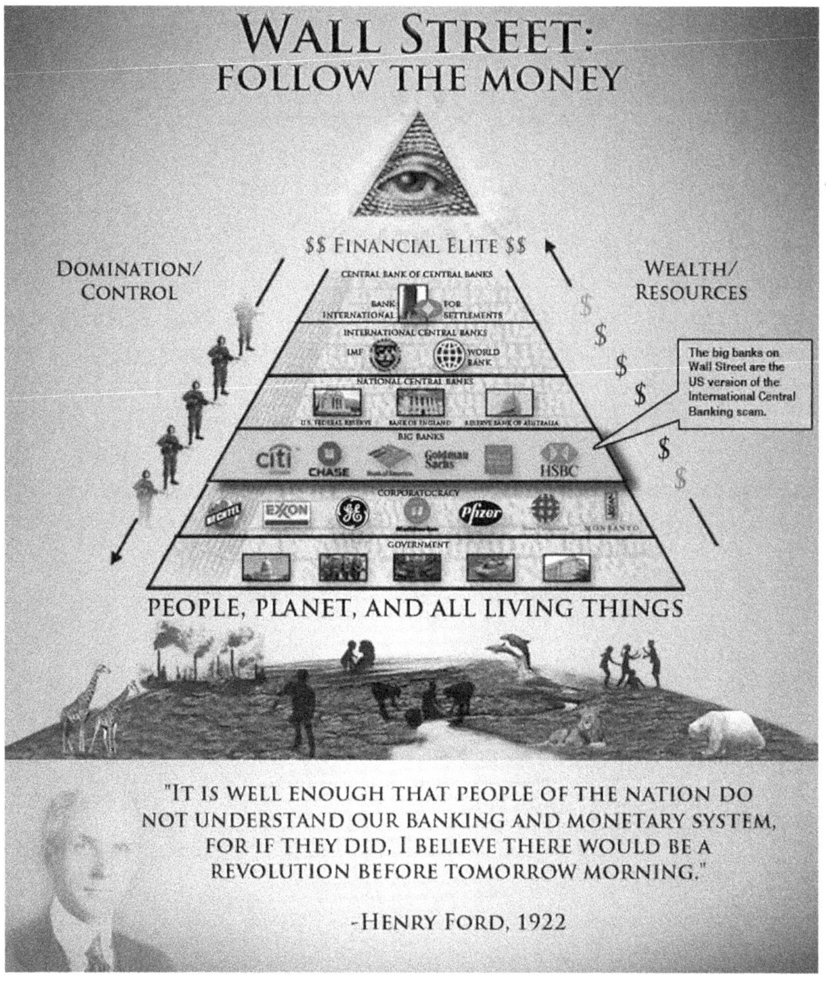

Follow the Money! [14] (https://www.thrivemovement.com/images/infographics/followthemoney.html)

It is the glory of God to conceal a matter;
to search out a matter is the glory of kings.
As the heavens are high and the earth is deep,
so the hearts of kings are unsearchable. (Proverbs 25:2)

All of this is not to be feared, but is to be exposed and brought down, as the kingdom of God is established. As we each press in, gates are secured, mountains are occupied and possessed. Through occupying positions in government to worshipping we will take the land. This will become the Church's finest hour. We decree and declare Isaiah 2:2 over these times.

In the last days
the mountain of the LORD's temple will be established
as the highest of the mountains;
it will be exalted above the hills,
and all nations will stream to it. (Isaiah 2:2)

Everyone can BE His expression of worship that shifts atmospheres, creating gateways for Revival. Dear friends of mine, Pastors Marcel and Ruth Langhorn created a portal of worship in the Bronx, NYC, not far from Yankee stadium, right in their backyard. As a private residence they didn't have to pull permits, pay exorbitant rental fees, etc. They had live, intensive, sustained worship and prayer. They literally opened the gates of their home. The sound of worship filled the night air in the Bronx. People came in from the street. His Presence was tangible; as a habitation for His Presence was established. You can make where you live His habitation. **Prepare the ground for Revival!**

and they will call him Immanuel" (which means "God with us")
(Matthew 1:23)

"and the government will be on his shoulders.
Of the greatness of his government and peace
there will be no end.
He will reign on David's throne
and over his kingdom,
establishing and upholding it
with justice and righteousness
from that time on and forever.
The zeal of the LORD Almighty
will accomplish this." (Isaiah 9:6-7)

CHAPTER 11

NOW – More Gates: Commerce, Arts & Entertainment, and Education

Taking Back the Gates

THE CHURCH IS AWAKENING SPIRITUALLY, with boldness. She's finding Her courage once again, to take back and secure our gates! For decades Christians were lax. We lost ground at key, invisible, access points. There has been profound moral decay in the fabric of our society.

Each one of us has a part! Focusing on the sphere God has placed us in, developing our gift/skill sets to bloom and be effective where He's placed us. We establish His authority over the environment around us, being engaged in the navigation of this nation.

The Business mountain controls the Media through those who fund it. Money, or mammon, is the element that makes the gate of Business/Marketplace such a powerful connecting gate with influence within many gates. All the other mountains have their inter-connectivity in how they relate to one another (Government, Education, etc.).

COMMERCE/Business
Gateway SHIFTS – Retail Buying and Social Media

> *A wise person should have money in their head, but not in their heart.* - Jonathan Swift

This is a season and era where Christians are called and given great favor to move into entrepreneurism. **God is pouring out a Joseph anointing on His Bride to prosper and steward prosperity.** Increase, insight, favor and blessing will be evident upon His people, they will rise to positions of prominence on the mountain of Business. Commensurate with Marketplace anointing (business, financial wealth) will be godly wisdom, as Joseph had. **God is giving us wisdom to not only gain wealth but for how to strategically store and disseminate it**. Believers will be in a place of leverage in future seasons of lack. The people of God (aka the Church) will not lack any good thing. Nations will come to them, as 'chief among the mountains'. (Isaiah 2:2)

We are called to take back the mountains of influence as the Reformation Army of the Lord. The Gate of Business holds the mammon. Mammon has the potential to buy power and influence – which likes to control. This Mountain of Marketplace controls the Mountain of Media. The Mountain of Media exerts influence on the other mountains. The Business mountain (or Marketplace) controls the Media through those who fund it. The mountains are all inter-connected. To know and understand what's really happening connect the dots and follow the money trail. They all need money for survival; even the mountains of Church and Family, although they're not as directly affected. The world of Finance/ Commerce has a direct tie-in and influence with all of the mountains.

A Gateway SHIFT toward E-Commerce

Skip over this section if you're not interested in money in e-commerce & trends. *Insight into leveraging current trends and tendencies gives entrepreneurs strategic advantage for success.*

Why talk about e-commerce in a book on securing our gates? Because God says, "My people perish for lack of knowledge." Not just any type of knowledge, revelation-knowledge. **We are to be the head and not the tail. A step ahead, not a step behind**. The USA and Europe have a wide-open, underdeveloped new frontier waiting to be harnessed in e-commerce. I believe savvy men and women of God will rise into prominence and wealth through e-commerce.

There is a shift already occurring in how Business is transacted. **The e-commerce market is a largely untapped market and is poised for growth**. There's gold in them thar hills!

To those who have been called to Marketplace ministry, do not miss the pivotal shift toward e-commerce! Do not suffer needlessly in this time of shifting and favor. In the current landscape, **an unwavering Christian perspective is more crucial than ever.**

Family Christian Stores (FCS), was the world's largest Christian bookstore and retailer of Christian-themed merchandise. They **closed ALL of their stores**

after 85 years, in 2017. "Publishing houses such as Tynedale's have said that the Christian publishing industry needs FCS. **Their closing is predominately a reflection of the shift in retail buying patterns.**[1]

I will miss them, I really liked the store. But let's learn from this and not allow there to be a void in the gates. Christians, we must MAKE THE SHIFT! In the marketplace and all mountains. See change coming from afar and strategically position yourself, with integrity, for the taking.

> "A prudent man foresees the difficulties ahead and prepares for them; the simpleton goes blindly on and suffers the consequences." (Proverbs 22:3, TLB)

The secret to success now is no longer to just 'get it out there and see how it performs'. The most successful retailers are strategic and targeted in their efforts, both offline and on. [2] **The power of the click is mighty**.

Effectively targeting a ready-to-buy audience, though, requires either tremendously solid data, statistics and analysis on your customers and/or a laser-like prophetic flow. **Research your market AND be prophetic!** For most small and mid-market ecommerce businesses, bandwidth is low and resources even sparser. Conducting high-level research to gain a full industry view of who buys what, where and why can be costly and time consuming.

Remember, the gateway portal and super highway for global communication is the Internet. As you must be aware most sites use cookies to track where you visit, what you purchase, what your interests are. There are literally corporations storing that data on you and millions of others to more effectively market themselves for your dollar. Analysts cull through it, analyzing trends to persuasively market you effectively. Public relations positions in Media are growing at a rate of 23% (vs. the growth rate of news correspondents, who research and report truth, is languishing at -8%. [23]

There is money to be had in analyzing PR trends, *as well as mindsets to influence.* <u>If you're interested in PR this is a time to market yourself and break into what has vast potential, particularly in the gates and mountains of Media, Marketplace, and Government</u>. God wants to use YOU as His 'secret agent' to BE part of His Reformation Army. Infiltrating business and media with salt and light and the fragrant aroma of Jesus Christ.

We need Christian and men and women of integrity to ready themselves to enter the PR arena. We MUST take back the mountain of Media and Commerce; **making our way to the top of PR will not only be very profitable, it will open pathways of great influence**. The danger, Christian be-ware, **don't get**

entangled in a corrupt system. Rather be the game-changer, cycle breaker. Don't compromise. Go in like a Ninja, covertly. Esther, occupied the position of Queen, but she didn't reveal her true identity as a Jew until *after* she had won the *heart* of the king. (Esther 2:10; 4:13-14)

For those in business general information on trends (job trends, e-commerce and more) is available to you, online, for free.

1. Do a google search,
2. Put in, e-commerce trends, as the search parameter for starters.
3. Read from a variety of sources. Be sure to check the dates of the reports. Get the most current data and information. Analyze it.
4. Prayerfully ask God for insight and revelation regarding it.

It won't be the same as having cookie trackers and your own company PR analyst(s). But you'll find ecommerce trends, data and statistics reporting on exactly how Americans shop online, why customers convert, why they don't and who your business should be targeting on the various online channels to optimize for a return on investment (ROI). You can then tap into the results of sophisticated software tracks the data on buying trends on millions of online shoppers, Internet browsers, etc. PR analysts study the data for resale/ retail purposes. This data gives a window into what consumers look for in an online shopping experience, showcasing the potential to adapt your ecommerce business to fit the modern shopper. These findings can percolate through every aspect of your business: product pages, emails, content marketing and much more.

In the world it's all connected to money. Money is power. **The one who takes the mountain of Business has great influence and sway in all of the mountains.** Secure the gates and get in on it! Gates and doors are opening!

Asia–Pacific is expected to lead in e-commerce. China is already #1 and all eyes are on Malaysia as the next e-commerce boomers. The United States and the United Kingdom pale in comparison.[3]

There are huge amounts of untapped growth potential in e-commerce. Surprisingly, Ecommerce sales account for just 8% of total retail sales in the US, and just 14% of retail sales in the UK.[4] If your business isn't online in some fashion you're losing untapped potential. (Seriously, if you own a small business, get it online. You don't need a web-developer. You can do it yourself. Most hosting sites offer templates to work with.)

Ecommerce tips: American consumers, although on their smartphones voraciously, **still prefer to make online purchases via a PC than a mobile device**, and they don't like paying shipping and handling. My recommendation is to pre-work that into the overall price rather than tack on another fee at the end. Or do as Amazon Prime has done, have an annual membership fee with the promise of free shipping & handling. Prediction – using mobile devices for e-commerce will increase radically over the next few years.

Now knowing this, how do you plan to take advantage of it this year? KNOW your target audience and follow their buying trends, likes, dislikes, etc. Ask God to give you revelation about your target audience. Those that do well in e-commerce are adept in marketing, branding, packaging, and selling to their target population.

Also, be sure to research the best options for payment gateways, such as: Authorize, PayPal, SecurePay, First Data, BluePay, etc. Choose the one that will fit your needs for your business.

A word of caution, knowing that cookies are tracking your every click, protect your privacy. Wall Street analyst, author, and pastor Silas Titus says, "The more access to information also means that it unfolded the accessibility of the commercial world into more privacy of users and their increased involvement in online activities. The rules of the game are changing as the internet services are now able to collect information of individuals like never before. Past dictators and distasteful regimes dreamed of having access to such information to enable their clandestine operations. The power of information, media, and economic reforms today has a profound influence on masses that makes the religious and imperial dictators of old look stupid. The blessing of information abundance also comes with the curse of information invasion."[5] Protect what you reveal of yourself and your assets.

Arts & Entertainment (A&E)

The various mountains of influence are inter-connected. Commerce, the world of Finance, is particularly entrenched in the affairs of government and the Arts. Wealthy advertising sponsors have vast influence, because of money, in A&E. There is a left-wing view prevalent in A&E.

America, sadly, is far removed from her roots and foundations. A nation established in honoring God, has become known for ungodliness. The Church was once THE mountain that shaped culture, government, legislation, family, et al. Even in the world of Finance, God was pre-imminent; with "In God We Trust" is on our currency. But, reality is that the love of money, seeking mammon, has replaced the love of God for many. A&E are now THE influence of pop-culture. A&E have taken on significant spiritual influence in our society. Stirring deep emotions, eliciting a sense of purpose, fueling passion and motivating the masses.

Artists of A&E often have strong ties with political figures and media. **The influence of A&E shapes our pop-culture.**

> *The plans of the righteous are just,*
> *but the advice of the wicked is deceitful.*
> *(Proverbs 12:5)*

Arts & Entertainment have taken on significant spiritual influence in our society. Stirring deep emotions, eliciting, provoking a sense of purpose, fueling passion and motivating the masses.

Dr. Ruth Westheimer is one of the world's most recognized authorities on sex. She has delivered her advice on TV, radio and the web for decades and has written numerous books. A sex therapist who became an icon in the '80's in syndicated programs such as; *Sexually Speaking, Good Sex With Dr. Ruth Westheimer*. The message that most identify her with is, "Always remember and never forget: *Anything two consenting adults do* in the privacy of their bedroom, living-room or kitchen counter is GOOD SEX!" That message took root in America as if it were a gospel verse from the Bible. That verse just isn't in the Bible. People used that as a license to rationalize all kinds of sexual behavior; 'swingers' groups emerged (where husbands and wives consent to swapping partners for a fling), same sex partners, infidelity, and more. Keep within God's best, His design for marriage is covenant. (Read Leviticus 18; 1 Corinthians 7:1-5 for God's basics.) Don't pollute your marriage bed. (Hebrews 13:4)

Be careful who and what you're listening to. Surround yourself with men and women of character, who won't compromise or rationalize away sound, godly, biblical principles. "The plans of the righteous are just, but the advice of the wicked is deceitful." (Proverbs 12:5)

Another message that left a negative, imprint on a generation was from the 90's, MTV's Beevis and Butthead, a cartoon series, that made its way into pop-culture. It was about two heavy-metal music fans who often did idiotic things because they were bored, and they sat around laughing all day. Their humor wasn't funny it was alarming. They put themselves in front of cars, to be injured, laughed at injured animals, laughed if an animal were going to die. It was sick, twisted humor.

The youth of America drank in their humor. Beevis and Butthead, heavy-metal music, mosh pits, became part of the youth culture, deriving gratification from harm to others and harm to themselves, including cutting. Psychology refers to that as sado-masochistic. The mindset is detrimental and anti-Christ.

Interestingly, bullying soon after became so prevalent that anti-bullying laws needed to be established in our schools.

Dr. Ruth, Beevis & Butthead, and others shaped recent generations. We, **the Church had left a void, BUT we are starting to fill it**!

I distinctly remember during the 90's fervently praying in corporate intercession that Christians would take back the Arts. Our God the Creator of all has made His people in His image – that means we're creative. We should be the leaders and influencers in the gates. I remember in 2000 being in the K-Mart and hearing a contemporary Christian song filled the air waves of the store. Then more songs continue to be played on secular radio as well as Christian channels. Veggie-Tales became cartoons that were embraced by secular society. Christian movies have gained in terms of quality, relevancy, and popularity. Most notably, Alex and Stephen Kendrick's with Provident Films: War Room, Courageous, FireProof and more. They've all been secular box-office hits.

Go through the gates and rise. Be relevant where you are, in your sphere of influence. You don't have to be a rock star or an actress. Shine where you are. For instance, where I get my hair done, the receptionist is born-again. One of her responsibilities is to put the music on. She plays a mix of contemporary Christian music with positive secular music. People, that otherwise would have no exposure, are hearing and being touched with the song of the Lord. His sound fills the atmosphere.

Other friends of mine own a secular ice cream store. She and her husband have contemporary Christian artists play live sets. After hours they open their doors for prayer. It's a hangout spot for teens in town. They have married the gates of A&E with Commerce. The Church is rising with relevant kingdom reformers, shining in the streets, not hiding behind religious brick walls.

> *"He who is faithful in a very little thing is faithful also in much;"*
> (Luke 16:10)

Often sports stars, actors and actresses become idolatrous icons and are given media time. Hats off to the ones that exalt Christ, and principles of the kingdom, such as Kirk Cameron, Tim Tebow, and so many more. **The views and character of A&E cultural heroes effect many for better or worse**.

- Kathy Griffin drew much attention as she held a bloodied, decapitated head of Donald Trump. It was reported that when Baron Trump, only 11 years old at the time, was upset as he saw the image of his father's head being held by the hair on tv. It looked very life-like. He feared for his father's life.

- Robert DeNiro interviewed said of Trump, "I want to smash his face." Why are violent comments like this being given air-time?
- Madonna – said she wanted to blow up the White House.
- *Julius Ceasar* (a Shakespeare in the Park play, funded by major corporations, including the New York Times, as well as the Bank of America) dramatizes the assassination of Trump and gets a standing ovation.
- Mel B., a judge on "America's Got Talent", as a contestant was about to present an impersonation of Trump, before he even opened his mouth she buzzed him. With hands raised in objection she vehemently exclaimed, "Stop! Are you kidding me?! Not him! No way! I can't believe you! I won't listen to this!" Shouting down the contestant before he had begun. (As it turned out he did a parody of President Trump, that shared her sentiments.)

The point is no matter which side of the coin we are on, promoting murderous imagery or shutting people down before they've even opened their mouth is wrong – on all sides! "**Love does no wrong to a neighbor. Therefore, love is the fulfillment of the law**." (Romans 10:13)

Day after day negative rhetoric and vivid imagery floods the air waves fueling dissension and discontent, or enamoring and alluring multitudes through the media. There are many people 'out there' who are not well balanced, and don't know how to process the onslaught of this type of profane Media coverage. **Whenever you see something that is driven by, or bearing fruit of hatred, anger, discord, bitterness, violence, etc. that is the litmus test to easily discern what spirit is in operation.**

> "Have nothing to do with the fruitless deeds of darkness, but rather expose them." (Galatians 5:11)
>
> The acts of the flesh are obvious: sexual immorality, impurity, and debauchery; idolatry and witchcraft; hatred, discord, jealousy, fits of rage, selfish ambition, dissensions, factions and envy; drunkenness, orgies, and the like. I warn you, as I did before, that those who live like this will not inherit the kingdom of God.
>
> But the fruit of the Spirit is love, joy, peace, forbearance, kindness, goodness, faithfulness, gentleness, and self-control. Against such things there is no law. Those who belong to Christ Jesus have crucified the flesh with its passions and desires. Since we live by the Spirit, let us keep in step with the Spirit. Let

> us not become conceited, provoking and envying each other. (Galatians 5:19-26)

The media bombardment has stirred the pot that has led to the culmination of heinous hate crimes. An inundation of hate-speech can have adverse effects on people. The violence and hatred in the atmosphere, fanned by the media and celebrity activists has incited anarchy and a murderous spirit, such as at the Democrat – Republican ball game where Republicans were used as target practice, riots in our cities, shootings of police officers, and more. Tragedy, like shock therapy, can jar us toward healing. As NY democratic representative Jeffries said, "I think we can all disagree without being disagreeable."

God is about to raise His people, even some who are reading this, to stardom. As celebrities you will have the opportunity to be His voice - emerging icons, that entertain, shape passions, emotions, with a sound and a message that influences culture for the kingdom of God in Jesus name. **We get to be part of the shifting of kingdoms!**

> "For the kingdoms of this world have become the kingdoms of our Lord and Savior." (Revelation 11:15)

EDUCATION – And the battle for a *mindset*!

Critical thinking is a learned skill. I've been an educator for over 40 years; teaching children, training, observing, evaluating staff, etc. Children must be taught to think. Questioning skills, such as Blooms taxonomy, Socratic reasoning, inductive vs. deductive reasoning, how to research, etc. and differing points of view, how to debate, must also be valued, taught and respected. Emotional intolerance is robbing us of these skills.

At Rutgers University many faculty and students decided that conservative values have no place in their vision of higher institutions of learning. Therefore, they've rejected many stellar public figures as their keynote speaker at their 2014 commencement; knowns such as; Condoleeza Rice, Erik Holder, and others. President Obama chided Rutgers students for their behavior. When such protests drive out potential speakers, they jeopardize free speech and diversity of opinions. Iron sharpens iron. (Proverbs 27:17)

Hence, the phrase 'the intolerant left' has become a term that will probably make its way into dictionaries, if not history books. Jokes already abound on it:

- Someecards has a cartoon card: You say you want tolerance and despise hate, but if I don't agree with everything you say, you call it intolerance and hate. Explain to me again how that works.

- One has a picture of Willy Wonka grinning. The caption reads, "And you won't eat there because the founder is a Christian? ... Tell me more about your tolerance and their bigotry."

Without realizing it our perspective, point of view and mindset are subtly being influenced toward a one-world view. It is very dangerous. It's a little like damming up tributaries in a river, in order for all of the water to flow in one stream and one direction. The whole ecosystem will suffer. The areas that the tributaries used to bring water to will dry up. If group-think and an 'all is one and one is all' mindset prevails then intolerance to differing or opposing views becomes the accepted norm, creativity is stifled; truth with 'iron sharpening iron' falters and fades.

NEA (National Education Association) vice-president Betsy Pringle urged students and teachers to skip school to protest President-elect Donald Trump's inauguration.[6] How can educators promote absenteeism from school?!

NEA president Lily Eskelsen refuses to sit down together at a discussion table with US Secretary of Education Betsy DeVos. [7] I'm not a big fan of DeVos' as there was much cause for concern in DeVos' lack of knowledge on issues, particularly on special education, BUT to refuse to talk with the US Secretary of Education? A person who win, lose or draw is sitting in a powerful position on behalf of education, is short-sighted. No one ever won a war by abdicating.

People of God seize the day! **Don't be emotional, be intentional. Go through the gates and ascend!** David ran to where Goliath was. This is a time to be heard in the mountain of education. If those in position of power have abdicated and won't meet or talk with the US Sec. of Education, then someone **step up and step in, fill the void with revelation and wisdom from God!**

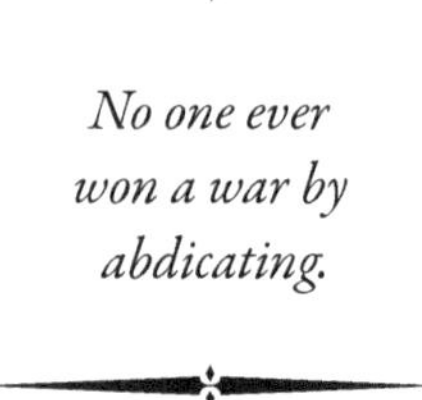

What's in your hand? The gates are your points of access. We can't all be the US Secretary of Education, but we can establish a proactive, godly influence where we are.

What a privilege, blessing, and honor it was for me to teach high school classes in US Government and World Geography in a Christian school! I was very careful to anchor them in the Word, not bias them with my viewpoints and opinions, but challenge them to research issues in light of His Word. Our classes were filled with life: debates on border issues, wars, the European Union, immigration, speeches, presentations, becoming registered voters, writing letters to Congressmen, and more. Wow! Such awesome students! Sitting before me were future lawyers, immigration specialists, technology network gatekeepers, politicians, educators and more. Young men and women grounded in His Word, prayer, with a spirit of courage and integrity! Equipped to shape the landscape of tomorrow and secure the gates!

Raise up through education youth that are trained, equipped and empowered to, securing our gates, scale the mountains, rule and reign here on earth as in heaven. Training camps and conferences, such as Lance Wallnau's "7m Gen" a camp for young adults, ages 14-24, the 'visionaries of today to become the leaders of tomorrow'. He's referred to it as training young adults how to 'raid Babylon'.[8]

And you thought I was going to focus on returning prayer to public schools! **The jury is out on whether we want to reinstate prayer in public schools or not. We are no longer a Judeo-Christian society.** Prayer in public schools will never again be what it was in the 50's. (Prayer was removed from public schools in 1962.) Until 1962 public school prayer usually was The Lord's Prayer and a reading of Psalm 23. **If prayer is reinstated in public education, prayers of *all* religions, and readings from a variety of sacred texts will be honored**. That includes eastern religions, Islam, and yes, even Satanism. Our students will be exposed to many belief systems, only one of which will be Judeo-Christian. Until we experience broad-sweeping reform, revival and legislative change, we do not want to see prayer reinstated in public schools.

The best way to secure our gates in education is to invest in our youth, at home and in the Church, and be prayerful, proactive watchdogs in guiding the curriculum and instructional content. There are many influences vying for our children's minds. It is our job to be in the know and not sleeping.

Meaningful and practical ways we can make a difference and shine where we are:

1. Be involved: in PTA's and PTO's,
2. attend board of education (BOE) meetings in your district,
3. serve on textbook selection committees,
4. look at your children's assignments, speak up if you see things that conflict with your value system (voice concerns at BOE meetings),
5. be your child's advocate and voice
6. serve as a BOE trustee,
7. PRAY for our children, teachers, schools and education.

Train and raise up our youth to be transformational leaders. The law DOES allow for student initiated and led Christian groups and prayer. Students may initiate 'clubs' that are youth fellowships and prayer meetings. A teacher can support them as an advisor, but it must be student led and initiated. Teachers are NOT allowed to initiate it. **In church and youth groups are we raising our youth *<u>to initiate and lead</u>* a Christian group in their school, with the assistance of an advisor?** One group I know of in a public high school calls themselves 'Refresh'.

In addition to times of prayer, Bible study and fellowship they are involved in projects that benefit the community. They are overtly Christian and are making a difference. And they are student led!

> Fighting flesh with flesh, or wickedness with wickedness is futile. **"The weapons we fight with are not the weapons of the world. On the contrary, they have divine power to demolish strongholds."** (2 Corinthians 10:4)

As we resist the devil (our flesh & worldly ways) and press into the Lord He will give us revelation, keys, wisdom and favor. "*The weapons we fight with are not the weapons of the world. They are contrary and contain divine favor and power to demolish strongholds. We demolish arguments and every pretension that sets itself up against the knowledge of God, and we take captive every thought to make it obedient to Christ.*" (2 Corinthians 10:4-5)

> *Pass through, pass through the gates!*
> *Prepare the way for the people.*
> *Build up, build up the highway!*
> *Remove the stones.*
> *Raise a banner for the nations. (Isaiah 62:10)*

Let's be all-in, like Patrick Henry, as he cried out, "Give me liberty or give me death!" and Dr. Martin Luther King who walked the talk, "If a man hasn't found something to die for, he isn't fit to live."

The Remnant is arising and coming forth, continually growing in wisdom. Good decisions come from experience and experience comes from both our good and bad decisions. We're moving forward, growing wiser with each new step.

Lanny Swaim declared prophetically, "While God's people have been busy with well-doing, they have been in a season of preparation, as the Lord has been maturing (growing within them the character of God/the fullness of Christ) and positioning them for that which lies just ahead. The Lord is now saying that a new season is upon us, when that which we have decreed, declared, prophesied and prayed for is about to burst forth in our lives and ministries and onto the world stage." [9]

Christians get organized. Business and the Marketplace control the Media through those the moguls who fund it. They are working their influence in A&E, and even Education into controlling government – working towards a one-world government control. Which will affect the Family and the Church. **Establish authority in the environment around you!**

The time for our silence is past. Bold, effectual, kingdom reformers move forward in every gate. Make your way to the top of each mountain of influence; as we continually secure, restore, occupy and possess!

Whatever we do, let all be done in love. These are tense and contentious times, rife with emotionalism. The pressure is on, God is positioning an army of reformers. Guard against group-think and over-zealous advocacy. We each must guard our heart, not just our mind. The scripture is clear,

> Where lawlessness increases, most people's love will grow cold. (Matthew 24:12, NASB)
>
> Above all else, guard your heart, for everything you do flows from it. (Proverbs 4:23)
>
> Beyond these things put on love, which is the perfect bond of unity. (Colossians 3:14, NASB)

Reform without love, misses the mark, it misses the heart of the Father. As we repair, rebuild, restore and secure our gates let us do so in love, or everything we do will be off-center. **Love should be the framework that each gate is set in.** Only love can heal to the depths that are needed in our gates.

> "Come, let us return to the LORD.
> For He has torn *us*, but He will heal us;
> He has wounded *us*, but He will bandage us.
> "He will revive us after two days;
> He will raise us up on the third day,
> That we may live before Him.
> "So let us know, let us press on to know the LORD.
> His going forth is as certain as the dawn;
> And He will come to us like the rain,
> (Hosea 6:1-3)

Arise, shine, for your light has come,
and the glory of the LORD rises upon you.
See, darkness covers the earth
and thick darkness is over the peoples,
but the LORD rises upon you
and his glory appears over you.
Nations will come to your light,
and kings to the brightness of your dawn.
(Isaiah 60:1-3, 11)

CHAPTER 12

MILITARY STRATEGIES

The LORD is a warrior;
the LORD is his name. (Exodus 15:3)

FIRST, I WANT TO TAKE a moment to thank those who have served, we salute you and thank you for your service. Our immediate family members have been active in 4 wars over 3 generations spanning almost 80 years: World War II, Vietnam, Iraq War, and Enduring Freedom – the war in Afghanistan. We have a great regard and appreciation for those who wear the uniform and serve our country.

Spiritual warfare is real and it's no joke! **The enemy is always contending at the gates.** We can learn from and apply military principles to our spiritual lives strengthening ourselves.

The military doesn't wonder if an enemy might attack one day – they presume there will be attacks and counter attacks from hostile forces, it is their reason for being. Armed forces anticipate, strategize, drill and prepare against possible attack(s) by enemy forces. We are engaged in spiritual warfare daily.

I personally have not served in our nation's armed forces, but I serve daily, at the pleasure of the King of Kings and Lord of Lords, Jesus Christ.

Once you are alive in Christ, you are in His Army! Whether you want to be, or not! We have a hostile enemy that's always on the prowl. (1 Peter 5:8) The warfare and the struggle is real!

Guerilla warfare, information warfare, cyber terrorism, troops, special ops, spies and espionage – it all goes on in spiritual warfare.

Stand, fight, secure the gates, 'hold the fort', advance & secure.

Protocols at the Gates

> *He also stationed gatekeepers at the gates of the LORD's temple so that no one who was in any way unclean might enter. (2 Chronicles 23:19)*

Since the Middle Ages "hold" in a military context has meant, *"to keep forcibly against an adversary; defend; occupy"*. If the commander of a fort decided to take some of his forces to make a foray against the enemy, he would always leave some of his men in the charge of a reliable officer, to hold the fort against any possible attack while they were away. [1] There are some basics to 'holding the fort' in daily practice by every branch; protocols at the gates is one.

The military has clear procedures for guarding our borders and their gates. Visiting a military base clearly reveals this before you even enter the base. Whether you are a civilian or military personnel, all will receive the same treatment at the gates. The gates are armed and protected; protocols are in place that apply to everyone. Everyone is checked and vetted.

<u>Guards</u>: Guards are posted at the gates 24/7, daily. Whenever we visited our sons on base we didn't drive through the gates on base casually. We stopped and presented our ID to armed guards for proper vetting. The ID is checked and run through data bases. Once vetted, we received a standard visitor's pass for, 24 hours.

If one tried to drive through the gates ignoring these procedures you would probably be shot at. If your ID is flagged, has an outstanding felony, or affiliations with gang or terrorist organizations you will not be visiting on base. However, one may be given a set of silver bracelets and detained until local civilian authorities pick you up.

This is an experience I had on the guarded border gate between the USA and Mexico:

I was part of a short-term mission team returning to the USA from Mexico. It was 118 degrees, we were in a van and the heat was making me ill. At the guarded checkpoint before entering the USA we were not allowed to exit the vehicle while guards were vetting us and checking the vehicle. I told our driver that I had to get out, I was about to be sick. He told me I could not. However, I was about to get violently ill, which would probably make the other 15 in our group ill. Finally, I couldn't hold back any longer. I burst out of the van, tried to get a couple of feet away, before throwing up. Little did I realize the guards had already drawn their guns, pointed in my direction. I think if I had tried to go any further they would have fired.

Food for thought:

How do you protect your personal gates, your heart? Who has access to you? Do you guard yourself? Check the character of others before allowing them into your home and your heart? Do you have healthy boundaries and limitations for 'visitors'?

Saluting: Each branch of the military has an established tradition of respect for country, flag and officers. This respect is shown through saluting. These customs aren't just basic politeness, but are important parts of morale-building and discipline. Military customs and courtesies are designed to ensure respect for the chain of command. If one is a civilian the protocol of saluting is not expected in return. When we worship we stand to honor the King of Kings. We don't have the same expectations of non-believers.

Bootcamp

He trains my hands for battle;
my arms can bend a bow of bronze.
You make your saving help my shield,
and your right hand sustains me;
your help has made me great. (2 Samuel 22:35; Psalm 18:34)

Basic training, or bootcamp prepares recruits for all elements of service: physical, mental and emotional. This training develops self-control, character, and a proper submission to authority.

Service members receive the basic tools necessary to perform the roles that will be asked of them for the duration of their time in the service. The objective of boot camp, is not to break recruits, but to make them strong and capable, to prepare young people to become warriors. By the end of bootcamp young soldiers have the tools to perform given tasks with the efficiency, courage and confidence to succeed in the face of adversity.

Basic training is also designed to teach the mentality of being part of a team. As the saying goes, there's no "I" in TEAM. If you fail, you fail as a team, and all share in the consequences. When you succeed, you succeed as a team.

Bootcamp tends to accelerate maturity, personal growth, and self-discipline. One of our children was called into a meeting with their Drill Instructor (DI). They had gone over their finances and noted an outstanding debt. The DI asked, "So what do you plan to do about it?" The recruit replied, "Well, my Dad usually takes care of that." The DI replied, "Daddy isn't here now. What do YOU plan to do about it?" They developed a payback plan, paid down their debt, and told us father about it *after* it was paid in full. They assumed full responsibility. Now *that* is growing in maturity!

> *Consider it pure joy, my brothers and sisters, whenever you face trials of many kinds, because you know that the testing of your faith produces perseverance.* ***Let perseverance finish its work so that you may be mature and complete, not lacking anything.*** *James 1:2-4)*

Bootcamp instills a high level of self-discipline. The following is an excerpt from an essay on military discipline:

"Discipline is a state of order that involves the ready subordination of the will of the individual for the good of the group. discipline demands habitual but reasoned obedience that preserves initiative and functions unfalteringly even in the absence of the commander. ... Discipline is created within a command by instilling a sense of confidence and responsibility in each individual. Discipline demands correct performance of duty. Self-discipline doesn't mean that you never get tired or discouraged after all, you're only human. It does mean that you do what needs to be done regardless of your feelings. ... Units that have solid discipline can take tremendous stress and friction yet persevere, fight through, and win." [1]

Military.com offers these tips for Bootcamp 'survival'. (I've included correlating biblical points in italicized print.):

- Boot camp is mostly a mind game. It's designed to take the civilian out of you and replace it with a top-notch military servicemember (Soldier, Sailor, Marine, or Airman). Thousands of young men and women have survived basic before you – just roll with it.
  When my husband arrived at Paris Island, for Marine bootcamp the bus driver remarked, "Welcome to Paris Island boys. I want to introduce you to your Momma, your Father and everything in between for the next several weeks." Then the DI began screaming non-stop in their face.
- Keep a good attitude. Remember, EVERYONE gets chewed out in boot camp, even when they have done well. It won't be this way after you graduate Basic.
  For everything that was written in the past was written to teach us, so that through the endurance taught in the Scriptures and the encouragement they provide we might have hope.
  May the God who gives endurance and encouragement give you the same attitude of mind toward each other that Christ Jesus had, so that with one

mind and one voice you may glorify the God and Father of our Lord Jesus Christ. (Romans 5:4-6)

- Never, ever, make excuses. Unless you are asked to explain yourself, explanations are seen as excuses, so just say "Yes, sir" and take the chewing out. *You were taught, with regard to your former way of life, to put off your old self, which is being corrupted by its deceitful desires; to* ***be made new in the attitude of your minds;*** *and to put on the new self, created to be like God in true righteousness and holiness." (Ephesians 4:22-24)*
- Do exactly what you're told to do, when you're told to do it, and how you're told to do it. Don't be inventive.
  To obey is better than sacrifice." (1 Samuel 15:22); "*You are my friends if you do what I command you."* (John 15:14)
- If you're "on time," then you're late. Always be where you're supposed to be five minutes early. *"Teach us to number our days that we may gain a heart of wisdom." (Psalm 90:12)*

It is important for Christians to have a foundation of 'basic training' in the faith. These foundations include: The Word, the blood of Christ, Name of Christ, baptism of the Holy Spirit, submission to authority, stewardship and giving, etc. Everyone wants 'deeper truth'. It doesn't get any deeper than the blood of Christ shed for us. Once we truly get a hold of our identity in Christ we are transformed. A knowledge that is made real, then we can 'run through a troop and leap over a wall' (2 Samuel 22:30; Psalm 18:29) and do all things through Christ who strengthens us (Philippians 4:13). **Our identity in Him is the key empowering us into who we are, how we function, and carry ourselves.** We were created to do great exploits in Him; **we are naturally supernatural because He is. Introductory basic training in Christ should anchor and transform us for a lifetime.**

In the schools where I worked I was part of the crisis management & preparedness team. Schools have become targets for attacks; we trained our staff and students in the event of possible crisis (active shooter, bomb threat, concealed weapon, etc.). One of the police officers on our team stated, "When the pressure is on in a crisis you always fall back on your training." That's why we have drills, and plans of action. We drill, visualize, de-brief, evaluate and continually improve upon our preparedness. You can't fall back on your training if you didn't have any!

MILITARY STRATEGIES of DEFENSE
Perimeter Security & In-Depth Security

> *You will say, "I will invade a land of unwalled villages; I will attack a peaceful and unsuspecting people—all of them living without walls and without gates and bars. (Ezekiel 38:11)*

Imagine this. You're now the commander of a special military base and it's your responsibility to protect it. What's your defense strategy? Do you put all your resources into building a massive barricade around the entire base? Or do you split your resources and invest in a variety of defensive options? It all depends on your objectives. Since in God we have unlimited resources, I'd opt for investing in both methods.

Perimeter security, refers to building one solid line of defense, such as a wall. *Depth security* refers to the practice of layering different types of defenses, one on top of the other.

Spiritually speaking perimeter security is analogous to united, 24/7 prayer networks across the nation (and ultimately the world) in key cities that geographically span territories and regions. In-depth are various other houses of prayer & strategies. A wall, and/or a firewall (front end and back end protection) involve the guards/ Watchmen on the Wall.

Walls are still one of the best methods of keeping the enemy out. Nehemiah knew what he was doing investing significant resources, of people, time, materials and the favor of the king in re-building the wall around Jerusalem. What does the Great Wall of China, the Berlin Wall, 13th century castle walls and other heavy barriers have in common? They're all walls, built at great cost monetarily and with back-breaking labor. **Walls are still the most difficult obstacles to penetrate or breach by humans without heavy destructive equipment, *but they also are the most expensive to build.***

In-Depth security assumes that a determined attacker will always be able to breach the perimeter. The devil is relentless. After tempting Jesus in the wilderness, the Scripture says, "When the devil had finished all this tempting, he left him *until an opportune time*." (Luke 4:13) We all have times when we are spiritually strong, as well as weak. The enemy smells weakness afar off and tries to exploit it. Military in-depth defense doesn't seek to prevent the advance of an adversary but, rather, seeks to delay their advance.

It is akin to the five-fold ministry each operating effectively in their assigned spheres; in respective areas of skill, giftedness AND territory.

Shared Intelligence, an understanding of the enemy's capability, strategy, *or afraid; do not panic or be terrified by them. For the Lord your God is the one who goes with you to fight for you against your enemies to give you victory." (Dt. 20:2-4)* **more the Church is united, acting as one, the greater the 'intel' of spiritual wisdom and insight and the more effective and strategic the defense stratagems.**

Take careful stock of your security's weak points and your own personal weak points – double your efforts there.

Call for help/ reinforcements as needed. *Great leaders know when to call for help and rely on allies.*

Defensive AND Offensive

The best defense is a good offense, an old adage, also known as *the strategic offensive principle of war*. The idea is that proactivity (a strong offensive action) instead of a passive attitude will preoccupy the opposition and ultimately hinder its ability to mount an opposing counterattack, leading to a strategic advantage. Greats such as Mao Zedong were of the opinion that «the only real defense is active defense», meaning defense for the purpose of counter-attacking and taking the offensive. **Often success rests on destroying the enemy's ability to attack.** Some martial arts, such as Kung-Fu emphasize attack over defense. One of their motto's is, "The hand which strikes also blocks." George Washington wrote in a letter dated 1799, "It is unfortunate when men cannot, or will not, see danger at a distance; or seeing it, are restrained in the means which are necessary to avert, or keep it afar off. ... **offensive operations, often times, is the surest, if not the only (in some cases) means of defence.**" [2] Securing the gates isn't just about defense, there must be an offensive plan and action as well. President George W. Bush said, "I think it's very hard to fight the war on terrorism if we're in retreat. I think we learned that lesson that if the United States decides to pull out before a free society emerges, it's going to be hard to defeat them. ... The enemy is very good at exploiting weakness. If we are serious about defeating ISIS we must project strength." [3] If we're serious about defeating Satan then we must be both offensive and defensive. *Invincibility lies in the defence; the possibility of victory in the attack. (Sun Tzu)*

If we're serious about defeating Satan then we must be both offensive and defensive.

SPECIAL FORCES

Elite special forces are formidable units of the best-trained men and women in the military. They go where other troops fear to tread, scoping out potential threats, taking out strategic targets, and conducting daring rescue missions. These are the best of the best. They've been through rigorous training that is geared to weed out only those who can attain to a high and exacting standard.

The sheer size of a country's military is not the only predictor of the outcome. These micro-groups of our elite forces, such as Navy Seals, Green Berets, Delta

Force, Night Stalkers, 75th Ranger Regiment, and several others make a huge difference. They are trained in larger numbers, but carry out and accomplish their missions in small units of 7-12 men and women These small units of elite, highly trained and disciplined forces are often the ones that 'get the job done'.

Micro groups of intercessors and worshippers are like teams of special forces. You and God are a majority! "The Lord their God is with them; the shout of the King is among them!" (Numbers 23:21)

3 Types of Modern Warfare – the Trilogy

Traditional, boots on the ground warfare is obviously alive and well all over the world. However, a trilogy of modern warfare has emerged. Modern warfare has changed and transitioned throughout the years. Like the contrast of Old Testament gates with 21st century gates, 'new' warfare methods are increasingly non-linear and non-lethal. However, they can cripple and bring down nations, without a shot fired.

Media is often used as a part of modern warfare. It feeds into a 'trilogy' of 3 types of warfare. Used together they can create strong influence and shifts in global society. Usually without realizing it our mind and emotions can be hi-jacked and manipulated when this 'trilogy' in action. This is the trilogy of modern warfare:

1. **Information Warfare**
2. **Psychological Warfare**
3. **Cyber Attack**

Information Warfare (IW) – Information warfare is a concept of information society conflicts and threats. Information warfare means the use of information, misinformation, or information technology during a time of crisis or conflict to achieve or promote specific objectives over a specific adversary or adversaries. IW is not in itself the technique but rather there are 5 forms of IW. They are: Command and Control Warfare, Intelligence-Based Warfare, Electronic Warfare, Hacker Warfare, Economic Information Warfare. Each form requires its own rules of engagement, own methods, objectives, and technologies.

> Ukraine's President Petro Poroshenko said, "Political pressure, blatant propaganda, interference with the electoral process, economic coercion, secret subversive and military operations, cyberattacks, misuse of diplomatic measures, these are modern and congenial methods of the undeclared war. ... The West must step up its efforts to combat and counter the information

> war being waged by its opponents. Countries like Russia are exploiting the freedom of the press in Western media to spread disinformation. They understand the weaknesses of our media in the post-Cold War environment: that we prioritize fairness over truth." ... the West must learn how to fight back." [4]

Psychological Warfare – the use of propaganda, threats, and other psychological techniques; arising from the mind or the emotions, to mislead, intimidate, demoralize, or otherwise influence the thinking or behavior of an opponent.

God used both Information Warfare and Psychological Warfare more than once when he brought the Israelites into victory. (More on that in a moment, when we examine Joshua and the Battle of Jericho.)

Cyber Warfare – Cyberwarfare is an assault on electronic communication networks. *Cyberwarfare* is Internet-based conflict involving politically motivated attacks on information and information systems. *Cyberwarfare* attacks can disable official websites and networks, disrupt or disable essential services, steal or alter classified data, and cripple financial systems — among many other possibilities.

Obviously, this wasn't something that Jesus had to worry about since He didn't have computers, but we DO today! To defend information systems today, it is crucial to assume that the network perimeter will be breached and **spend time planning for what happens after *and how to stay in control.*** We've got to be practical as well as spiritual.

> Literally in the midst of writing about cyber attack the United Kingdom (UK) was hit with a sustained cyber attack (6/24/17). "The government's National Security Strategy said in 2015 that the threat from cyber-attacks from both organized crime and foreign intelligence agencies was one of the "most significant risks to UK interests". [5]

> Then there's the classified information contained in Hillary Clinton's e-mails while she was Secretary of State. Before and after this book goes to publication, there will be others, with more on the horizon. **We must proactively secure our gates, by investing in cyber-security**. The Internet is a major communication, information gateway. Disaster recovery plans are a must for taking measures to minimize damage from cyber-attacks. The USA government has released a Defcon scale (released in August 2016) as a guide for cyberattacks. Corporations have

network security systems as their most important method of protection against cyber-attack.

Have a plan in place. In addition to anti-virus software individuals and corporations must back up, back up, back up! We've all learned that one the hard way. I was almost done with my dissertation that I'd worked over a year on. My computer got a virus which caused the loss of *all* of my files, including my dissertation. My back up flash drive became infected too. I wanted to cry. Months of work lost! Fortunately, I had a friend who is a computer genius. He was able to get the ghost files off of my hard drive. Yay!!! My dissertation was saved, and many other files. Since then, I have back up for my back up: a flash drive *and* an external hard drive. (Personally, I do not trust cloud computing and online storage. That works well for the sharing of files, but I don't trust it as a primary storage method or back up.)

The more multi-layered your disaster recovery plan the better it will mitigate potential damage. It's not a matter *IF* one gets attacked, it's a matter of when. It's not the punch that hits you the hardest that takes you out – it's the one you didn't see coming. Proactively prepare and plan ahead of time in order to minimize the impact of a surprise attack. This applies to spiritual matters as well as practical ones. You can't plan for everything, unforeseeable 'stuff' happens, but plan for obvious, potential attacks.

It's not a matter IF one gets attacked, it's a matter of when. It's not the punch that hits you the hardest that takes you out – it's the one you didn't see coming.

Let's be practical as well as spiritual in securing gates. We don't want to be so heavenly minded that we're no earthly good!

GOD the MASTER WARFARE STRATEGIST

God is absolutely amazing! He strategically sets up coups (brilliant, sudden, and usually highly successful set ups or acts leading to takeovers). He is THE divine strategist! In Joshua and the battle of Jericho God utilized Information Warfare, Psychological Warfare, Spiritual Warfare long before the actual battle. The results were an overwhelming victory for the Hebrews.

Even the selection of Jericho as their first official battle in the Promised Land was strategic. Jericho was considered THE most formidable, impregnable, unconquerable fortress in the land. To take Jericho was a coup paving the way for broad-sweeping takeover throughout the land.

> Now, when all the Amorite kings west of the Jordan and all the Canaanite kings along the coast heard how the LORD had dried up the Jordan before the Israelites until they had crossed over, their hearts melted in fear and they no longer had the courage to face the Israelites. (Joshua 5:1)

Joshua and the Battle of Jericho shows how shrewd, wise, and Masterful God is!

Background: The Israelites were worn out from about 400 years of heavy labor as slaves. God miraculously parted the Red Sea and they passed through on dry land. Then they found themselves in a desert, wandering on a 40 year journey in pursuit of the Promised Land.

> "When Pharaoh let the people go, God did not lead them on the road through the Philistine country, though that was shorter. For God said, "*If they face war, they might change their minds and return to Egypt.* So God led the people around by the desert road toward the Red Sea. The Israelites went up out of Egypt ready for battle." (Exodus 13:17-18)

They thought they were ready for battle, but they didn't have the right mindset.

> "Thirty-eight years passed from the time we left Kadesh Barnea until we crossed the Zered Valley. By then, that entire generation of fighting men had perished from the camp, as the LORD had sworn to them. The LORD'S hand was against them until he had completely eliminated them from the camp." (Deuteronomy 2:14-15)

[Note: If you're waiting upon breakthrough, you may be in the middle of a divine set up. Be patient, He's lining everything up; including your mindset, outlook, perspective AND who stands with you. **Not everyone who's with you now will finish with you**. Don't throw away your confidence. He's readying everything for you.]

The set up: *A lot* of preparation and divine 'set up' took place before Jericho. God had to weed out the old mindset/ generation and build up His people; as He was doing that he began an elaborate 2 year information/propaganda campaign with the Israelites' enemies, those nations that occupied the land promised to them.

There is no place for fear on the battlefield. The enemy can smell fear and will leverage it against you. The essence of basic training is to raise warriors, not fearful children. Fear is paralyzing and debilitating. **Fear doesn't win wars, faith and courage do.** The longest distance in the world is the 18 inches between your head and your heart. Confidence and faith (the opposite of fear) are not head knowledge fruits. They reside in the heart – an unshakable knowledge that has been made real.

The curse of fear was reversed. Instead of Israel being afraid of enemy strongholds, they were feared by all the nations in the Promised Land, even before they entered it. God the Master Strategist/ Warrior initiated information and psychological warfare among the nations, *2 years before attacking Jericho*.

> "See, I have given into your hand Sihon the Amorite, king of Heshbon, and his country. Begin to take possession of it and engage him in battle. **This very day I will begin to put the terror and fear of you on all the nations under heaven. They will hear reports of you and will tremble and be in anguish because of you.**" (Deuteronomy 2:24-25)

No mercy on the enemy: "The LORD said to me, "See, I have begun to deliver Sihon and his country over to you. Now begin to conquer and possess his land. ... At that time we took all his towns and completely destroyed them—men, women and children. We left no survivors. But the livestock and the plunder from the towns we had captured we carried off for ourselves." (Dt. 2:31, 34-35)

The real battle, the battle of the mind, of identity, knowing and resting in His sovereignty, took place long before they ever began marching around Jericho.

Victorious warriors win first and then go to war, while defeated warriors go to war first and then seek to win. (Sun Tzu. *Art of War.*) As a man thinks in his heart, so he is. (Proverbs 23:7)

The Lord also taught His people how to fight spiritually, to listen to Him and to know the awe of His Presence that was with them, for them. The priests of the Lord weren't just gatekeepers and ministers in the temple, they were warriors on the frontlines as well.

> *When you are about to go into battle, the priest shall come forward and address the army. He shall say: "Hear, Israel: Today you are going into battle against your enemies. Do not be fainthearted or afraid; do not panic or be terrified by them. For the LORD* your God is the one who goes with you to fight for you against your enemies to give you victory." (Dt. 20:2-4)

Before coming against the stronghold of Jericho the Israelites consecrated themselves at Gilgal. This consecration was no small thing. Grown men were circumcised with flint knives. Ouch! These men were 'all-in' and fully committed! What do you need to do to consecrate yourself? Are there soul ties to be cut? Is there anything that needs to be cut away or removed? They remained at Gilgal until they were completely healed.

Here's an example of modern-day consecration and being all-in:

There was a man named Brother Andrew. He visited a church in Russia; during the days when the KGB seized pastors, imprisoned and tortured them for their faith. Brother Andrew walked into a church, shouting, "Anyone not prepared to die for your faith get out now!" With that many ran for the door and cleared out. Then Brother Andrew shook the pastor's hand saying, "Hi, I'm Brother Andrew. I just wanted you to know where your congregation stood."

Before Gilgal Joshua sent out his elite special forces of 2 spies to do reconnaissance on Jericho and gather intel. (Joshua 2) These spies were top notch. They had to find their own way across the Jordan, gain access into the fortress of Jericho, gather intel and make it back safely. The intel they procured, from Rahab the prostitute, was invaluable; they gained information and perspective straight from the stronghold of the enemy. The bigger picture of what God had woven together since Egypt came clearly into focus. The Israelites didn't even realize the fame of their God and the fear of them that already filled the land. Sometimes the enemy sees the bigger picture better than we do.

> Rahab said to them, "I know that the LORD has given you this land and that a great fear of you has fallen on us, so that all who live in this country are melting in fear because of you. We have heard how the Lord dried up the water of the Red Sea for you when you came out of Egypt, and what you did to Sihon and Og, the two kings of the Amorites east of the Jordan, whom you completely destroyed. When we heard of it, our hearts melted in fear and everyone's courage failed because of you, for the Lord your God is God in heaven above and on the earth below." (Joshua 2:9-11)

My, my how the Israelites perspective shifted! 37 years earlier when Moses sent out 12 spies 10 of them saw themselves as grasshoppers. "We seemed like grasshoppers in our own eyes, and we looked the same to them." (Numbers 13:33) How we see ourselves changes with 2 things:

a. when we understand who we truly are, how He sees us
b. when we realize how the enemy sees us!

Prior to the marches around Jericho Joshua was so 'ballsy' he was dangerous, in a good way. He almost rushed an angel that had come to visit him.

"Now when Joshua was near Jericho, he looked up and saw a man standing in front of him with a drawn sword in his hand. Joshua went up to him and asked, "Are you for us or for our enemies?"

"Neither," he replied, "but as commander of the army of the LORD I have now come." Then Joshua fell facedown to the ground in reverence, and asked him, "What message does my Lord have for his servant?"

The commander of the LORD's army replied, "Take off your sandals, for the place where you are standing is holy." And Joshua did so. (Joshua 5:13-15)

It was in that angelic visitation that Joshua received the specifics of God's strategy for battle. (Joshua 6:2-5)

The Jews didn't concern themselves with the barred, 40 foot high, 25 foot thick walls, manned with guards and an army. Jericho's reputation of being impregnable didn't alarm them. Their reality was rooted and anchored in the reputation of the Lord God Almighty. They envisioned victory, tasted and smelled it. In their minds they had already won, theirs was simply to obey His marching orders. At the sound of the shofar, probably with the 'Tekiah' – one long blast, signifying the King's coronation, and a shout the walls of Jericho collapsed. After that the army didn't hesitate, they rushed in and took the city and word spread throughout the land.

All of the walls of Jericho collapsed at the shout of the King; <u>except for the north side of the wall where Rahab and her family lived</u>.

By faith the walls of Jericho fell, after the army had marched around them for seven days.

By faith the prostitute Rahab, because she welcomed the spies, was not killed with those who were disobedient. (Hebrews 11:30-31)

Other Military Strategies Given by God

Each battle in the Old Testament was unique. There was only 1 Jericho. We don't see Him carrying out the same battle plans over and over. Someone else's 'how to' won't bring results, if we didn't 'pay the price' of faith. Prophetic revelation leads us into victory. "Have faith in the LORD your God and you will be upheld; have faith in his prophets and you will be successful." (2 Chronicles 20:20) Not by might, not by power, but by His spirit! (Zech. 4:6)

Awesome God! Who else but the Lord mighty in battle would give the following strategies for battle and victory?

- As the Captain of the Hosts He commanded His people to simply stand still "The LORD will fight for you; you need only to be still." (Exodus 14:14)
- Selected which soldiers would fight arbitrarily by how they drank water. (Judges 7:1-8)
- Strike the ground, not people, with arrows for complete victory. (2 Kings 13:15-18)
- Smashing jars, carrying torches and blowing trumpets to route an enemy force of 132,000.
- Act like a madman and drool to avoid capture by the enemy. (1 Samuel 21:12-14)
- Worship (2 Chronicles 20:21-22)
- A warrior and a priest upholding an old man's arms until victory was won. (Exodus17:9-13)

> *"For my thoughts are not your thoughts,*
> *neither are your ways my ways,"*
> *declares the LORD.*
> *"As the heavens are higher than the earth,*
> *so are my ways higher than your ways*
> *and my thoughts than your thoughts." (Isaiah 58:8-9)*

God's ways surely aren't our ways; the principles of His kingdom are contrary to the ways of the world, but His ways are sure. In the kingdom of God:

- the ultimate triumph comes through surrender, even through death on a cross; (Phil. 2:8)
- as one gives they receive, (2 Cor. 9:6-9)
- the greatest is the least and the least is the greatest; (Mat. 23:11-12)
- the first is last and the last is first; (Mat. 19:30)
- in weakness one is strong (2 Cor. 12:9)
- the meek shall inherit the earth (Mat. 5:5)
- He trades beauty for ashes (Is. 61:3)
- mercy triumphs over judgment (James 2:13)

It took faith and gutsiness to obey and follow Him fully! Can you imagine going out with Jehoshaphat and facing well- armed hostile multitudes with only a song and a trumpet? Or like Gideon how would you like to march into the odds of 300 to 132,000? Yikes!

"But my righteous one will live by faith.
And I take no pleasure
in the one who shrinks back."
But we do not belong to those who shrink back and are destroyed,
but to those who have faith and are saved." (Hebrews 10:38-39)

Worship a Primary Weapon of War

"For though we live in the world, we do not wage war as the world does. The weapons we fight with are not the weapons of the world. On the contrary, they have divine power to demolish strongholds. We demolish arguments and every pretension that sets itself up against the knowledge of God, and we take captive every thought to make it obedient to Christ." (2 Corinthians 10:3-5)

There are many spiritual weapons that He gives us, such as; peace, unity, humility, repentance, etc. The most vital weapons are worship and prayer. Why is praise such a powerful weapon of war? Because praise & worship:

- Bring us into His presence – He inhabits, the praises of His people (Psalm 91:1; 100:4),
- Fills our territory with His glory and favor as we behold Him (Isaiah 6:1-3),
- His throne is established upon praise (Psalm 22:3)
- Worship lifts our countenance and vision higher (Psalm 108:3-5),
- Aligns us in agreement with His character and nature, (1 John 3:2)
- Activates divine protection over us (Psalm 5:10-12; Psalm 140:7)
- Produces joy and strength (Psalm 63:7; 92:4-5)
- Prompts the Lord to fight victoriously on our behalf (Numbers 23:21; 2 Chronicles 20:21-22)

There is a type of treatment for cancer involving music, with favorable results. (It is called Sound Healing or Sonotherapy.)

Spiritually there is a frequency of heaven that aligns, heals and restores things to their rightful order. Let's fill the atmosphere with the sound of heaven. (Literally electro-magnetic frequencies have detected a sound in the DNA of cells. In cancerous cells there is a discordant sound frequency that is heard in the electro-magnetic resonance.) I received a prophetic word that angels were singing over me at the frequency of heaven, and that the frequency of heaven was coming down and literally shifting things in my body. Shortly afterward profound pain and motion limitation in my shoulder was healed. May our worship release the sound and frequency of heaven.

God wants to form habitations for the occupation of His presence!

A Biblical Example – There's no limit to what He can do as he inhabits the praises of His people. The battle becomes the Lord's and He sets ambushes against the enemy.

> "Then the Spirit of the LORD came on Jahaziel son of Zechariah, the son of Benaiah, the son of Jeiel, the son of Mattaniah, a Levite and descendant of Asaph, as he stood in the assembly.
>
> He said: "Listen, King Jehoshaphat and all who live in Judah and Jerusalem! This is what the LORD says to you: 'Do not be afraid or discouraged because of this vast army. For the battle is not yours, but God's. Tomorrow march down against them. They will be climbing up by the Pass of Ziz, and you will find them at the end of the gorge in the Desert of Jeruel. You will not have to fight this battle. Take up your positions; stand firm and see the deliverance the Lord will give you, Judah and Jerusalem. Do not be afraid; do not be discouraged. Go out to face them tomorrow, and the Lord will be with you.'"
>
> Jehoshaphat bowed down with his face to the ground, and all the people of Judah and Jerusalem fell down in worship before the LORD.
>
> ... Jehoshaphat stood and said, "Listen to me, Judah and people of Jerusalem! Have faith in the Lord your God and you will be upheld; have faith in his prophets and you will be successful."
>
> After consulting the people, Jehoshaphat appointed men to sing to the LORD and to praise him for the splendor of his holiness as they went out at the head of the army, saying:
>
> "Give thanks to the LORD,
>
> for his love endures forever."
>
> *As they began to sing and praise, the LORD set ambushes against the men of Ammon and Moab and Mount Seir who were invading Judah, and they were defeated.*
>
> (2 Chronicles 20:14-18, 21-22)

Be Strategic: Hear Him – Do What He Says Do

God is also calling us to be strategic, as the sons of Issachar were; to know the times and the season that we are in. The more strategic we are the more impactful and effective we will be ; as the saying goes, "Work smarter, not harder."

The more strategic we are the more impactful and effective we will be.

Mary said to the servants when Jesus performed His first miracle of turning water into wine, "Whatever He says do – DO IT!" It's time to be strategic in terms of:

a. Venue
b. Location
c. Timing

VENUE: Whenever possible hold venues/events outside of a church building, preferably under an open sky, where there are no walls. Penetrate, infiltrate, and permeate the air. Filling the air with His Presence (He inhabits the praises of His people) and the essence of the attributes of God; love, hope, justice, righteousness, obedience. Sow fruits of the Spirit (love, joy, peace, righteousness, self-control, patience, faithfulness, gentleness, humility).

TIMING: Hear Him in the timing. "Like apples of gold in settings of silver, is a word spoken at the right time/ in due season." (Proverbs 25:11, AMP/Darby) What makes something prophetic isn't just that it's accurate, but that it's spoken in God's timing. Also, there are simply times that are more optimum than others, when God is closer and more attentive. "Seek the LORD while he may be found; call on him while he is near." (Isaiah 55:6)

Strategic times and seasons were selected for events: Awaken the Dawn during the feast of Tabernacles, in tents, prayer walks in Wall Street (NYC) and Liberty State Park during the Hebrew month of Elul, during a historic solar eclipse (on the eve of Rosh Hashanah).

Whether the event is large or small, ask Him the what, when, and where you're supposed to be.

Be bold, fearless and assertive, do not hold back! Move in the breadth of freedom that God has granted us in this nation. Be atmosphere changers.

Securing Gates Through Reformation

It's not church as usual any longer. We are moving out of the four walls and into every stratosphere of society. Justice isn't a gavel in a courtroom. It's restoring the world to 'right'. That's reformation.

This type of reformation has yielded very favorable results throughout history when one ruler took over from another or rebuilt after war. Here are 2 examples from the pages of history:

1. During the Norman Conquest (in 1066), the newly formed kingdom of England was secured through reform; through occupying and establishing positive change. the military conquest of England by William, duke of Normandy was primarily affected by his decisive victory at the Battle of Hastings. Although William's main rivals were gone, he still faced rebellions over the following years and was not secure on his throne until after 1072. The lands of the resisting English elite were confiscated; some of the elite fled into exile. To control his new kingdom, William granted lands to his followers and built castles commanding military strongpoints throughout the land; resulting ultimately in profound political, administrative, and social changes in the British Isles.
2. Post World War II, Japan had been ravaged by the atomic bomb that had just been dropped on them by the USA. As in any war the USA occupies any country they have been at war with that has experienced heavy losses. The purpose of occupation was to assist in rebuilding and stabilizing the country. In September, 1945, the U.S. occupying forces, led by General Douglas A. MacArthur, enacted widespread military, political, economic, and social reforms. The occupation of Japan (1945-1952) can be divided into three phases: the initial effort to punish and reform Japan, the work to revive the Japanese economy, and the conclusion of a formal peace treaty and alliance. Obviously, the occupation/reformation had its desired result in that we continue to enjoy positive relations with Japan today and their economy is thriving.

Occupation of a land *with* reformation brings effectual, lasting change. It is a vital aspect of securing our gates, simultaneously advancing the kingdom. **We are His remnant, reformation army in every gate and mountain of influence!**

Occupation of
a land with
reformation
brings effectual,
lasting change

CHAPTER 13

Our Future

"We did not choose to be guardians of the gate, but there is no one else." (Lyndon B. Johnson)

For he chose us in Him before the creation of the world! (Ephesians 1:4)

IF THE CHURCH DOESN'T MANIFEST kingdom, then we won't change culture." [1] **If we do not see manifest change in culture then our influence failed to impact.** If everything we do goes uncontested and with ease, we're probably ineffective. If we see conflict and controversy then we're probably making an impact. That means the status quo is being shaken. People don't like change. They don't want their comfort zones and 'golden calves' touched or ruffled – especially when there are opposing kingdoms diametrically opposed and at war with one another. As Winston Churchill said, "You have enemies? Good. That means you've stood up for something, sometime in your life."

In the book of James (chapter 1:22-25) **we're exhorted to be effectual doers, not forgetful hearers.** If we failed to impact it may be because of a combination of the following:

- other influences contending against us for the gates – A need to stand, fight and prevail!
- our manifestation of kingdom needs adjustment,
- moving out of wrong motive (self-interests or religiosity) instead of love
- void of prophetic revelation
- or we need a personal revival – a fresh in-filling of the Holy Spirit in order to move in His revelation and power

We know, understand and internalize kingdom through knowing the King, hearing, sensing, discerning by the kingdom of God that is within us. **The**

kingdom of God is made manifest by our actions and words. When we find our voice, we speak into our spheres His truth in love with a demonstration of power in the Holy Spirit.

How you respond to adversity defines what you believe. What you believe is manifested in your actions. **People will know you by the decision you make. Not deciding is a decision.**

As Chuck Pierce says, "God is using how we developed in this past season to provide the access to what He is opening up in the year ahead. We must manifest who we have become; the sword He has made us into must be used. This is the time of cutting off, and gaining strength and power. Prepare to be extended through and into a place that God has promised, but where we have yet to gain our footing. Set your hearts to receive the revelation to go through the gate and gain access!" [2]

> *Be very careful, then, how you live—not as unwise but as wise, making the most of every opportunity, because the days are evil. (Ephesians 5:15-16)*

<u>BUILD to LAST</u>: Teachers & the Gift of Discernment

There will be a new birthing of Teachers arising in this season as the five-fold ministry is secured, balanced and established in the Church. Prophetic teaching, fresh revelation, with solid biblical principles, to build, establish and empower the saints to be the influence of Christ in the earth today. The Word of God carries authority. **Teachers, rightly dividing the Word of truth, will walk in and impart the authority of righteousness and truth; which will cleanse and establish the land and its people.**

> In Ezra and Nehemiah's day, "Teachers: were key to turn the tide of iniquity, idolatry and depravity and reversed the effect of the mindset of captivity in the land. A generation had grown accustomed to the ways of Babylon and grown comfortable and fatalistic to the reality of captivity. Hopelessness, compromise and comfortability with captivity, had captured their hearts. God was releasing a decree through Cyrus for the opportunity to take back the systems of education of a generation that had led them into bondage.
>
> What happens in our academic and educational systems, both public and private, will set the tone of the values and morals of a generation." [3] (Tom Hamon)

Today's millennial generation is strong in worship, and the supernatural, but there is a need for training, teaching, mentoring, self-discipline, discernment, soundness so that what is being built will last and perpetuate from one generation to future generations. We need the mantle of the teacher and the gift of discernment of spirits to arise and flourish in greater dimension. **Revelation, wisdom, knowledge, and discernment are precious commodities for the builders and reformers of this day.**

The Lord already warned us that deception and apostasy would be great in the end times. (1 Timothy 4:1) We must be vigilant to secure gateways of soundness, balance and truth. These things increase the risk of deception, error and potential demonic attack:

- A lack of the knowledge of the Word
- Isolating or not being connected to a body
- Not being submitted to authority
- Rebellion
- Unforgiveness
- Emotionalism

Diverse generations embracing the wisdom and perspective of one another will keep us growing in knowledge, understanding our history and in discernment. Good decisions come from experience and experience comes from bad decisions. We can avoid the errors of previous generations as we are open to and receive from those who have gone before us. Older generations need the fire, zeal and freshness that millennials have. Millenials need the wisdom and depth, learned through the 'school of hard knocks' that older generations have. Together we're a winning team!

Your greatest strength can also be your greatest weakness. This generation is passionate, spontaneous, bold, and loves to worship. Let's be all in, not just wanting to be entertained by good music and 'vibes' but rooted, grounded, and established in His Word. As an older song says, "When the music fades, and all is swept away; I'll give You more than a song, for a song in itself is not what You have desired. You look much deeper within, to the way things have been; You're looking into my heart."

As we walk in the Spirit and listen for *His voice* let's press in to:

- Be of sound doctrine; grounded and established in the Word of God
- Develop the gift of discernment.

Discernment is one of the 9 gifts of the spirit listed in 1 Corinthians 12. The times that we are in call for something greater than finite reasoning.

"In this season, you must be able to discern your Judas, from your Peter...... Peter had a bad day, Judas had a bad heart. .... Peter you restore, Judas you release." [4] In order to determine whether to restore or release we need to *know* the Word and have cultivated the gift of discernment. The more pure your spirit, the keener and more sensitive your discernment is.

Without His gift of discernment/ distinguishing of spirits, we will not be able to tell a real threat from a rumor and or doctrine that sounds good but is in error. Charles Spurgeon said, "Discernment is not knowing the difference between right and wrong. It's knowing the difference between right and almost right." **Discernment is the ability to judge well, without being judgmental.** One judges the truth and the spirit of a matter, not the people.

Compromise will blunt one's discernment. A.W. Tozer says, "One compromise here, another there, and soon enough the so-called Christian and the man in the world look the same."

> "*Many false prophets will appear and deceive many people. Because of the increase of wickedness, the love of most will grow cold, but the one who stands firm to the end will be saved. And this gospel of the kingdom will be preached in the whole world as a testimony to all nations, and then the end will come.*" (Matthew 24:6-14)

We all need to continually grow in discernment, but there are 5 types of Christians that are most at risk for deception:

1. Those who have become corrupt and compromised, rationalizing truth to fit their corrupt lifestyle.
2. Those who have been hurt that didn't heal properly. (They see everything through the lens of their hurt and pain, becoming like what they came out of. Hurt people hurt people.)
3. Those that are ignorant of the Word and foundations of the faith.
4. Those prone to emotionalism and/or easily swayed by a crowd.
5. Those who are mentally or emotionally off balance and unstable.

Discernment is the ability to see things as they really are, not for what we want them to be. God give us grace to be governed by the Spirit and Your Word, not our emotions. "There's only one kind of person who is worse than a fool: The impetuous one who speaks without thinking first." (Proverbs 29:20, CEB) Paraphrased, you can recognize fools by the way they give full vent to their rage and let their words fly! But the wise bite their tongue and hold back all they could say.

<u>THE TIMES WE ARE IN</u> – Where will they lead us?

We're in a season of mighty outpouring, on the cusp of the greatest revival of all time. Then will come an apostasy of such a dimension that the Church has never known or endured before. You may be thinking to yourself can't we just enjoy this season? Absolutely! Enjoy it, but know what is coming. Now is the time to secure the gates for future generations! **That a generation yet to be born, will be anchored in soundness and truth, inheriting a strong and healthy kingdom.** That is what securing the gates is all about.

Having said all that, I'm in agreement with Johnny Enlow, "This is not the age of the beast, the antichrist, the false prophet, the great tribulation, a one world government, "perilous times", or whatever other foreboding that you may be inclined to give attention to. We are rather in a multi-decades period of advanced kingdom activity. It is the beginning of the age of the kingdom. We are in the days of the restoration of all things. An extended era of renaissance in the knowledge of God is upon us."[5]

This is a period of an unprecedented release of His glory, causing His people to infiltrate and re-establish kingdom dominion and principles in all areas of society. Rebuild, restore, establish and secure!

As the spirit of the Lord said through Chuck Pierce, "This is a time that I am realigning the lands and the people of the lands. Lay down your prejudices and your political gleanings—what I am doing is way above this. I am creating a government in the earth that will shake things in a new way. I am working both the heavens and the earth. These next 10 years are critical to aligning the heavens, the earth and the nations of the earth."[6]

It is the time to give all of our life and labor to be co-workers together with Christ in demonstrating and enforcing His Kingdom in all the earth."

A DREAM & A VISION

<u>I had a dream/vision, snapshot</u>:

It was a warm and beautiful sunny day, with clear, blue skies. I was standing in a field between NJ & NYC, overlooking the Hudson River. Tall NY skyscrapers were across the river in the background. There, in the harbor, were several wind turbines.

The image was very clear and left a lasting impression on me. The Holy Spirit began revealing what He was saying in the dream.

Interpretation:

Location, location, location! – The setting of this vision is known as the 'Gateway of America'. **What emanates in the Gateway of America flows throughout the land.** NYC and NJ are like a mirror for what happens within the country, because of their diversity and many cultures represented.

This dream was situated on the Hudson, in the harbor, between prime real estate in NY & NJ. It overlooks 2 iconic American landmarks, the Statue of Liberty and the WTC. It is ground that has also been prepared in prayer. I've had the opportunity to participate in corporate prophetic prayer meetings, both large and small; at Liberty State Park, NJ (by the Statue of Liberty), and at the World Trade Center memorial (NYC) as well as numerous prayer walks. Multitudes from many nations have immigrated through this gateway. As a banner of declaration at the base of the Statue of Liberty, the inscription reads, "Give me your huddled masses yearning to breathe free, The wretched refuse of your teeming shore. Send these, the homeless, tempest-tossed to me, I lift my lamp beside the golden door!" This gateway, in the east, has also witnessed the trauma and tragedy of 9-11. Intercession has risen before the throne of God for America and He has heard our cry!

America you have yet another chance to align with God's kingdom! A chance to uproot, over-turn corruption, and for the spirit of greed, pride and mammon to fall.

Planted in the river of His Spirit we will continually ascend. As we ascend He will flow into every area of society. There will be an increase of prosperity and true freedom. (Both the wind and the river are symbols of the Holy Spirit.) Psalm 1 is all about being planted by the river.:

> "Blessed is the one
> who does not walk in step with the wicked
> or stand in the way that sinners take
> or sit in the company of mockers,
> but whose delight is in the law of the Lord,
> and who meditates on his law, day and night.
> That person is like a tree planted by streams of water,
> which yields its fruit in season
> and whose leaf does not wither—
> whatever they do prospers." (Psalm 1:1-3)

There will be an increase of prosperity. **Entrepreneurial anointing will arise and usher in a new wave of prosperity**, bringing back wealth, restoring foundations, restoring prosperity. Kingdom entrepreneurs with the anointing and wisdom of Joseph, who in times of plenty will reserve a portion for the future. People, nations, will stream to the Church. She will arise as the chief cornerstone. **A new breed of leader is emerging from the Church, with apostolic, entrepreneurial anointing and mandate for the marketplace.** Ethics and integrity will be their hallmark – and SUCCESS!

Wind turbines, such as the ones in the dream, are able to harness and store the power of the wind, releasing and directing it with purposeful, measured, intention and duration for maximum effectiveness.

The presence of wind turbines in the Hudson indicates the ability of sustained, renewable power, energy and prosperity. The turbines were facing East in the direction of the Statue of Liberty. The wind of the Spirit, is blowing on liberty/freedom in the Gateway of America, flowing throughout the land.

Facing the direction of the East also parallels significance of the Eastern gate in Old Testament Jerusalem; a very prophetic gate, also referred to as *the golden gate*. (Interestingly remember the inscription on the Statue of Liberty, "I lift my lamp beside *the golden door*!")

First the natural, then the spiritual. (1 Corinthians 15:46) I didn't know, but discovered as I researched, that in the natural there are multi-million dollar plans afoot to engineer wind turbines between 2 shipping lanes for NY harbor. The potential of the turbines could generate as much power as a mid-size nuclear generating station! Construction could begin in the 2020's. In the spiritual realm God is already establishing wind turbines of His Holy Spirit the Gateway of America – the revival that is on its way, globally.

Moving In Reformation

And the Spirit is asking, "Where are YOU located? Which Gateway have you been strategically placed in?" What are the gates in your life and in your city? Are you near mountains, cornfields, deserts, swamps, cities or farmlands? You are strategically placed. Dr. Melodye Hilton eloquently declares, "Our inheritance as reformers equips us with a prophetic edge to dominate the spiritual environment setting us apart to be the best in our field. I am not called to compete with others, but I am commissioned by Heaven to be the best that I can be. At this time in history, we have an opportunity to rescue from error and return systems, structures and lives back to their original course. We have been placed here by God, at this time, for this purpose." [7] Rise up to be the influence of Christ on earth as it is in heaven! There's a fresh and powerful wind of the Spirit blowing in the Gateway of America throughout the land, one that will be sustained. You and I are called to be part of it.

As Tom Hamon points out, "This is all exciting and wonderful stuff, ... However, not without great conflict.

Reformation is often messy, complicated and full of conflict. That was true of reformation in Jesus' day in the first reformation. It was definitely true during the 2nd Reformation in Martin Luther's day. This was definitely also true in Nehemiah's day and in our day as well: what happened when the people began to operate to rebuild under the new Cyrus decree in their generation?" [8] They were mocked, falsely accused, and discredited. Be prepared to fight the good fight. The warfare can be intense.

> "Hear us, our God, for we are despised. *Turn their insults back on their own heads.* ... Don't be afraid of them. Remember the Lord, who is great and awesome, *and fight for your families*, your sons and your daughters, your wives and your homes.
>
> When our enemies heard that we were aware of their plot and that God had frustrated it, we all returned to the wall, each to our own work.
>
> From that day on, half of my men did the work, while the other half were equipped with spears, shields, bows and armor." (Nehemiah 4:4, 14-16)

They worked, like we will work, with a sword in one hand and a trowel in the other. (BTW – It's ok in prayer to "turn your enemies insults back on their own heads.")

> *"Vindicate me, my God, and plead my cause against an unfaithful nation. Rescue me from those who are deceitful and wicked. You are God my stronghold." (Psalm 43:1-2)*

Where is it that you are stationed 'on the wall', in life? Are you a Mom, a member of a Home & School Association? A business executive in the gateway of commerce? A student in college? Can you imagine if ALL believers began moving with God-given boldness, authority and power – dunamis, in their sphere of influence?! Faithfully praying one for another and those in authority. Wow! What an impact the body of Christ, the Church will have when we arise as one in every stratosphere of society!!!

The Era of 3 R's is upon us!

It's more than a season, it's an era. A season is a short segment of time related to climate. An era is a longer span of time, usually associated with a period of history. Many seasons are contained within an era. **The Era of the 3 R's has begun**, and we're *not* talking about Reading, wRiting & aRithematic)!

God's 3 R's in this era are:

- **Remnant**
- **Reformation**
- **Revival**

God always reserves a remnant. "Then it will happen on that day that the Lord will again recover the second time with His hand, the remnant of His people, who will remain" (Isaiah 11:11) He delights in working through the least likely and the humble. "So too, at the present time there is a remnant chosen by grace." (Romans 11:5) This is a time that those who have been hidden and 'passed by' will arise! There is a large multitude that this pertains to.

Your effectiveness in doing great exploits in God will be directly linked to your obedience having nothing to do with your numbers, means, or notoriety. It's a 'Gideon-like' time. (Judges 7:2-9) A time where numbers and natural circumstances aren't in your favor, when your only boast can be in the awesome strength of God; the One who makes a way where there is no way. Flesh doesn't get any glory, only God.

God is full of surprises. Get ready, be ready. Do what He says do – especially in non-traditional things in this season. He's in the small whisper! **Reformation is being birthed by a Remnant of pioneers willing to do what He says do**. It's not business as usual. If you're part of the remnant than you're not just a Sunday bench-warmer.

The Remnant will usher in Reform – going into all the world, *filling society with kingdom culture*; "that the earth will be filled with the knowledge of the glory of the Lord, just as the waters cover the sea." (Habakkuk 2:14, AMP) The face of the Church is changing. No longer will it look like brick buildings with steeples, but it will be the Marketplace, the Arts, the Media and the Streets. **He will place the remnant in strategic places, using them to lift up His standard** just as it is written in the context of the remnant, "And He will lift up a standard for the nations." (Isaiah 11:12, NIV)

God is placing His people in strategic positions at the entry and exit points, or gates of influence. It will not always be easy. The Builder/Reformers will be gaining ground and often 'going against the grain' as they bring a standard of righteousness. We have witnessed an intense clashing of kingdoms. We will be taking back territory, pushing back the enemy, and advancing. There will be push-back, but the Lord says, "Listen to Me, you who know righteousness, A people in whose heart is My law; **Do not fear the reproach of man**, Nor be dismayed at their revilings." (Isaiah 51:7).

The Reformation led by the Remnant will birth the greatest Revival the earth has ever seen! **This Revival will NOT be a 'fire and fizzle' revival. It will be more of a 'slow burn' – sustained and maintained *because of a societal reformation which establishes a culture of kingdom.*** Kingdom will be woven into the very fabric of society.

> "Come, let us go up to the mountain of the Lord,
> To the house of the God of Jacob;
> That He may teach us concerning His ways
> And that we may walk in His paths."
> For the law will go forth from Zion
> And the word of the Lord from Jerusalem. (Isaiah 2:3)

The Presence, pleasure and favor of the Lord will overshadow the land as godly principles and standards overtake, displace and replace corrupt, decadent spiritual influences. He's raising up a Remnant to Reform and take the gates. Revival will be marked by Repentance, Reform, prayer and worship. This will bring about a huge Revival. **Because of Reformation, in every area of society, Revival will be maintained and sustained for a long while.**

Be vigilant to keep the gates that you have access to secure. (Your personal life, family, work, etc.)

We must secure our gates to sustain and maintain the ground we gain in on-going reform and revival. **Securing our gates begins with us in personal reform in identity, self-discipline and self-governance, extending to all gates of influence around us:** Family, Education, Government, Commerce, Media, Arts & Entertainment, and the Church. We've been given the keys and authority of the Kingdom of heaven. The gates of hell will not prevail. (Matthew 16:18)

What an awesome time to be alive!

About the Author

A PASSIONATE, PROPHETIC TEACHER AND intercessor, Dr. Janet Shuler is an apostolic leader, founder of His Kingdom Ministries, public speaker, itinerant minister, webinar presenter, and author. Dr. Shuler has also had an extensive career in education, with over 40 years as a: principal, asst. principal, literacy coordinator, staff developer, teacher and adjunct professor for graduate students at Seton Hall University.

Her mission is to establish, equip and empower believers to be an influence for Christ on earth. Her core value is to empower others – equipping and encouraging them to be effective in their call and attain their destiny. Dr. Janet works with leaders and their people in building teams of powerful, prophetic intercessors.

Dr. Janet is particularly thankful for her husband Jim's love and support. He is the wind beneath her wings. They have 8 adult children, and several grandchildren. Family is near and dear to their heart.

Contact her for training, activation, and impartation for you and your people – receive the Father's heart, with transforming truths!

- Webinar courses soon to be available.

To learn more about Dr. Janet Shuler or to contact her:

Contact her by email at:
HKMdrJanet@gmail.com
Visit her web site at:
www.jshuler.blog

Follow her on social media at:
FaceBook
www.facebook.com/janetshuler2
Instagram
www.instagram.com/HKMdrJanet

NOTES

Chapter 1 – Advance and Secure – Secure and Advance

[1] LeClaire, Jennifer. "The Lord is Mantling Underground Intercessors With New Boldness". http://www.elijahlist.com/words/display_word.html?ID=17947 . 5/9/17. Accessed: 6/21/17.

[2] Wallnau, Lance. "*The Year of the Clashing of Swords and Taking New Ground*". 1/4/17. http://www.elijahlist.com/words/display_word.html?ID=17245.

[3] Rodriguez, Cindy. Bush ties to Bin Laden haunt grim anniversary. Denver Post. http://www.denverpost.com/2006/09/11/bush-ties-to-bin-laden-haunt-grim-anniversary/ . 9/11/2006. Accessed: 8/10/17.

[4] Marsh, Warwick. 4/26/17. "Australian Prayer Leaders Call the World to Pray and Fast for America". http://www.elijahlist.com/words/display_word.html?ID=17872 . (Accessed 4/26/17).

[5] Sunil, Isaac. *Codebreakers: Trump and the Media – What's Really at Stake?* . 3/16/17. http://elijahlist.com/words/display_word.html?ID=17631.

[6] Buis, Alan. "Japan Quake May Have Shortened Earth's Days, Moved Axis". 3/14/11. https://www.nasa.gov/topics/earth/features/japanquake/earth20110314.html . Accessed 5/4/17.

[7] Pitre, Isaac. https://www.youtube.com/watch?v=p-WxNJx5iK-0. 1/12/11. Accessed: 5/4/17.

[8] Titus, Silas. Fading Capitalism, Socialism, and True Economy: A Sustainable Response to Global Financial Crisis. Publisher: Pronoun. Available on Kindle, Loc. 517/3192. Copyright: 12/27/16.

[9] Ibid. Loc. 636/3192.

[10] Pierce, Chuck. 2017. "*Ten Days of Decreeing Your Land and Boundaries Will Rejoice*!". http://elijahlist.com/words/display_word.html?ID=17557. 3/1/17. Accessed: 3/1/17.

Chapter 2 – THEN: Old Testament Gates and Gatekeepers

[1] Vaughn, Jane. The Promise to Abraham. http://www.ivernainternational.com/teaching/pdf/ThePromisetoAbraham.pdf. January 2006. Accessed: 9/23/17.

[2] Hilton, Melodye. Instagram informal post on 7/2/17. Accessed: 7/2/17.

[3] Liles, Valerie. *How to Secure Yard Gates – Home Guide – how-to's.* http://homeguides.sfgate.com/secure-yard-gates-58332.html.

Chapter 3 – Prayer

[1] Hayford, Jack. *Election Outcome Could Be Prophetic Announcement.* http://www.charismanews.com/opinion/34504-jack-hayford-election-outcome-could-be-prophetic-announcement . 11/8/2012. Accessed: 6/3/17.

[2] Silvoso, Ed. Presentation at IGAP conference. Destiny Church, Santa Rosa, Fl. 10/20/16.

[3] Pierce, Chuck. *Times of Chaos.* http://www.kingdomwatchmen.org/prayer-targets-chuck-pierce-word-worship-prayer-gathering. July, 2016. Accessed: 4/2017.

[4] Sanders, Andy. *America: I'm Sending My Eagles Up Into The Sky.* http://elijahlist.com/words/display_word.html?ID=18832 . 9/23/17. Accessed: 9/23/17.

[5] Hayford, Jack. *Election Outcome Could Be Prophetic Announcement.* http://www.charismanews.com/opinion/34504-jack-hayford-election-outcome-could-be-prophetic-announcement . 11/8/2012. Accessed: 6/3/17.

[6] Anonymous. Witches Cast Mass Spell With Hopes of Removing Trump From Office. 2/25/17. http://insider.foxnews.com/2017/02/25/witches-cast-spell-donald-trump-crescent-moon-removal-office. Accessed: 3/23/17.

[7] LeClaire, Jennifer. *The Lord is Mantling Underground Intercessors With Boldness.* 5/9/17. http://www.elijahlist.com/words/display_word.html?ID=17947. Accessed: 5/9/17.

[8] Silvoso, Ed. http://adopt.transformourworld.org/en/adopt-your-street/create . Accessed: 9/25/17.

[9] Strand, Paul. Awaken the Dawn: A weekend of worship fills the national mall. http://www1.cbn.com/cbnnews/us/2017/october/awaken-the-dawn-a-weekend-of-worship-fills-the-national-mall. 10/8/17. Accessed: 10/13/17.

[10] Hamon, Tom. A New Prophetic Season for America: The Cyrus Decree and Breaking Resistance. http://elijahlist.com/words/display_word.html?ID=18894. 10/4/17. Accessed: 10/4/17.

[11] Herd, Aimee. *Awaken the Dawn Moved Us Forward.* http://www.elijahlist.com/words/display_word.html?ID=18966. *10/13/17. Accessed: 10/14/17.*

[12] *Ibid.*

Chapter 4 – SELF

[1] Hilton, Melodye. Higher Living Leadership. (USA: Outskirts Press, 2017). p 156.

[2] Ruell, Peter. When brains overvalue immediate rewards. http://news.harvard.edu/gazette/story/2017/07/why-psychopathic-brains-overvalue-immediate-rewards/ . 7/27/17. Accessed: 8/12/17.

[3] Anonymous. Train your brain to let go of habits: 10 Methods for creating new neural pathways. http://themindunleashed.com/2014/03/train-brain-let-go-habits-10-methods-creating-new-neural-pathways.html . 3/2/2014. Accessed: 8/12/17.

[4] Johnson, Keith. Informal Facebook post on 6/27/17. Accessed: 6/27/17.

[5] Lackie, Paul. Informal Facebook post on 6/30/17. Accessed: 6/30/17.

[6] Mast, Dale. Informal Facebook post on 5/29/17. Accessed: 5/29/17.

[7] Johnson, Keith. Informal Facebook post on 6/22/17. Accessed: 6/22/17.

[8] Hilton, Melodye. Higher Living Leadership. (USA: Outskirts Press, 2017). p 64.

[9] Williamson, Marianne. *A Return To Love: Reflections on the Principles of A Course in Miracles*. Harper Collins, 1992. From Chapter 7, Section 3 (Pg. 190-191).

[10] Goll, James. *Values Anchored Believers*. Streaming video: https://www.godencounters.com/videos/?zoombox=0 **. March 2016.**

Chapter 5 – FREEDOM

[1] Chuck Pierce. *Ten Days of Decreeing Your Land and Boundaries Will Rejoice*! http://elijahlist.com/words/display_word.html?ID=17557. 3/1/17. Accessed: 3/27/17.

[2] Papa, Juliet. Remembering the 'Son of Sam' case 40 years after serial killers arrest. http://newyork.cbslocal.com/2017/08/10/son-of-sam-arrest-40th-anniversary/. 8/10/17. Accessed: 8/28/17.

[3] Milloy, Rose. *Bodies identified as those of missing atheist and kin.* http://www.nytimes.com/2001/03/16/us/bodies-identified-as-those-of-missing-atheist-and-kin.html?rref=collection%2Ftimestopic%2FO'Hair%2C%20Madalyn%20Murray&action=click&contentCollection=timestopics®ion=stream&module=stream_unit&version=latest&contentPlacement=1&pgtype=collection . 3/16/2001. Accessed: 8/16/17.

[4] Pierce, Chuck. *10 days of decreeing your land and boundaries will rejoice.* http://www.elijahlist.com/words/display_word.html?ID=17557 . 3/1/17. Accessed: 3/23/17.

[5] Smith, Larry. The African Diaspora to the Bahamas. http://www.bahamapundit.com/2013/02/the-african-diaspora-to-the-bahamas.htm_ 2/19/13. Accessed: 6/1/17.

[6] Sherfinski, David. *Hard to fight the war on terror if we're in retreat.* Washington Times. http://www.washingtontimes.com/news/2017/feb/27/george-w-bush-hard-fight-war-terror-if-were-retrea/. 2/27/17. Accessed: 3/1/17.

[7] Freed, Sandie. *Jezebel and Athaliah at the gate.* http://www.elijahlist.com/words/display_word/3986. 4/13/06. Accessed: 8/15/17.

[8] Prophetic Presbytery. Giving Light. Elizabethville, Pa. 3/16/14.

Chapter 6 – FAMILY & RELATIONSHIPS

[1] National Estimates of Marriage: Dissolution and Survivorship US. https://www.cdc.gov/nchs/data/series/sr_03/sr03_019.pdf. Accessed: 6/14/17.

[2] Living Arrangements of Children Under 18. https://www.census.gov/library/visualizations/2016/comm/cb16-192_living_arrangements.html . 11/17/16. Accessed: 6/14/17.

[3] Institute of Family Studies. *The Family World Map 2015: Mapping Family Change and Child Well-Being Outcomes.* http://worldfamilymap.ifstudies.org/2015/articles/world-family-indicators/family-structure. 2015. Accessed: 6/27/17.

[4] McCarthy, Justin. *Majority in US Still Say Moral Values Getting Worse.* http://www.gallup.com/poll/183467/majority-say-moral-values-getting-worse.asp. 6/2/15. Accessed: 6/25/17.

[5] National Survey of Family Growth. https://www.cdc.gov/nchs/data/nhsr/nhsr049.pdf . 3/2012. Accessed: 6/14/17.

[6] Care-net. Facts on Abortion and Related Issues in the United States – Top 40 Abortion Statistics in America: Abor-

tion At-A-Glance. (a compilation of multiple studies). https://www.care-net.org/free-resources . Accessed: 6/19/17.

[7] Ibid.

[8] The Fatherless Generation. https://thefatherlessgeneration.wordpress.com/statistics/ . Accessed: 6/17/17.

[9] Ibid.

[10] Hamon, Tom. A New Prophetic Season for America: The Cyrus Decree and Breaking Resistance. http://elijahlist.com/words/display_word.html?ID=18894 . 10/4/17. Accessed: 10/4/17.

[11] Francis, Rebecca. *7 Key Standards for the Body of Christ to Advance.* http://www.elijahlist.com/words/display_word.html?ID=17504. 2/20/17. Accessed: 6/14/17.

[12] Castro, Valerie. *Hungry For Love? A dinner date might not satisfy your appetite.* http://newyork.cbslocal.com/2016/12/30/dinner-dates/. 12/30/16. Accessed: 4/15/17.

[13] Silk, Danny. *Life Academy Promo Video*. www.loplifeacademy.com. Accessed 4/26/17.

[14] Titus, Silas. *Fading Capitalism, Socialism, and True Economy: A Sustainable Response to Global Financial Crisis.* Publisher: Pronoun. Available on Kindle, Loc. 485/3192. Copyright: 12/27/16.

[15] Greenfield, David. https://www.psychalive.org/cell-phone-addiction/. Accessed: 4/26/17.

[16] Jumio. Chart: 2013 Smartphone Use. https://www.washingtonpost.com/news/the-intersect/wp/2014/07/14/why-you-should-really-seriously-permanently-stop-using-your-smartphone-at-dinner/?utm_term=.2b5e275d4938 . 7/14/14. Accessed: 5/27/17.

Chapter 7 – Prejudice in the Gates

[1] Stansfield, Katie. Informal FaceBook post. 9/26/17. Accessed: 9/26/17.

[2] Edwards, Malik. Informal Facebook post on 8/12/17. Accessed: 8/13/17.

[3] Seiger, Theresa. Father of Charlottesville victim forgives. ww.ajc.com/news/national/father-charlottesville-victim-heather-heyer-says-forgives-james-fields/s1pU0YOSxABpPuFvCIDu6I/ . 8/15/17. Accessed: 8/23/17.

[4] Pierce, Chuck. Times of chaos! This is a time when America determines its future. http://www.elijahlist.com/words/display_word.html?ID=16331 . 7/8/16. Accessed: 5/28/17.

[5] Hilton, Melodye. Informal Facebook post 9/15/17. Accessed: 9/15/17.

[6] Kunneman, Hank. Prophetic word given 3/19/17. http://www.elijahlist.com/words/display_word.html?ID=18201. Accessed: 6/19/17.

[7] *Herd, Aimee. Awaken the Dawn Moved Us Forward.* http://www.elijahlist.com/words/display_word.html?ID=18966. *10/13/17. Accessed: 10/14/17.*

[8] Wallnau, Lance. *Lessons From Kim on Warfare and Worship.* https://www.facebook.com/LanceWallnau/posts/10154782503909936:0 . 11/25/16. Accessed: 12/12/16.

Chapter 8 – NOW: 21st Century Gates, Gatekeepers, the Internet & Media

[1] Gunelius, Susan. *The History and Evolution of the Internet in 5 InfoGraphics.* https://aci.info/2013/10/24/the-history-and-evolution-of-the-internet-media-and-news-in-5-infographics/ . 10/24/13. Accessed: 7/5/17.

[2] Business Dictionary. Online: http://www.businessdictionary.com/definition/gatekeeper.html_. Accessed: 3/15/17.

[3] Tashman, Brian. *America Will Fall Apart, East and West Coast Will Be Ruled By Demons.* http://www.rightwingwatch.org/post/chuck-pierce-america-will-fall-apart-east-and-west-coasts-will-be-ruled-by-demons/_. 11/14/12. Accessed 1/15/17.

[4] Barzilai-Nahon Karine, 2008, "Towards a Theory of Network Gatekeeping: A Framework for Exploring Information Control", Journal of the American Society for Information Science and Technology (JASIST), Vol. 59(9), p. 1501. As noted on https://en.wikipedia.org/wiki/Gatekeeping_(communication). Accessed: 1/15/17.

[5] Ibid. pp. 1493–1512.

[6] Wallnau, Lance. 5777: The Year of the Clashing Swords._https://lancewallnau.com/2016/10/5777 . 10/10/16. Accessed: 2/17/17.

[7] Wallnau, Lance. Spiritual Warfare – This month is key! (Streaming video. 3/5/17, https://www.youtube.com/watch?v=5zEyushNUFc. Accessed 3/15/17).

[8] Vinton, Kate. *These 15 Billionaires Own America's News.* https://www.forbes.com/sites/katevinton/2016/06/01/these-15-billionaires-own-americas-news-media-companies/#7ba14fad660a_. 6/1/16. Accessed 2/25/17.

[9] Lutz, Ashley. These 6 Corporations Control 90% of the Media. http://www.businessinsider.com/these-6-corporations-control-90-of-the-media-in-america-2012-6 . 6/14/12 Accessed 2/25/17.

[10] Ibid.

[11] Gunelius, Susan. *The History and Evolution of the Internet in 5 InfoGraphics.* https://aci.info/2013/10/24/the-history-and-evolution-of-the-internet-media-and-news-in-5-infographics/ . 10/24/13. Accessed: 7/5/17.

[11] Ibid.

[12] Ibid.

[13] Ibid.

[14] Johnson, Keith. Informal Facebook post. 8/19/17. Accessed: 8/19/17.

[15] Gunelius, Susan. *The History and Evolution of the Internet in 5 InfoGraphics.* https://aci.info/2013/10/24/the-history-and-evolution-of-the-internet-media-and-news-in-5-infographics/ . 10/24/13. Accessed: 7/5/17.

[16] Lam, Katherine. *Chaos Breaks Out at Jersey Garden Mall.* http://pix11.com/2016/12/26/chaos-at-jersey-gardens-mall-as-police-respond-to-report-of-shooting/. 12/26/16. Accessed: 3/5/17.

Chapter 9 – SHIFTS in Immigration and Borders

[1] Dane, Bob. *Davis-Oliver Act could make Trump's immigration agenda law of the land.* http://thehill.com/blogs/pundits-blog/immigration/335933-davis-oliver-act-would-make-trumps-immigration-agenda-law-of?amp . 6/1/17. Accessed: 7/10/17.

[2] Martinelli, Ron. *The truth about crime, illegal immigrants and sanctuary cities.* http://thehill.com/blogs/pundits-blog/crime/329589-the-truth-about-crime-illegal-immigrants-and-sanctuary-cities . 4/19/17. Accessed: 7/11/17.

[3] Carranza, Rafael. How much does it cost to deport one immigrant? It depends. http://www.azcentral.com/story/news/politics/immigration/2017/04/28/deportation-costs-illegal-immigration/99541736/ . 4/27/17. Accessed: 7/11/17.

[4] Chuck Pierce. *Ten Days of Decreeing Your Land and Boundaries Will Rejoice*! http://elijahlist.com/words/display_word.html?ID=17557. 3/1/17. Accessed: 3/27/17.

[5] Oduntan, Gbenga. *Africa's border disputes are set to rise – but there are ways to stop them*! http://theconversation.com/africas-border-disputes-are-set-to-rise-but-there-are-ways-to-stop-them-44264 . 7/14/15. Accessed: 5/20/17.

[6] MacDowall, Andrew. *Rumbling Balkans threaten foreign-policy headache for Trump.* https://www.theguardian.com/world/2017/feb/27/balkans-foreign-policy-headache-trump-kosovo-serbia-bosnia-montenegro . 2/27/17. Accessed: 6/27/17.

[7] Mast, Dale. FaceBook, informal post made on 6/4/17. Accessed: 6/4/17.

Chapter 10 – OUR GOVERNMENT

[1] Hamon, Tom. A New Prophetic Season for America: The Cyrus Decree and Breaking Resistance. http://elijahlist.com/words/display_word.html?ID=18894. 10/4/17. Accessed: 10/4/17.

[2] Wallsion, Peter J. *Why We Need the Electoral College.* http://www.realclearpolitics.com/articles/2016/12/06/why_we_need_the_electoral_college_132499.html . 12/6/16. Accessed 5/29/17.

[3] Schulman, Marc. *Why the Electoral College.* http://www.historycentral.com/elections/Electoralcollgewhy.html. Accessed 5/29/17.

[4] Wallnau, Lance. *God's Chaos Candidate: Donald J. Trump and the American Unraveling.* Killer Sheep Media: Keller, Tx. Copyright: 2016.

[5] Landry, Curt. *Is Donald Trump a Cyrus or a Nebuchadnezzer*? https://www.curtlandry.com/is-donald-j-trump-a-cyrus-or-a-nebuchadnezzar/. 11/20/16. Accessed: 7/13/17.

[6] Hamon, Tom. A New Prophetic Season for America: The Cyrus Decree and Breaking Resistance. http://elijahlist.com/words/display_word.html?ID=18894. 10/4/17. Accessed: 10/4/17.

[7] Wallnau, Lance. *A Call to Courage.* (Streaming video: http://www.elijahlist.com/words/display_word.html?ID=17485. 2/14/17, Accessed 2/21/17.

[8] Garcia, Carlos. *CNN host slaps down liberal intolerance and close-mindedness.* http://www.theblaze.com/news/2017/05/29/cnn-host-slaps-down-liberal-intolerance-and-close-mindedness/. 5/29/17. Accessed: 6/2/17.

[9] Brown, Michael. Left wing intolerance, right wing hypocrisy. https://stream.org/leftwing-intolerance-rightwing-hypocrisy/. 2/11/17. Accessed: 2/15/17

[10] Walia, Arjun. *The Deep state institutions that control America.* 6/1/17. http://www.collective-evolution.com/2017/06/01/the-deep-state-institutions-that-control-america-they-dont-care-who-you-vote-for/. Accessed: 6/1/17.

[11] Strassel, Kimberley A. *Anatomy of a Deep State.* https://www.wsj.com/articles/anatomy-of-a-deep-state-1495753640. 5/25/17. Accessed 6/1/17.

[12] Rodriguez, Cindy. Bush ties to bin Laden haunt grim anniversary. Denver Post. http://www.denverpost.com/2006/09/11/bush-ties-to-bin-laden-haunt-grim-anniversary/. 9/11/06. Accessed: 8/10/17.

[13] Gamble, Foster. *Thrive, what on earth will it take*? www.thethrivemovement.com. Accessed: 6:15/17.

[14] Anonymous. Follow the Money. https://www.thrivemovement.com/images/infographics/followthemoney.html. Accessed: 7/17/17.

Chapter 11 – MORE GATES

[1] Martin, Mark. *How Will Family Christian Stores Closing Affect You?* http://www1.cbn.com/cbnnews/us/2017/february/how-will-family-christian-stores-closing-affect-you. 2/25/17. Accessed 2/25/17.

[2] Wallace, Tracey. *E-commerce trends: 139 stats regarding how modern customers shop in 2017.* https://www.bigcommerce.com/blog/ecommerce-trends/. Accessed: 7/7/17.

[3] Anonymous. Top 10 E-Commerce Markets. https://www.brainsins.com/en/blog/top-10-ecommerce-markets-statistics-and-trends-infographic/4022. 1/2016. Accessed: 7/7/17.

[4] Ibid.

[5] Titus, Silas. Fading Capitalism, Socialism, and True Economy: A Sustainable Response to Global Financial Crisis. Publisher: Pronoun. Available on Kindle, Loc. 485/3192. Copyright: 12/27/16.

[6] Anonymous. *Organization Urges Students to Skip School to Protest Trump's Inauguration.* http://insider.foxnews.com/2017/01/19/nea-urges-teachers-students-protest-trump-schools. 1/19/17. Accessed: 7/12/17.

[7] Strauss, Valerie. *Teachers Union Leader Won't Work with Trump or DeVos.* https://www.washingtonpost.com/news/answer-sheet/wp/2017/07/03/teachers-union-leader-we-wont-work-with-trump-and-devos-because-i-do-not-trust-their-motives/?utm_term=.1ba148f65885. 7/3/17. Accessed: 7/12/17.

[8] Wallnau, Lance.7M Gen Camp 2017. https://lancewallnau.clickfunnels.com/optin13903931. Accessed: 7/13/17.

[9] Swaim, Lanny. *The Remnant Will Experience the Fullness of Christ.* http://www.elijahlist.com/words/display_word.html?ID=1822. 6/24/17. Accessed: 7/4/17.

Chapter 12 – Military Strategies

[1] Anonymous. Military Discipline Essay. https://www.cram.com/essay/Military-Discipline/PK6PCH35 . 11/1/05. Accessed: 10/12/17.

[2] Washington, George. Informal letter to John Trumball. 6/25/1799. https://founders.archives.gov/documents/Washington/06-04-02-012 . Accessed: 10/5/17.

[3] Bush, George W. *Fighting the War on Terrorism.* http://www.washingtontimes.com/news/2017/feb/27/george-w-bush-hard-fight-war-terror-if-were-retrea/. Accessed 3/1/17.

[4] Ridgwell, Henry. NATO Warns West 'Losing Information War Against Russia'. http://www.voanews.com/a/nato-russia-information-war-propaganda/3526780.html . 9/27/16. Accessed: 8/20/17.

[5] Anonymous. Parliament hit by sustained cyber-attack. http://www.bbc.com/news/uk-40394074. Accessed: 6/25/17 6/25/17.

[6] Strand, Paul. Awaken the Dawn: A weekend of worship fills the national mall. http://www1.cbn.com/cbnnews/us/2017/october/awaken-the-dawn-a-weekend-of-worship-fills-the-national-mall. 10/8/17. Accessed: 10/13/17.

[8] Sullivan, Peter. *In-Depth Security Planning.* http://searchsecurity.techtarget.com/tip/Defense-in-depth-strategy-Growing-cyberthreat-intelligence. Accessed: 6/20/17.

Chapter 13 – the Future

[1] Hamon, Tim. IGAP conference presentation. 10/20/16.

[2] Pierce, Chuck. Head to the Future 5778. http://www.elijahlist.com/words/display_word.html?ID=18635 . 8/29/17. Accessed: 8/29/17.

[3] Hamon, Tom. A New Prophetic Season for America: The Cyrus Decree and Breaking Resistance. http://elijahlist.com/words/display_word.html?ID=18894. 10/4/17. Accessed: 10/4/17.

[4] White, Jamillah. Informal FaceBook post. May 2017.

[5] Enlow, Johnny. FaceBook page: https://www.facebook.com/JohnnyEnlow77/?hc_ref=SEARCH&fref=nf . (Written: 3/22/17. Accessed 3/25/17.

[6] Pierce, Chuck. *Short, 10 Year Window in the Nation.* Charisma News. http://www.charismanews.com/opinion/watchman-on-the-wall/61541-chuck-pierce-prophesies-short-10-year-window-in-the-nations. 11/30/16.

[7] Hilton, Melodye. Informal Facebook post, from *Higher Living Leadership Biblical Edition.* 8/19/17. Accessed: 8/20/17.

[8] Hamon, Tom. A New Prophetic Season for America: The Cyrus Decree and Breaking Resistance. http://elijahlist.com/words/display_word.html?ID=18894 . 10/4/17. Accessed: 10/4/17.

Recommended Reading

Deliverance

Parkes, Bob & Sharon. *Prophetic Healing & Deliverance Manual.* (Isaiah 62:4 Ministries: Santa Rosa, Florida, 2011).

Wagner, Doris M. *How to Cast Out Demons.* (Regal Books from Gospel Light: Ventura, California, 2000).

Dreams

Thompson, Adam F. & Beale, Adrian. *The Divinity Code to understanding your dreams and visions.* (Destiny Image: Shippensburg, Pa., 2011).

Healing from Spiritual Abuse

Williams, Harold. *Dancing with Wolves.* (Kelly Publishers: USA, 2017).

Identity

Mast, Dale. *And David Perceived He Was King – Identity the key to your destiny.* (Xulon Press: USA, 2017).

Mast, Dale. *Two Sons and a Father.* (Xulon Press: USA, 2017).

Leadership

Hilton, Dr. Melodye. *Higher Living Leadership.* (Outskirts Press: USA. 2017).

Kreider, Larry. *21 Tests of Effective Leadership.* (Destiny Image: Shippensburg, Pa., 2010).

Prayer

Eastman, Dick. *No Easy Road.* (Baker Book House: Grand Rapids, Mi., 1971).

Eivaz, Jennifer. *The Intercessors Handbook.* (Chosen: Bloomington, Minn., 2016).

Hamon, Bill. *70 Reasons for Speaking in Tongues.* (Parsons Publishing House: Stafford, Va, 2010).

Jacobs, Cindy. *Possessing the Gates of the Enemy*. (Chosen Books: Grand Rapids, Mi., 1994).

Jacobs, Cindy. *The Voice of God*. (Regal: Ventura, Ca., 1995).

Olukoya, Dr. Daniel. *Prayer Passport to Crush Oppression*. (Mountain of Fire and Miracles Ministries. Nigeria, 2006).

Reformation

Hamon, Bill. *The Day of the Saints*. (Destiny Image: Shippensburg, Pa., 2002).

Silvoso, Ed. *Transformation*. (Chosen: Bloomington, Minn., 2007).

Silvoso, Ed. *Ekklesia*. (Chosen: Bloomington, Minn., 2014, 2017).

Spiritual Mothers & Fathers

Kreider, Larry. *The Cry for Spiritual Mothers & Fathers*. (Regal: Ventura, Ca., 2014).

Warfare

Frangipane, Francis. *The Stronghold of God*. (Charisma House: Lake Mary, Fl., 1998).

Freed, Sandie. *Breaking the Threefold Demonic Cord*. (Chosen: Grand Rapids, Mi., 2008).

Freed, Sandie. *Destiny Thieves*. (Chosen: Grand Rapids, Mi., 2007).

Freed Sandie. *The Jezebel Yoke*. (Chosen: Bloomington, Minn., 2012).

Jackson, Eric. *Sun Tzu's 31 Best Pieces of Leadership Advice*. https://www.forbes.com/sites/ericjackson/2014/05/23/sun-tzus-33-best-pieces-of-leadership-advice/#42b9eef15e5e . Accessed: 5/30/17.

Jackson, John Paul. *Needless Casualties of War*. (Streams Publishing House: Coleyville, Tx., 1999).

Jackson, John Paul. *Unmasking the Jezebel Spirit*. (Streams Publishing House: Coleyville, Tx., 2002).

LeClaire, Jennifer. *The Spiritual Warriors Guide to Defeating Jezebel*. (Chosen: Bloomington, Minn., 2013).

LeClaire, Jennifer. *Waging Prophetic Warfare*. (Charisma House: Lake Mary, Fl., 2016).

Meyers, Joyce. *Battlefield of the Mind*. (FaithWord: NY, NY, 2011.)

Tzu, Sun. *The Art of War*. [An ancient Chinese military treatise from 5th century BC that is still used as a military text today. It has had an influence on Eastern and Western military thinking, business tactics, legal strategy and more.]

CPSIA information can be obtained
at www.ICGtesting.com
Printed in the USA
BVHW04s1331130818
524340BV00017B/556/P

9 781545 622001